When should I travel to get the best airfare?
Where do I go for answers to my travel questions?
What's the best and easiest way to plan and book my trip?

frommers.travelocity.com

Frommer's, the travel guide leader, has teamed up with **Travelocity.com**, the leader in online travel, to bring you an in-depth, easy-to-use resource designed to help you plan and book your trip online.

At **frommers.travelocity.com**, you'll find free online updates about your destination from the experts at Frommer's plus the outstanding travel planning and purchasing features of Travelocity.com. Travelocity.com provides reservations capabilities for 95 percent of all airline seats sold, more than 47,000 hotels, and over 50 car rental companies. In addition, Travelocity.com offers more than 2,000 exciting vacation and cruise packages. Travelocity.com puts you in complete control of your travel planning with these and other great features:

> **Expert travel guidance from Frommer's** - over 150 writers reporting from around the world!

> **Best Fare Finder** - an interactive calendar tells you when to travel to get the best airfare

> **Fare Watcher** - we'll track airfare changes to your favorite destinations

> **Dream Maps** - a mapping feature that suggests travel opportunities based on your budget

> **Shop Safe Guarantee** - 24 hours a day / 7 days a week live customer service, and more!

Whether traveling on a tight budget, looking for a quick weekend getaway, or planning the trip of a lifetime, Frommer's guides and Travelocity.com will make your travel dreams a reality. You've bought the book, now book the trip!

Also available from IDG Books Worldwide:

Beyond Disney: The Unofficial Guide to Universal, Sea World, and the Best of Central Florida, by Bob Sehlinger and Amber Morris

Inside Disney: The Incredible Story of Walt Disney World and the Man Behind the Mouse, by Eve Zibart

Mini I as Vegas: The Pocket-Sized Unofficial Guide to Las Vegas, by Bob Sehlinger

The Unofficial Guide to Bed & Breakfasts in California, by Mary Anne Moore and Maurice Read

The Unofficial Guide to Bed & Breakfasts in New England, by Lea Lane

The Unofficial Guide to Bed & Breakfasts in the Northwest, by Sally O'Neal Coates

The Unofficial Guide to Branson, Missouri, by Bob Sehlinger and Eve Zibart

The Unofficial Guide to California with Kids, by Colleen Dunn Bates and Susan LaTempa

The Unofficial Guide to Chicago, by Joe Surkiewicz and Bob Sehlinger

The Unofficial Guide to Cruises, by Kay Showker with Bob Sehlinger

The Unofficial Guide to Disneyland, by Bob Sehlinger

The Unofficial Guide to Florida with Kids, by Pam Brandon

The Unofficial Guide to the Great Smoky and Blue Ridge Region, by Bob Sehlinger and Joe Surkiewicz

The Unofficial Guide to Golf Vacations in the Eastern U.S., by Joseph Mark Passov with C.H. Conroy

The Unofficial Guide to Hawaii, by Lance Tominaga

The Unofficial Guide to Las Vegas, by Bob Sehlinger

The Unofficial Guide to London, by Lesley Logan

The Unofficial Guide to Miami and the Keys, by Bob Sehlinger and Joe Surkiewicz

The Unofficial Guide to New Orleans, by Bob Sehlinger and Eve Zibart

The Unofficial Guide to New York City, by Eve Zibart and Bob Sehlinger with Jim Leff

The Unofficial Guide to Paris, by David Applefield

The Unofficial Guide to San Francisco, by Joe Surkiewicz and Bob Sehlinger with Richard Sterling

The Unofficial Guide to Skiing in the West, by Lito Tejada-Flores, Peter Shelton, Seth Masia, Ed Chauner, and Bob Sehlinger

The Unofficial Guide to Walt Disney World, by Bob Sehlinger

The Unofficial Guide to Walt Disney World for Grown-Ups, by Eve Zibart

The Unofficial Guide to Walt Disney World with Kids, by Bob Sehlinger

The Unofficial Guide to Washington, D.C., by Bob Sehlinger and Joe Surkiewicz with Eve Zibart

Mini Mickey

the Pocket-Sized Unofficial Guide® to Walt Disney World® 2001

Bob Sehlinger

Acknowledgments:

Mary Ellen Botter edited this guide. Starting with a tome delivered by forklift and as big as a bale of hay, she chopped, slashed, burned, and purged every nonessential word. The final product is so portable that a Southern lady can tote it all day without a hint of perspiration.

Thanks also to Holly Cross, Steve Jones, Laura Didyk, Chris Mohney, and Shannon Dobbs, who turned what Mary Ellen left into a book.

Dedicated to the Dirty Dozen:

Georgia Goff	Steve Jones	Budd Zehmer
Molly Merkle	Marie Hillin	Brenda Robbins
Annie Long	Chris Mohney	Patricia Parks
Tiffany Prewitt-McClain	Holly Cross	Grant Tatum

IDG Books Worldwide, Inc.

An International Data Group Company
909 Third Avenue
New York, New York 10022

Produced by Menasha Ridge Press

UNOFFICIAL GUIDE is a registered trademark of IDG Books Worldwide, Inc.

ISBN 0-7645-6250-9

ISSN 1089-8042

Manufactured in the United States of America

10 9 8 7 6 5 4 3 2 1

Contents

List of Maps

Introduction

Why This Pocket Guide?

The optimum stay at Walt Disney World is seven days, but many visitors don't have that long to devote to Disney attractions. Some are on business with only a day or two available for Disney's enticements. Others are en route elsewhere or want to sample additional attractions in Orlando and central Florida. For these visitors, efficient, time-effective touring is a must. They can't afford long waits in line for rides, shows, or meals. They must determine as far in advance as possible what they really want to see.

This guide distills information from the comprehensive *Unofficial Guide to Walt Disney World* to help short-stay or last-minute visitors decide quickly how best to spend their limited hours. It will help these guests answer questions vital to their enjoyment: What are the rides and attractions that appeal to me most? Which additional rides and attractions would I like to experience if I have any time left? What am I willing to forgo?

DECLARATION OF INDEPENDENCE

The author and researchers of this guide are totally independent of Walt Disney Co. Inc., Disneyland Inc., Walt Disney World Inc., and all other members of the Disney corporate family. We represent and serve the consumer.

The material in this guide originated with the author and researchers and hasn't been reviewed or edited by the Walt Disney Co., Disneyland, or Walt Disney World.

Ours is the first comprehensive critical appraisal of Walt Disney World. It aims to provide the information necessary to tour

Walt Disney World with the greatest efficiency and economy. The authors believe in the wondrous excitement of the Disney attractions, but we recognize that Walt Disney World is a business.

THE DEATH OF SPONTANEITY

When it comes to touring Walt Disney World, we researchers agree that you absolutely must have a plan. We aren't saying you can't have a great time without one. We're saying you need one.

HOW THIS GUIDE WAS RESEARCHED AND WRITTEN

Little written about Disney World has been comparative or evaluative. Many guides parrot Disney's promotional material. In preparing this guide, however, we took nothing for granted. Each theme park was visited at different times throughout the year by trained observers. They conducted detailed evaluations and rated each park, with its component rides, shows, exhibits, services, and concessions, according to a formal, pretested rating method. Interviews were conducted to determine what tourists—of all ages—enjoyed most and least during their Disney World visit.

The essence of this guide consists of individual critiques and descriptions of each feature of the Magic Kingdom, Epcot, Disney-MGM Studios, and the Animal Kingdom, along with detailed touring plans to help you avoid bottlenecks and crowds. Also included are descriptions for Typhoon Lagoon, Blizzard Beach, Pleasure Island, and the nearby Universal theme parks.

Walt Disney World: An Overview

There's nothing on earth like Walt Disney World. Incredible in its scope, genius, beauty, and imagination, it's a joy and wonder for all ages. Disney attractions are a quantum leap beyond most man-made entertainment we know. We can't understand how anyone could visit Florida and bypass Walt Disney World.

WHAT WALT DISNEY WORLD ENCOMPASSES

Walt Disney World encompasses 43 square miles, an area twice as large as Manhattan Island. In this expanse are the Magic Kingdom, Epcot, Disney-MGM Studios, and the Animal Kingdom theme parks, three water parks, two night-life areas, a sports complex, golf courses, hotels and campgrounds, more than 100 restaurants, four interconnected lakes, a shopping complex, three convention venues, a nature preserve, and a transportation system.

The formal name is Walt Disney World, but most tourists refer to the entire Florida Disney facility simply as Disney World. The Magic Kingdom, Epcot, Disney-MGM Studios, and the Animal Kingdom are thought of as being "in" Disney World.

THE MAJOR THEME PARKS
The Magic Kingdom

The Magic Kingdom is the heart of Disney World. It's the collection of adventures, rides, and shows symbolized by the Disney cartoon characters and Cinderella Castle. The Magic Kingdom is divided into seven subareas or "lands," six of which are arranged around a central hub. First encountered is Main Street, U.S.A. Moving clockwise around the hub, other lands are Adventureland, Frontierland, Liberty Square, Fantasyland, and Tomorrowland. Mickey's Toontown Fair, the first new land in the Magic Kingdom since the park opened, is along the Walt Disney Railroad on three acres between Fantasyland and Tomorrowland. Access is through Fantasyland, Tomorrowland, or via the railroad. The Contemporary Resort, Polynesian Resort, and Grand Floridian Beach Resort are close to the Magic Kingdom and connected to it by monorail and boat. Shades of Green and the Wilderness Lodge Resort and Villas are nearby but aren't served by the monorail.

Epcot

Epcot (Experimental Prototype Community of Tomorrow) Center opened in October 1982. Divided into two major areas, Future World and World Showcase, it's twice as big as the Magic Kingdom. Future World consists of futuristic pavilions, each with a different theme relating to human creativity and technological advancement. World Showcase, arranged around a 41-acre lagoon, presents the architectural, social, and cultural heritages of 11 nations, each represented by famous landmarks and local settings. Epcot is more educational than the Magic Kingdom and has been characterized as a permanent World's Fair entity.

Epcot has five hotels: Beach Club, Yacht Club, BoardWalk Resort, Swan, and Dolphin. All are within a 5- to 15-minute walk

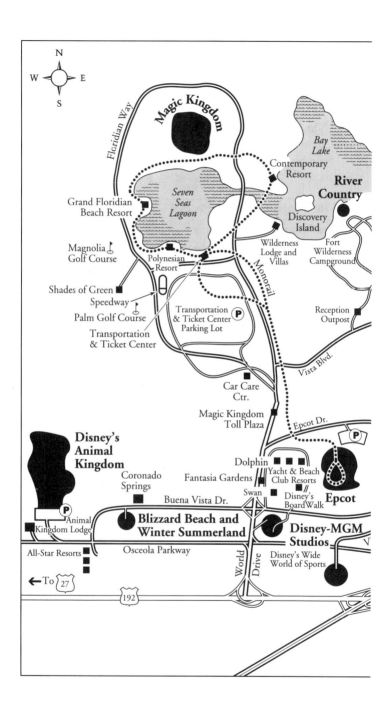

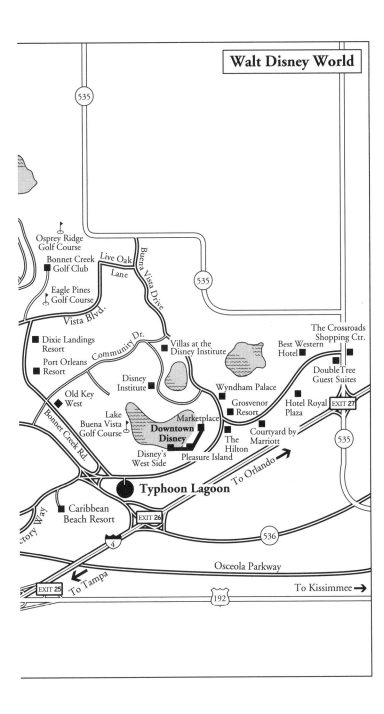

Walt Disney World

535

Osprey Ridge
Golf Course

Bonnet Creek
Golf Club

Live Oak
Lane

Buena Vista Drive

535

Eagle Pines
Golf Course

Vista Blvd.

Dixie Landings
Resort

Community Dr.

Villas at the
Disney Institute

The Crossroads
Shopping Ctr.

Best Western
Hotel

Port Orleans
Resort

Disney
Institute

Wyndham Palace

DoubleTree
Guest Suites

EXIT 27

Old Key
West

Lake
Buena Vista
Golf Course

Bonnet Creek Rd.

Marketplace

Downtown
Disney

Grosvenor
Resort

Hotel Royal
Plaza

535

Disney's
West Side

Pleasure Island

The
Hilton

Courtyard by
Marriott

Typhoon Lagoon

To Orlando

Victory Way

Caribbean
Beach Resort

EXIT 26

I-4

536

Osceola Parkway

EXIT 25

To Tampa

192

To Kissimmee →

of the International Gateway entrance to Epcot. The hotels are also linked by canal and tram. The monorail links Epcot to the Magic Kingdom and its hotels.

Disney-MGM Studios

This $300 million, 100-plus-acre attraction opened in 1989 and has two areas. The first is a theme park relating to the past,   present, and future of the movie and television industries. It   contains movie-theme rides and shows and covers about half the complex. The remaining half is a working motion-picture and television production facility made up of three soundstages, a backlot of streets and sets, and creative support services.

Disney-MGM is connected to other Disney World areas by highway and canal but not by monorail. Guests can park in the Studios lot or commute by bus. Epcot hotel guests can arrive by boat.

Disney's Animal Kingdom

More than five times the size of the Magic Kingdom, the Animal Kingdom combines zoological exhibits with rides, shows, and live entertainment. A lush rain forest funnels visitors to centrally located Safari Village, dominated by the 14-story-tall, hand-carved Tree of Life. The village encompasses guest services, shopping, and dining. From here you can access the theme areas: Africa, DinoLand U.S.A., Asia, and Camp Minnie-Mickey. A fifth land should come on line over the next couple of years. The 100-acre Africa has herds roaming in a re-creation of the Serengeti Plain.

Animal Kingdom has its own pay parking lot and is connected to other Disney World destinations by the Disney bus system. Although it has no hotels, the All-Star, Animal Kingdom Lodge, and Coronado Springs Resorts are nearby.

WATER THEME PARKS

Disney World has three water theme parks: Typhoon Lagoon, River Country, and Blizzard Beach. Typhoon Lagoon has a wave pool capable of producing six-foot waves. The much smaller River Country is a pioneer among water theme parks. Blizzard Beach, the trio's newest, features more slides than the other two swimming parks combined. Typhoon Lagoon and Blizzard Beach have their own parking lots. River Country can be reached on foot by campground guests or by boat or bus for others.

OTHER DISNEY WORLD VENUES

Downtown Disney

Downtown Disney is a large shopping, dining, and entertainment complex encompassing Downtown Disney Marketplace on the east, six-acre Pleasure Island nighttime entertainment venue (tickets required) in the middle, and Disney's West Side on the west. The Marketplace has the world's largest Disney-merchandise store. Pleasure Island includes eight nightclubs and several upscale restaurants and shops. The West Side combines night life, shopping, dining, and entertainment. It includes a permanent showplace for the extraordinary *Cirque du Soleil;* DisneyQuest, a high-tech interactive virtual reality and electronic games venue; and a 24-screen cinema.

You can access Downtown Disney by bus from most Disney World locations.

Disney's BoardWalk

Near Epcot, the BoardWalk is an idealized replication of an East-Coast turn-of-the-century waterfront resort. Open all day, it features restaurants, shops, and galleries; a brew pub; an ESPN Sports Bar; a nightclub with dueling pianos; and a swanky dance club. Clubs levy a cover charge at night. Also on-site are a 378-room deluxe hotel and a 532-unit time-share development.

The BoardWalk is within walking distance of Epcot's resorts and International Gateway. Boats link it to Disney-MGM Studios, and buses transport guests to other Disney World locations.

Disney's Wide World of Sports

The 200-acre Wide World of Sports is a competition and training facility consisting of a 7,500-seat ballpark; a field house; and venues for baseball, softball, tennis, track and field, beach volleyball, and 27 other sports. It's the home of spring training for the Atlanta Braves, and it hosts numerous professional and amateur competitions. Spectators must pay. Guests may not use the facilities unless they're in one of the competitions.

The Disney Institute

The Disney Institute offers professional-development courses for private groups and corporations. The campus, located near Downtown Disney Marketplace, is connected to other Disney locations by Disney bus service.

Part One

Planning Before You Leave Home

Gathering Information

In addition to this guide, if you have time, obtain copies of:

1. The Walt Disney Travel Co. Walt Disney World Vacations Brochure Describes Walt Disney World and vacation packages and lists rates for all Disney resort hotels and campgrounds. Call your travel agent or Walt Disney Travel Company at (800) 327-2996 or (407) 934-7639. Be prepared to hold; you may have a long wait.

2. The Disney Cruise Line Brochure If you are contemplating a vacation package that combines a Disney cruise with a stay at Walt Disney World, this brochure will provide all the particulars. It is available from travel agents, by calling the Walt Disney Travel Company at (800) 327-2996, or at **www.disneycruise.com.**

3. Orlando MagiCard Provides eligibility for discounts at hotels, restaurants, and attractions outside Disney World. Get a card, Vacation Planner, and Orlando Official Accommodations Guide from the Orlando Visitors Center by calling (800) 255-5786 or (407) 363-5872. On the internet, see **www.go2orlando.com.**

4. Florida Traveler Discount Guide Good source of lodging, restaurant, and attraction discounts throughout Florida. Call (352) 371-3948, Monday–Friday, 8 a.m.–5 p.m. EST. Cost is $3 ($5 USD if mailed to Canada).

5. Kissimmee–St. Cloud Tour & Travel Sales Guide Directory of hotels and attractions; one of the most complete guides available. Call the Kissimmee–St. Cloud Convention and Visitors Bureau at (800) 327-9159, or check out **www.floridakiss.com.**

6. The Eclectic Gourmet Guide to Orlando   Researched and written by the same team that produces this *Unofficial Guide,* the *Eclectic Gourmet* is the best resource for finding great restaurants outside Walt Disney World. It evaluates more than 150 restaurants and is available for $11.95 plus shipping by calling (800) 243-0495.

Request all information far in advance, if possible, and allow four weeks for delivery.

Facts Online

Recent Walt Disney World vacationers and employees supply late-breaking news online. A newsgroup on Usenet **(www.usenet.com)** called rec.arts.disney provides current information and answers questions about the park. There is a $10 per month fee to access information.

Disney's official Web page offers much of the same information as the Walt Disney Travel Company's vacation guidebook, but the guidebook has better pictures. Though the Web page is supposedly updated daily, we found a number of errors. You can purchase theme park admissions and make resort and dining reservations on the Internet. The Web page also offers shopping, weather forecasts, and events information. The address is **www.disney.com.** Also visit **www.themeparks.com/wdw/wdwphone** for a comprehensive and generally accurate directory of Walt Disney World phone

---

Important Walt Disney World Addresses

Walt Disney World Information/Guest Letters
P.O. Box 10040
Lake Buena Vista, FL 32830-0040

Walt Disney World Central Reservations
P.O. Box 10100
Lake Buena Vista, FL 32830-0100

Walt Disney World Educational Programs
P.O. Box 10000
Lake Buena Vista, FL 32830-1000

Merchandise Mail Order (Guest Service Mail Order)
P.O. Box 10070
Lake Buena Vista, FL 32830-0070

numbers. Universal Studios Florida also offers a home page at **www.usf.com**.

Private individuals also maintain Disney-related pages that disseminate both information and misinformation. A lot of it is fun and some is useful, but the best way to obtain facts without a long wait is to call Disney at (407) 824-4321.

Important Telephone Numbers

Information on Walt Disney World is available at public libraries, travel agencies, AAA, or by calling Walt Disney World directly.

Important Phone Numbers	
General Information	(407) 824-4321
Accommodations / Reservations	(407) 934-7639
	or (407) 824-8000
Cirque du Soleil	(407) 939-7600
Dining Priority Seating	(407) 939-3463
Disney Institute Programs	(407) 827-1100
Lost and Found	(407) 824-4245
Disabled Guests Special Request	(407) 939-7807

When to Go to Walt Disney World

WALT DISNEY WORLD AND THE MILLENNIUM

Walt Disney World will continue to celebrate the millennium through January 1, 2001. The millennium includes special versions of *IllumiNations* at Epcot; *Fantasmic!* at Disney-MGM Studios; and parades, fireworks, and live entertainment at all parks. Epcot, as Walt Disney World's millennium headquarters, features a World's Fair–type exhibit hall in World Showcase. Disney's millennium press and advertising blitz continues in full swing as you read this guide, so you can expect much larger than usual crowds through January 2001.

SELECTING THE TIME OF YEAR FOR YOUR VISIT

Walt Disney World is busiest Christmas Day through New Year's Day, Thanksgiving weekend, Washington's Birthday week, Martin Luther King holiday weekend, college spring break, and the two weeks around Easter.

The slowest time is after Thanksgiving weekend until the week before Christmas. Next are November through the weekend before Thanksgiving, January 4 through the first week of February, and the week after Easter through early June. Late February, March, and early April are dicey. Disney promotions boost crowds during September and October, but these months remain good for weekday tours at the Magic Kingdom, Disney-MGM, and the Animal Kingdom, and for weekends at Epcot. We would never choose to go in summer or during a holiday period.

The Downside of Off-Season Touring

We strongly recommend visiting Disney World in fall or spring, but there are trade-offs. The parks often open late and close early then. When they open as late as 9 a.m., everyone arrives about the same time; it's hard to beat the crowd. Late opening coupled with early closing drastically reduces touring hours. Even with small crowds, it's difficult to see the Magic Kingdom or Epcot between 9 a.m. and 6 p.m. Closing before 8 p.m. also eliminates evening parades or fireworks. Also, some attractions may be closed for maintenance or renovation. And temperatures fluctuate wildly during late fall, winter, and early spring; daytime highs in the 40s and 50s aren't uncommon.

Avoid the Magic Kingdom and Animal Kingdom on Saturday and Epcot on weekdays in September, October, and November to bypass crowds of locals. We must warn you that the difference between high and low season has blurred considerably in recent years. Even during off-season, crowd size can vary enormously. With Walt Disney World promotional hype in perpetual overdrive, huge crowds can materialize anytime.

As if the crowds aren't enough, you must also consider the weather. September, October, and November are pleasant enough, but December and January can hit you with just about anything. And thunderstorms and pouring rain are not uncommon at any time of year.

SELECTING THE DAY OF THE WEEK FOR YOUR VISIT

Most summer vacationers arrive in the Orlando area on Sunday and visit the Magic Kingdom on Monday and Animal Kingdom on Tuesday; Epcot and Disney-MGM on Wednesday and Thursday; and Typhoon Lagoon, Blizzard Beach, or a non-Disney attraction on Friday. Those who travel by car often reserve Friday for heading home. If this were all we had to consider, we could recommend Fridays and Sundays as the best days all year to avoid crowds.

However, off-season promotions attract locals on weekends at the Magic Kingdom, Animal Kingdom, and Disney-MGM. Crowds at Epcot, particularly in September and October, are almost always larger on weekdays. Disney brings thousands of school children to Epcot in March, September, and October. In late spring, teenagers fill the parks on "senior days" or prom nights, many on weekdays.

The most significant shift in attendance patterns results from the early-entry program for guests at Disney resort hotels and campgrounds (but not guests at Disney Village hotels). Each day, Disney World lodging guests are invited to enter a designated theme park one hour before the general public. The early-entry park will be more crowded that day, the others less crowded. During holiday periods and summer, when Disney hotels are full, the early-entry park fills by about 10 a.m. and is practically gridlocked by noon. At any season, whether you're eligible or not, avoid the early-entry park. Or, exercise your early-entry privilege, enjoy the attractions there, and move to another park when crowds build.

Least-Crowded Days

During summer, Saturday and Sunday are least crowded because locals stay home and out-of-staters travel on those days. September through May (excluding holidays and spring break), the opposite's true.

Magic Kingdom   In summer, Sunday and Friday are least crowded. Friday and Wednesday are least crowded at other times.

Disney-MGM Studios   In summer, Monday and Friday are best. Off-season, go Thursday and Friday.

Epcot   Monday, Wednesday, and Thursday are least crowded January through May, November, and December. During summer, crowds are smaller Saturday and Sunday. In September and October, visit on Saturday or Sunday.

Animal Kingdom   High- or low-season, on Monday, Friday, or Sunday.

E-Ride Night

In 1999, Disney instituted a program called E-Ride Night, where multiday pass-holding Disney resort guests could (for an extra $10) remain in the Magic Kingdom after official closing time and ride all the biggies with little or no waiting. Offered exclusively in the off-seasons, E-Ride Night is described in more detail on pages 130–131.

THE CRUELEST TIMES OF ALL: SUMMER AND HOLIDAYS

We advocate avoiding summer and holidays but understand that many folks have no choice concerning the time of year they visit Walt Disney World. Much of this book, in fact, is dedicated to making sure those readers who visit during the busier times of year enjoy their Walt Disney World experience. Sure, off-season touring is preferable, but, armed with a little knowledge and some basic strategy, you can have a great time whenever you visit.

To put it in perspective, early summer (up to about June 15) and late summer (after August 15) are not nearly as crowded as the intervening period. And even the crowds of midsummer pale in comparison to the vast hordes that invade during holiday periods.

Whatever the season, if you roll out of bed early and get yourself to one of the parks not scheduled for early entry an hour or so prior to official opening time, you are practically certain to be admitted. Regardless of the time of year, if you aren't eligible for early entry, stay clear of the early-entry park.

The Disney folks, however, feeling bad about those long, long lines and the nearly impossible touring conditions on packed holidays, compensate their patrons with a no-less-than-incredible array of first-rate live entertainment and happenings. Shows, parades, concerts, and pageantry continue throughout the day. In the evening, particularly, so much is going on that you have to make some tough choices. Concerts, parades, light shows, laser shows, fireworks, and dance productions occur almost continually. Admittedly, it isn't the ideal situation for a first-timer who really wants to experience the attractions, but for anyone else it's a great party.

Epcot is usually the least crowded park during holiday periods, unless it's scheduled for early entry. Expect the other parks to be mobbed. To save time in the morning, purchase your admission in advance. Also, consider bringing your own stroller or wheelchair instead of renting one of Disney's. If you are touring Epcot or the Magic Kingdom and plan to spend the day, try exiting the park for lunch at one of the nearby resort hotels. Above all, bring your sense of humor and pay attention to the morale of your party. Bail out when it gets to be more work than fun.

Part Two

Making the Most of Your Time and Money

Allocating Money

How much you spend depends on how long you stay at Walt Disney World. But even if you only stop by for an afternoon, be prepared to drop a bundle. In Part Three we'll show you how to save money on lodging, and in Part Eight you'll find lots of tips for economizing on meals. This section will give you some sense of what you can expect to pay for admission, as well as which admission option will best meet your needs.

WALT DISNEY WORLD ADMISSION OPTIONS

Here are the admissions options the short-stay parkgoer is most apt to use:

1-Day/One-Park Only Ticket   Good for admission and same-day, unlimited use of attractions at your choice of one of the four major theme parks.

1-Day/One-Park Bounce-Back Pass   A good deal for anyone wanting to visit the theme parks over a 3- or 4-day period without hopping from park to park on the same day.

If you purchase a 1-Day/One-Park Pass at the regular price, you are eligible to buy a 1-Day/One Park Bounce-Back Pass at a discounted rate, *but you must buy it on the same day you bought the original pass.* If you purchase a 1-Day/One-Park Pass and a discounted 1-Day/One-Park Bounce-Back Pass, you are also eligible to buy a third and fourth 1-Day/One-Park Bounce-Back Pass at an even greater discount. *All passes must be bought on the same day.*

A 1-Day/One-Park Pass and three 1-Day/One-Park Bounce-Back Passes are approximately $16 per adult and $12 per child less than a 4-Day Park-Hopper Pass. For the savings you forfeit the right to visit more than one park in a single day and the possibility of using the passes in the future (Bounce-Back passes expire, whereas Park-Hopper Passes are good forever).

4- and 5-Day Park-Hopper Passes Provides same-day admission to the Magic Kingdom, Animal Kingdom, Epcot, and Disney-MGM Studios. With it, you can tour the Studios in the morning, eat at Epcot, safari in the afternoon in the Animal Kingdom, and see the evening parades at the Magic Kingdom. Five-, 6-, and 7-Day Park-Hopper Plus Passes include the water parks, Pleasure Island, DisneyQuest, and the Wide World of Sports.

The 4-, 5-, 6-, and 7-Day Park-Hopper Passes needn't be used on consecutive days and are good forever.

Unlimited Magic Pass For Disney resort and campground guests. It can be purchased for *any* stay two days or longer and includes admission to all major and minor parks. The pass is good only during your stay. This convenient pass functions as a park pass and credit card. Use the card at restaurants, shops, and other facilities World-wide; purchases will be charged to your room.

WHICH ADMISSION SHOULD YOU BUY?

If you have only one day at Walt Disney World, select the park that most interests you and buy the 1-Day/One-Park Ticket. If you have two days and don't plan to return to Florida soon, buy two 1-Day tickets, a Bounce-Back Pass, or an Unlimited Magic Pass if you're a Disney resort guest. If you think you'll return soon, spring for a 4- or 5-Day Pass. Use two days of admission and save the remaining days for another trip.

WHERE TO BUY YOUR ADMISSION IN ADVANCE

Tickets are available at a Disney Store before you leave home or, if you're driving, at Disney's Ocala Information Center at Exit 68 on I-75. If you fly to Walt Disney World, purchase tickets at the Orlando airport Disney Store. Most Disney hotels also sell them.

Buy tickets by mail from Walt Disney World Ticket Mail Order Service, P.O. Box 10100, Lake Buena Vista, FL 32830, and via the Internet at **www.disney.com.**

Allocating Time

WHICH PARK TO SEE FIRST?

Children who see the Magic Kingdom first expect more of the same type of entertainment at Epcot and Disney-MGM. At Epcot, they're often disappointed by the educational orientation and more serious tone (adults are, too). Disney-MGM offers some wild action but also is generally educational and adult. Most children enjoy zoos, but they may not find the Animal Kingdom as exciting as the Magic Kingdom or Disney-MGM.

First-time visitors and groups with children should see Epcot first. You'll tour without having been preconditioned to think of Disney entertainment solely as fantasy or adventure. Next, see the Animal Kingdom. Like Epcot, it's educational, but it features live animals. Then go to Disney-MGM. The Studios help younger and older visitors make a fluid transition from imposing Epcot to the fanciful Magic Kingdom. Also, because the Studios is smaller, you won't have to walk as much or stay as long. Save the Magic Kingdom for last.

OPERATING HOURS

Disney runs a dozen or more schedules during the year; call (407) 824-4321 for the *exact* hours of operation before you arrive. Generally:

From September through mid-February and during May, excluding holiday periods, the Magic Kingdom is open from 9 a.m. to 7 or 8 p.m. and on some weekends until 9, 10, or even 11 p.m. During the same period, Epcot is open from 9 a.m. to 9 p.m., Disney-MGM is open from 9 a.m. to 7 or 8 p.m., and the Animal Kingdom is open from 7 or 8 a.m. until 7 or 8 p.m.

During summer, expect the Animal Kingdom to remain open until 8 p.m.; Epcot and Disney-MGM until 9 or 10 p.m.; and the Magic Kingdom sometimes as late as 1 a.m.

At day's end, all attractions shut down near the official closing time. Main Street in the Magic Kingdom remains open a half hour to an hour after the rest of the park closes.

OFFICIAL OPENING TIME VS. REAL OPENING

Disney publishes "official" hours. The parks actually open earlier, depending on projected crowds. If the official hours are 9 a.m.– 9 p.m., for example, Main Street in the Magic Kingdom will open at 8 or 8:30 a.m. and the remainder of the park will open at 8:30 or 9 a.m.

If you don't have early-entry privileges, tour a park where early entry *is not* in effect and arrive 50 minutes before official opening during the off-season. In mid-summer arrive 70 minutes before official opening. If you go on a major holiday, arrive one hour and 20 minutes early.

If you're a Disney resort guest and want to take advantage of early entry, arrive at the early-entry park one hour and 40 minutes before it's scheduled to open. Buses, boats, and monorails to the early-entry park start operating about two hours before the general public is admitted.

CARDINAL RULES FOR SUCCESSFUL TOURING

Even the most efficient plan won't allow visitors to tour two or more major theme parks in one day. Allocate at least an entire day to each park (except when the theme parks close at different times, allowing visitors to tour one park until closing and then go to another). If your schedule permits just one day of touring, concentrate on only one theme park.

One-Day Touring

A comprehensive tour of the Magic Kingdom, Animal Kingdom, Epcot, or Disney-MGM in one day requires knowledge of the park, good planning, and plenty of energy and endurance. One-day touring leaves little time for sit-down meals in restaurants, prolonged shopping, or lengthy rests. One-day touring can be fun and rewarding, but allocating two days per park, especially for the Magic Kingdom and Epcot, is always preferable. Successful one-day touring of the major theme parks hinges on *three rules:*

1. Determine in Advance What You Really Want to See

This book describes and evaluates the theme parks. Attractions are rated in stars. Five stars is the best rating.

Because attractions range from midway-type rides to high-tech extravaganzas, we've developed categories for them:

Super Headliners   The best attractions in the theme parks. Mind-boggling in size, scope, and imagination. The cutting edge of attraction technology and design.

Headliners   Full-scale, multimillion-dollar themed adventures and theater presentations. Modern in technology and design, employing a range of special effects.

Major Attractions   Themed adventures on a more modest scale but incorporating the newest technologies. Or, larger-scale attractions of older design.

Minor Attractions   Midway-type rides, small "dark rides" (cars on a track zig-zagging in the dark), small theater presentations, transportation rides, and elaborate walk-through attractions.

Diversions   Passive and interactive exhibits. Includes playgrounds, video arcades, and street theater.

2. Arrive Early! Arrive Early! Arrive Early!

This is the critical key to touring efficiently and avoiding long lines. The earlier a park opens, the greater your advantage, because most vacationers won't wake up early and go to a park before it opens. Take advantage of early-entry privileges if you're eligible.

3. Avoid Bottlenecks

Crowds create time-gobbling bottlenecks. To avoid them: Eat off-hours. Don't shop near closing time when throngs moving toward the exit fill shops en route. Reconsider taking new or slow-loading rides; both have long lines.

TOURING PLANS: WHAT THEY ARE AND HOW THEY WORK

General Overview of the Touring Plans

Our touring plans are step-by-step guides for seeing the maximum with a minimum of time in line. All were tested by our staff and everyday Disney World patrons. When the two groups were compared, visitors touring without the plan *averaged* 3⅔ hours more waiting per day than people using our plan, and they experienced 37% fewer attractions.

Touring plans for the Magic Kingdom begin on page 127; Epcot, page 175; and Disney-MGM, page 239. The Animal Kingdom touring plan starts on page 210. For your convenience, one-day touring plans for Universal Florida appear on pages 261 and 281.

What You Can Realistically Expect from the Touring Plans

There are more attractions at the Magic Kingdom and Epcot than you can see in one day, even if you never wait in line. The one-day touring plans, however, allow you to see as much as possible. Depending on circumstances, you may not complete the plan. For the Magic Kingdom and Epcot, the two-day plans are more comprehensive, efficient, and relaxing. Disney-MGM or the Animal Kingdom can be seen in a day.

Variables That Will Affect the Success of the Touring Plans

Factors affecting the plans' success are how quickly you move between rides; when and how many food and rest room breaks you take; where and how you eat; your ability to navigate the parks; how fast rides are brought to capacity; and the time you arrive for a theater performance. Small groups almost always move faster than large ones, and adults generally move faster than families with young children. Switching off (see page 54) slows families. Plus, some children simply can't meet the "early-to-rise" dictate of the plans.

Tour continuously and expeditiously until around noon. After that hour, breaks and setbacks won't affect the plans significantly.

Finally, if you have young children in your party, be prepared for character encounters. The appearance of a Disney character is usually sufficient to stop a touring plan dead in its tracks. What's more, while some characters continue to stroll the parks, it is becoming more the rule to assemble characters in some specific venue (like the Hall of Fame at Mickey's Toontown Fair) where families must line up for photos and autographs. Meeting characters, posing for photos, and collecting autographs can burn hours of touring time. If your kids are into character autograph collecting, you will need to anticipate these interruptions to the touring plan and negotiate some understanding about when you will follow the plan and when you will collect autographs.

If You Lose the Thread

Anything from a blister to a broken attraction can derail a touring plan. If the plan is interrupted:

1. Skip one step for every 20 minutes you're delayed.
   or

2. Forget the touring plan and organize the remainder of your day using the optimum touring times given in the attraction profiles.

FASTPASS

In 1999 Disney launched a new system for moderating the wait for popular attractions. FASTPASS was originally tried at the Animal Kingdom and then subsequently expanded to cover attractions at the other parks. Here's how it works.

Your handout park map and signage at respective attractions tell you which attractions are included. Attractions operating FASTPASS have a regular line and a FASTPASS line. A sign at the entrance tells you how long the wait is in the regular line. If the wait is acceptable hop in line. If the wait seems too long, insert your park admission pass into a special FASTPASS machine and receive an appointment time (for sometime later in the day) to come back and ride. When you return at the appointed time, you will enter the FASTPASS line and proceed directly to the attraction's preshow or boarding area with no further wait. FASTPASS works well and can save a lot of time standing in line. There is no extra charge to use FASTPASS.

Here's an example of how to use FASTPASS: Let's say you have only one day to tour the Magic Kingdom. You arrive early and ride Space Mountain and experience *Alien Encounter* with only minimal waits. Then, following our touring plan, you head across the park to Splash Mountain and find a substantial line. Because Splash Mountain is designated as a FASTPASS attraction, you can insert your admission pass into the machine and receive an appointment time to come back and ride, thus avoiding a long wait.

Because each park offers six or fewer FASTPASS attractions, you still need to get an early start if you want to see as much as possible in a single day. Plus, there is a limited supply of FASTPASSES available for each attraction. If you don't show up until the middle of the afternoon, you might find that all the FASTPASSES have been distributed. FASTPASS does make it possible to see more with less waiting than ever before. It also allows you to postpone wet rides, like Kali River Rapids at the Animal Kingdom or Splash Mountain at the Magic Kingdom, until the warmer part of the day.

You can obtain a FASTPASS anytime after a park opens, but the FASTPASS Return lines do not begin operating until about an hour after opening. Whatever time you obtain a FASTPASS, you can be assured of a period of time between when you receive your FASTPASS and the period to report back. The interval can be as short as 30 minutes or as long as several hours. The earlier in the day you secure a FASTPASS, the shorter the interval between time of issue and your one-hour return window.

Touring Plans and the Obsessive/Compulsive Reader

We suggest that you follow the touring plans religiously, especially in the mornings, if you're visiting Disney World during busier, more crowded times of year. The consequence of touring spontaneity in peak season is literally hours of otherwise avoidable standing in line. During quieter times, there's no need to be compulsive about the plans.

A Clamor for Customized Touring Plans

We've been asked for itineraries to suit specific groups. We believe they're unnecessary. Our touring plans are flexible; adapt them to your group's preferences. If you don't like scary rides, skip them. If you want to ride Space Mountain three times in a row, go for it. Will the plan be less effective? Sure, but it was created only to help you have fun.

Part Three

Selecting Your Hotel

The Basic Considerations

Whether short-timer or full-vacationer, every Disney World visitor needs a place to stay. The basic question is whether or not to stay in Walt Disney World. Luxury accommodations can be found in and out of the World; budget lodging is another story.

Beyond affordability is convenience. There's no real hardship in staying outside the World and driving (or taking the hotel shuttle, if available) to the theme parks. Meals can be less expensive, and rooming outside leaves you more receptive to other Orlando attractions. Universal Studios, Universal's Islands of Adventure, Kennedy Space Center, Sea World, Gatorland, and Cypress Gardens, among others, are well worth your attention.

If there are young children in your party, review Walt Disney World with Kids (pages 51–59) before choosing your lodging. Similarly, seniors, honeymooners or romantics, and disabled guests should refer to the applicable sections of Special Tips for Special People (pages 60–65) before choosing a hotel.

BENEFITS OF STAYING IN THE WORLD

Walt Disney World resort hotel and campground guests have exclusive privileges. Some are advertising gimmicks; others are real and potentially valuable. Here are the privileges and what they mean:

1. Convenience   The commute is short, and connections by Disney's bus, boat, and monorail are frequent. This is especially advantageous if you stay in a hotel connected by the monorail or by boat. There are, however, dozens of hotels just outside Disney

World that are within five minutes of theme park parking lots.

2. Early Entry at Theme Parks   Guests at Walt Disney World resorts (excluding those at the independent hotels of Disney Village Hotel Plaza) may enter a designated theme park one hour earlier than the general public each day. Disney guests are also offered specials on admission, among them a passport good for the duration of their visit.

Early-entry privileges can be quite valuable during peak season, when the theme parks are mobbed. If you're willing to get up before sunrise and get to the park as early as 6:30 a.m., you'll be rewarded with uncrowded, stress-free touring. Early entry is also handy off-season, when the parks open late and close early.

Disney has also been running a program called E-Ride Night that (for an extra $10) allows resort guests with certain multiday passes to remain in the park two to three hours after official closing time. For more on this program see pages 130–131.

3. Baby-sitting and Childcare Alternatives   Baby-sitting, childcare, and children's programs are offered to Disney resort guests. Each hotel connected by the monorail, as well as several other Disney hotels, offers "clubs" —themed childcare centers where potty-trained children ages 3–12 can stay while parents go out.

Though somewhat expensive, the clubs are highly regarded by children and parents. On the negative side, they're open only in the evening, and not all Disney hotels have them. If you're staying at a Disney hotel without a childcare club, use one of the private, in-room baby-sitting services (pages 58–59). In-room baby-sitting is also available at hotels outside the World.

4. Guaranteed Theme Park Admissions   This is useful on days of unusually heavy attendance. In practice, no guest is ever turned away from a theme park until its parking lot fills. This privilege does not extend to Blizzard Beach, Typhoon Lagoon, or River Country.

5. Children Sharing a Room with Their Parents   There's no extra charge for children under age 18 to stay in a room with their parents. Many hotels outside the World also offer this.

6. Free Parking in Theme Park Lots   This saves about $6 per day.

7. Recreational Privileges   Disney resort guests get preferential treatment for tee times at golf courses.

How to Get Discounts on Lodging at Walt Disney World

There are so many guest rooms in and around Walt Disney World that competition is brisk, and everyone, including Disney, deals to keep them filled. This has led to a more flexible discount policy for Disney World hotels. Here are tips for getting those breaks:

1. Seasonal Savings   You can save $15–50 per night on a Walt Disney World hotel room by scheduling your visit during the slower times of the year. Disney uses so many adjectives (regular, holiday, peak, value, etc.) to describe its seasonal calendar, however, that it's hard to keep up without a scorecard. To confuse matters more, the dates for each "season" vary from resort to resort. Our advice, if you're set on staying at a Disney resort, is to obtain a copy of the Walt Disney Travel Company's Vacations Brochure, described on page 8.

2. Ask about Specials   When you talk to Disney reservationists, inquire specifically about specials. Ask, "What special rates or discounts are available at Disney hotels during the time of our visit?" One reader saved $440 by asking about discounts "for that room" during her stay.

3. Ocala Disney Information Center   Ocala Disney Information Center off I-75 in Ocala, FL, routinely books Disney hotel rooms at discounts of up to 43%! The discounts are offered as an incentive to walk-in travelers who may not have considered lodging at a Disney property or even going to Disney World. The rooms available vary according to date and season, but you can almost always count on a good deal. You must reserve your room in person at the center, but if you call in advance (phone (352) 854-0770) and say you're on your way, they'll usually tell you what discounts are available. You can also arrange priority seatings for dining. The center is open daily 9 a.m.–6 p.m.

4. Travel Agents   Once ineligible for commissions on Disney bookings, travel agents now are active players and good sources of information on specials.

5. Magic Kingdom Club   Membership in this club is offered as a benefit by employers, credit unions, and organizations and includes a 10–20% discount on Disney lodging and 5% off theme park tickets. Ask your personnel department if the club is offered. Two-year individual memberships in the program are about $50. For information, call (800) 49-DISNEY or write:

> Magic Kingdom Club Gold Card
> P.O. Box 3850
> Anaheim, CA 92803-9832

6. Organizations and Auto Clubs   Disney works with programs with several auto clubs and organizations. Recently, for instance, AAA members were offered a 10–20% discount on Disney hotels.

7. Room Upgrades   Sometimes an upgrade is as good as a discount. If you visit during a slower time, book the least expensive room your discounts will allow. Checking in, ask very politely about being upgraded to a "water-" or "pool-view" room. Often, you'll be accommodated at no additional charge.

8. Extra-Night Discounts   During slower times, book your Disney hotel for half as long as you intend to stay. The hotel often offers extra nights at a discount to get you to stay longer.

WALT DISNEY WORLD LODGING

The Grand Floridian, Polynesian, Contemporary, Wilderness Lodge and Villas, and Shades of Green Resorts are near the Magic Kingdom. The Swan and Dolphin hotels, Yacht and Beach Club Resorts, and Disney's BoardWalk Inn and Villas are near Epcot. The Villas at the Disney Institute are on the far northeast side of Disney World; the All-Star, Coronado Springs, and Animal Kingdom Lodge Resorts occupy a similar position on the far southwest side. Centrally located are the Caribbean Beach, Old Key West, Port Orleans, and Dixie Landings Resorts.

Choosing a Walt Disney World Hotel

Refer to this section if you want to stay in Walt Disney World but don't know which hotel to choose.

1. Cost   Look at your budget, then the price listings in this section. BoardWalk Villas, Wilderness Lodge Villas, Old Key West Resort, and Villas at the Disney Institute offer condo-type lodging with one-, two-, and three-bedroom units complete with kitchens, living rooms, VCRs, and washers and dryers. Prices range from about $295 per night for a one-bedroom townhouse at the Disney Institute to over $1,150 per night for a three-bedroom villa at the

What It Costs to Stay in a Disney Resort Hotel	
Grand Floridian	$329–955
Polynesian Resort	$304–500
Animal Kingdom Lodge	$300–1,150
Swan (Westin)	$295–465
Dolphin (Sheraton)	$295–465
Beach Club Resort	$294–1,175
Yacht Club Resort	$294–500
BoardWalk Inn	$294–530
BoardWalk Villas (studio)	$294–329
Contemporary Resort	$289–430
Old Key West Resort (studio)	$254–289
Wilderness Lodge and Villas	$210–685
Villas at the Disney Institute (bungalow)	$205–275
Coronado Springs Resort	$140–375
Caribbean Beach Resort	$140–180
Dixie Landings Resort	$140–180
Port Orleans Resort	$140–180
All-Star Resorts	$95–105

BoardWalk Villas. Fully equipped house trailers are available at the Fort Wilderness Campground for $180 to $275. A limited number of suites are available at the more expensive Disney resorts, but they don't have kitchens.

Rooms in the seven hotels of Disney Village Hotel Plaza are commodious, but can be more expensive than those at hotels served by the monorail. We find few bargains there, and it's less exciting than being inside the World. Plaza guests don't have early-entry privileges or free parking at the theme parks, but the hotels do operate their own buses to the parks.

Not included in this discussion is Shades of Green. It was leased by the U.S. Department of Defense in 1994 for use by active-duty and retired service personnel. Rates at Shades of Green, one of the nicest Disney World hotels, are based on the guest's rank: the higher the rank, the greater the cost. All rooms, however, go for a fraction of what military personnel would pay at other Disney resorts.

What It Costs to Stay at the Village Hotel Plaza			
Hotel	**How Many Rooms**	**Bus Service**	**Cost per night**
DoubleTree Guest Suites	229	Yes	$200–300
The Hilton	814	Yes	$195–659
Hotel Royal Plaza	396	Yes	$170–210
Wyndham Palace	1,028	Yes	$170–210
Courtyard by Marriott	323	Yes	$160–180
Grosvenor Resort	630	Yes	$135–220
Best Western Resort	325	Yes	$120–140

2. Location   If you use your own car, the location of your Disney hotel isn't especially important unless you plan to spend most of your time at the Magic Kingdom. (In this case, Disney transportation is always more efficient than your car, because it bypasses the Transportation and Ticket Center and deposits you at the theme park entrance.) If you plan to use Disney transportation:

Grand Floridian, Contemporary, and Polynesian are conveniently linked to the Magic Kingdom by monorail.

Contemporary Resort is also a 10- to 15-minute walk from the Magic Kingdom. Contemporary Resort guests reach Epcot by monorail, but must transfer at the Transportation and Ticket Center. Buses connect the resort to Disney-MGM Studios and the Animal Kingdom.

The Polynesian Resort is served by the monorail and is within walking distance of the Transportation and Ticket Center (TTC), where you can catch an express monorail to Epcot. This makes the Polynesian the only Disney resort with direct monorail access to both Epcot and the Magic Kingdom. To minimize your walk to the TTC, reserve a room in the Pago Pago, Moorea, or Oahu buildings.

Most convenient to Epcot and Disney-MGM are the BoardWalk Inn, BoardWalk Villas, Yacht and Beach Club Resorts, and the Swan and Dolphin. Though all are within easy walking distance of Epcot's International Gateway, boat service is also available. Vessels also connect to Disney-MGM. Epcot hotels are best for guests planning to spend most of their time at Epcot and/or Disney-MGM Studios.

If you plan to use Disney transportation to see all four major parks and the swimming parks, book a centrally located resort with good transit connections. Recommended are the Epcot resorts and the Polynesian, Caribbean Beach, Dixie Landings, and Port Orleans Resorts.

Though not centrally located, the All-Star, Coronado Springs, and Animal Kingdom Lodge Resorts have very good bus service to all Walt Disney World destinations and are nearest to the Animal Kingdom. Wilderness Lodge and Villas and Fort Wilderness Campground have the most convoluted transportation.

If you plan to play golf, the Villas at the Disney Institute and the Old Key West Resort are built around courses. Shades of Green, the Armed Forces Recreation Center, is adjacent to a golf course. Near but not on a course are the Grand Floridian, Polynesian, Dixie Landings, and Port Orleans Resorts. For boating and water sports, book the Polynesian, Contemporary, Grand Floridian, or Wilderness Lodge and Villas. The Lodge is also the best choice for hikers, cyclists, and joggers.

3. Room Quality   Most Disney guests don't spend much time in their hotel rooms, though they're among the best-designed and best-appointed anywhere. Plus, they're meticulously maintained. Top of the line are the spacious and luxurious rooms of the Grand Floridian. Bringing up the rear are the small, garish rooms of the All-Star Resorts. But even these are sparkling clean and livable.

Here's how rooms at Disney hotels (along with the Swan and Dolphin, which are Westin and Sheraton hotels, respectively) stack up for quality:

Hotel	Room Quality Rating
1. Grand Floridian Resort	96
2. BoardWalk Villas (studio)	95
3. Old Key West Resort (studio)	94
4. BoardWalk Inn	93
5. Beach Club Resort	92
6. Yacht Club Resort	92
7. Polynesian Resort	90
8. Contemporary Resort	87
9. Coronado Springs Resort	86

Hotel	Room Quality Rating
10. Dolphin (Sheraton)	86
11. Swan (Westin)	86
12. Wilderness Lodge	86
13. Dixie Landings Resort	84
14. Port Orleans Resort	84
15. Villas at the Disney Institute	82
16. Caribbean Beach Resort	76
17. All-Star Resorts	73

The new Animal Kingdom Lodge, a luxury hotel, and the Wilderness Lodge Villas will be rated in the next edition.

Groups and larger families should ask how many persons can be accommodated in a guest room. Groups requiring two or more rooms should consider condos or villas in or out of the World.

The most cost-efficient lodging in Walt Disney World for groups of five or six are the cabins or wilderness homes at Fort Wilderness.

4. Theme All Disney hotels are themed to make you feel you're in a special place or a period of history.

Hotel	Theme
All-Star Resorts	Sports, music, and movies
Animal Kingdom Lodge	African game preserve
Beach Club Resort	New England beach club of the 1870s
BoardWalk Inn	East Coast boardwalk hotel of the early 1900s
BoardWalk Villas	East Coast beach cottage of the early 1900s
Caribbean Beach Resort	Caribbean islands
Contemporary Resort	The future as perceived by past and present generations
Coronado Springs Resort	Northern Mexico and the American Southwest
Dixie Landings Resort	Life on the Mississippi in the antebellum South
Dolphin	Modern Florida resort

Hotel	Theme
Grand Floridian Beach Resort	Turn-of-the-century luxury hotel in Florida
Old Key West Resort	Key West
Polynesian Resort	Hawaiian / South Sea islands
Port Orleans Resort	Turn-of-the-century New Orleans and Mardi Gras
Swan	Modern Florida resort
Villas at the Disney Institute	Combination rustic villas and country-club atmosphere
Wilderness Lodge	National-park grand lodge of the early 1900s in the American Northwest
Yacht Club Resort	New England seashore hotel of the 1880s

5. Dining   Epcot resorts are best for quality and selection in dining. Each is within an easy walk of the others and of the ten ethnic restaurants in World Showcase at Epcot.

The only other place in Disney World where restaurants and hotels are similarly concentrated is Disney Village Hotel Plaza. The Hilton, Courtyard by Marriott, Best Western Grosvenor, and Buena Vista Palace offer dining and are in walking distance of dining at Downtown Disney.

Guests at the Contemporary, Polynesian, and Grand Floridian Resorts can eat there or commute to restaurants in the Magic Kingdom (not recommended) or to restaurants in other monorail-linked hotels. Riding the monorail among hotels (or to the Magic Kingdom) takes about ten minutes each way, not counting the wait for the train.

All other Disney resorts are somewhat isolated. This means you dine at your hotel unless you have a car and can go elsewhere. Or, you can eat in the theme parks or Downtown Disney. Disney transportation works fine for commuting from the hotels to the parks and Downtown Disney, but it's hopelessly time-consuming for moving among hotels not connected by the monorail.

Of the more isolated resorts, the Wilderness Lodge and Villas and Animal Kingdom Lodge serve the best and most varied food. Next is the Villas at the Disney Institute, but food there is expensive. The Coronado Springs, Port Orleans, Dixie Landings, Old Key West, and Caribbean Beach Resorts have full-service restaurants of acceptable quality, food courts, and in-room pizza delivery. None of the isolated resorts offers enough variety for the average person to be happy eating in his/her hotel daily. The All-Star Resorts don't have a full-service restaurant, only three food courts.

6. Amenities and Recreation   All Disney resorts provide elaborate swimming pools, themed shops and stores, restaurants or food courts, bars or lounges, and access to the five Disney golf courses. The more you pay, the more you get.

Seven resorts offer evening childcare: Swan and Dolphin, Grand Floridian, Animal Kingdom Lodge, Yacht and Beach Club, Polynesian, Wilderness Lodge and Villas, and BoardWalk Inn and Villas. All other Disney resorts offer in-room baby-sitting.

7. Nightlife   The boardwalk at BoardWalk Inn and Villas has an upscale dance club, a New Orleans club with dueling pianos and sing-along, a brew pub, and a sports bar. BoardWalk clubs are within easy walking distance of all the Epcot resorts. Some of the Villas at the Disney Institute are within walking distance of Downtown Disney. Other Disney resorts offer only lounges that stay open late.

Camping at Walt Disney World

Disney's Fort Wilderness Campground is a spacious resort for both tent and RV campers. Fully equipped, air-conditioned trailers are also for rent, as are newer prefab log cabins. The cabins are essentially the same size as the trailers, but are newer, more aesthetically appealing, and have an elevated outdoor deck. Fort Wilderness has economy sites, a group camping area, evening entertainment, horseback riding, bike and jogging trails, swimming, and a petting farm. River Country is nearby. Access to the Magic Kingdom is by boat; access to other destinations is by private car or shuttle.

SELECTING AND BOOKING A HOTEL OUTSIDE WALT DISNEY WORLD

There are three primary "out-of-the-World" areas to consider:

1. International Drive   This area, about 15–20 minutes east of Walt Disney World, parallels I-4 on its southern side and offers a wide selection of hotels and restaurants. Accommodations range

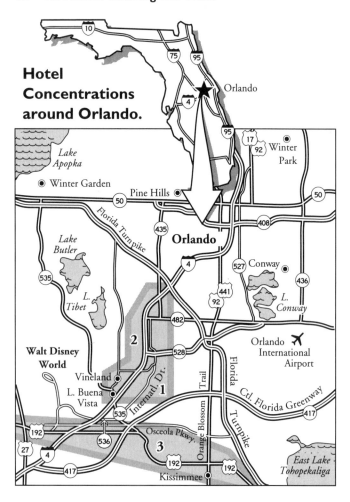

Hotel Concentrations around Orlando.

from $35 to $320 per night. The chief drawbacks of the International Drive area are its terribly congested roads, numerous traffic signals, and inadequate access to westbound I-4. The biggest bottleneck is the intersection of International Drive and Sand Lake Road. In some sections of International Drive, the traffic can be circumvented by using local streets one or two blocks to the southeast.

Stores, restaurants, and entertainment facilities are within walking distance from many International Drive hotels.

Hotels in the International Drive area are listed in the *Orlando Official Accommodations Guide* published by the Orlando/

Orange County Convention and Visitors Bureau. For a copy, call (800) 255-5786 or (407) 363-5872.

2. Lake Buena Vista and the I-4 Corridor   There are a number of hotels along FL 535 and north of I-4 between Walt Disney World and I-4's intersection with the Florida Turnpike. These properties are easily reached from the Interstate and are near numerous restaurants. Driving time from here to Disney World is 5–15 minutes. Most hotels in this area are listed in the *Orlando Official Accommodations Guide*.

3. US 192   This is the highway to Kissimmee, southeast of Walt Disney World. In addition to a number of large, full-service hotels there are many small, independent motels that are a good value. Several dozen properties on US 192 are closer to Disney theme parks than the more expensive hotels in Walt Disney World Village and the Disney Village Hotel Plaza. Traffic on US 192 is extremely heavy, but usually moves smoothly. Though the situation is improving, US 192 is somewhat inferior in the number and quality of restaurants.

Hotels on US 192 and in Kissimmee are listed in the Kissimmee–St. Cloud Visitor's Guide. Call (800) 327-9159 or access the Web at **www.floridakiss.com.**

Driving Time to the Theme Parks for Visitors Lodging outside Walt Disney World

See our chart on page 34 for the approximate commuting time to the major theme parks' parking lots from several off-World lodging areas. Add a few minutes to pay your parking fee and park. Once parked at the Transportation and Ticket Center (Magic Kingdom parking lot), it's an average of 20–30 minutes more to the Magic Kingdom. To get to the main entrance from Epcot's lot, add 7–10 minutes. At Disney-MGM and the Animal Kingdom, expect to spend 5–10 minutes getting from your car to the entrance. If you haven't bought your theme park admission in advance, tack on another 10–20 minutes.

GETTING A GOOD DEAL ON A ROOM OUTSIDE WALT DISNEY WORLD

Hotel development at Walt Disney World has sharpened the competition among lodgings throughout the Disney World/ Orlando/Kissimmee area. Hotels outside the World struggle to

Driving Time to the Theme Parks				
Minutes From	To Magic Kingdom Parking Lot	Epcot Parking Lot	Disney-MGM Studios Parking Lot	Animal Kingdom Parking Lot
Downtown Orlando	35	31	33	37
North International Dr. and Universal Studios	24	21	22	26
Central International Dr.–Sand Lake Road	26	23	24	27
South International Dr. and Sea World	18	15	16	20
FL 535	12	9	10	13
FL 192, north of I-4	10–15	7–12	5–10	5–10
FL 192, south of I-4	10–18	7–15	5–13	5–12

fill their rooms. Unable to compete with Disney on convenience or perks, off-World hotels lure patrons with bargains. The extent of the bargain depends on the season, the day of the week, and area events. Here are tips and strategies for getting a good deal on a room outside Walt Disney World.

1. Orlando MagiCard   Orlando MagiCard is a discount program sponsored by the Orlando/Orange County Convention and Visitors Bureau. Cardholders are eligible for discounts of 20–50% at about 50 participating hotels. The MagiCard is also good for discounts at area attractions. It's free, valid for up to six persons, and available to anyone age 18 or older.

To obtain a MagiCard and a list of participating hotels and attractions, call (800) 255-5786 or (407) 363-5874. It's also available at the CVB at 8723 International Drive in Orlando.

2. Exit Information Guide   EIG (Exit Information Guide) publishes a book of discount coupons for bargain rates at hotels throughout Florida. The book is free in many restaurants and motels along interstate highways leading to Florida. The guide is available in advance of your trip for $3 (credit cards accepted; $5 USD for Canadian delivery) by contacting:

Exit Information Guide
4205 NW 6th Street
Gainesville, FL 32609
(352) 371-3948

3. Wholesalers, Consolidators, and Reservation Services   Whole-salers and consolidators buy rooms, or options on rooms, from hotels at a low rate. They then resell the rooms at a profit through travel agents or tour packagers or directly to the public. When wholesalers and consolidators deal directly with the public, they frequently represent themselves as "reservation services." Here are three that frequently offer substantial discounts:

Accommodations Express	(800) 444-7666
Hotel Discounts	(800) 715-7666 or
	www.hoteldiscounts.com
Hotel Reservations Network	(800) 964-6835

4. Hotel Shopping on the Internet   Hotels are increasingly using the Internet to fill rooms during slow periods and advertise specials. If you enjoy cyber shopping, have at it, but hotel shopping on the Internet is not as quick or convenient as using your travel agent. You'll be hard-pressed to find a deal on the Internet that is not also available through your agent. And often your agent will be able to beat the deal or improve on it. Although a good travel agent working alone can achieve great things, the same agent working with a savvy, helpful client can work wonders.

5. If You Make Your Own Reservation   Always call the specific hotel, not the chain's national 800 number. Reservationists at the 800 number often don't know about local specials. Always ask about specials before you inquire about corporate rates. Don't be reluctant to bargain. If you're buying a hotel's weekend package, for example, and want to stay longer, you can often obtain at least the corporate rate for the extra days. Bargain, however, before you check in.

6. Condominium Deals   A large number of condo resorts, time-shares, and all-suite properties in the Kissimmee/Orlando area rent to vacationers for a week or less. Look for bargains, especially during off-peak periods. Reservations and information can be obtained from:

Condolink	(800) 733-4445
Holiday Villas	(800) 251-1112
Kissimmee–St. Cloud Reservations	(800) 333-5477
Vistana Resort	(800) 877-8787
Ramada Suites by Sea World	(800) 633-1405
Holiday Inn Family Suites	(877) 387-KIDS

Hotels and Motels:
Rated and Ranked

ROOM RATINGS

To evaluate properties according to relative quality, style, state of repair, cleanliness, and size of their *standard rooms,* we have grouped the hotels and motels into classifications denoted by stars. Star ratings in this guide apply to Orlando-area properties only and don't necessarily correspond to ratings awarded by other travel critics. We have tied our ratings to levels of quality established by specific American hotel corporations.

Star ratings apply to *room quality only* and describe the property's standard accommodations. At most hotels and motels, a "standard" room has either one king or two queen beds. In an all-suite property, the standard accommodation is either a one- or two-room suite. Star ratings are assigned without regard to whether a property has restaurant(s), recreational facilities, entertainment, or other extras.

In addition to stars, we also use a numerical rating system. Our rating scale is 0–100, with 100 as the best possible rating and zero (0) as the worst. Numerical ratings are presented to show the difference we perceive between one property and another.

The location column identifies the area around Walt Disney World where you will find a property. The designation "WDW" means the property is inside Walt Disney World. A "1" means the property is on or near International Drive. Properties on US 192 (a.k.a. Irlo Bronson Memorial Highway, Vine Street, and Space Coast Parkway) are indicated by "3." All others are marked "2" and for the most part are along the I-4 corridor.

Properties on US 192 also carry location designations with their names, such as the Holiday Inn Maingate East. The consensus in Orlando seems to be that the main entrance to Walt Disney World is the broad interstate-type road that runs from US 192. This is called Maingate. Coming from US 27 toward the Maingate area, properties before the Maingate turnoff are called Maingate West; properties after the Maingate turnoff are called Maingate East.

Room Star Ratings		
★★★★★	*Superior Rooms*	Tasteful and luxurious by any standard
★★★★	*Extremely Nice Rooms*	What you would expect at a Hyatt Regency or Marriott
★★★	*Nice Rooms*	Holiday Inn or comparable quality
★★	*Adequate Rooms*	Clean, comfortable, and functional, without frills— like a Motel 6
★	*Super Budget*	

How the Hotels Compare

Cost estimates are based on the hotel's published (rack) rates for standard rooms. Each "$" represents $50. Thus a cost of "$$$" means that a room (or suite) will be about $150 a night.

Here's a hit parade of the nicest rooms in town. It was compiled by checking several rooms randomly at each hotel, but not all. If you arrive and are assigned a room inferior to what you were led to expect, demand to be moved.

How the Hotels Compare					
Hotel	Location	Room Star Rating	Room Quality Rating	Cost ($=$50)	Phone (A/C 407)
WDW Grand Floridian Resort	WDW	★★★★★	96	$$$$$$$–	934-7639
WDW Boardwalk Villas	WDW	★★★★½	95	$$$$$$–	934-7639

		Room	Room		
		Star	Quality	Cost	Phone
Hotel	Location	Rating	Rating	($=$50)	(A/C 407)

How the Hotels Compare *(continued)*

Hotel	Location	Room Star Rating	Room Quality Rating	Cost ($=$50)	Phone (A/C 407)
WDW Old Key West Resort	WDW	★★★★½	94	$$$$$+	934-7639
Shades of Green	WDW	★★★★½	93	na	824-3400
WDW Boardwalk Inn	WDW	★★★★½	93	$$$$$–	934-7639
Marriott Orlando World Center	2	★★★★½	92	$$$+	239-4200
Renaissance Orlando Resort	1	★★★★½	92	$$$+	351-5555
WDW Beach Club Resort	WDW	★★★★½	92	$$$$$–	934-7639
WDW Yacht Club Resort	WDW	★★★★½	92	$$$$$–	934-7639
Peabody Orlando	1	★★★★½	91	$$$$$–	352-4000
Celebration Hotel	WDW	★★★★½	90	$$$$$+	566-6000
Hyatt Regency Grand Cypress	2	★★★★½	90	$$$$	239-1234
WDW Polynesian Resort	WDW	★★★★½	90	$$$$$$+	934-7639
Crowne Plaza Resort	1	★★★★	87	$$$+	239-1222
WDW Contemporary Resort	WDW	★★★★	87	$$$$$–	934-7639
Embassy Suites Orlando Int'l	1	★★★★	86	$$$$–	352-1400
Radisson Twin Towers Hotel	1	★★★★	86	$$$–	(800) 327-2110
WDW Coronado Springs Resort	WDW	★★★★	86	$$$–	934-7639
WDW Dolphin	WDW	★★★★	86	$$$$$–	934-7639
WDW Swan	WDW	★★★★	86	$$$$$–	934-7639

How the Hotels Compare *(continued)*

Hotel	Location	Room Star Rating	Room Quality Rating	Cost ($=$50)	Phone (A/C 407)
WDW Wilderness Lodge	WDW	★★★★	86	$$$$+	934-7639
Embassy Suites Resort	2	★★★★	85	$$$	239-1144
Hotel Royal Plaza (tower rooms)	WDW	★★★★	85	$$$–	828-2828
The Castle Hotel (Doubletree)	1	★★★★	84	$$+	345-1511
Hilton Disney Village	WDW	★★★★	84	$$$$+	827-4000
WDW Dixie Landings Resort	WDW	★★★★	84	$$$–	934-7639
WDW Port Orleans Resort	WDW	★★★★	84	$$$–	934-7639
Embassy Suites Plaza Intl	1	★★★★	83	$$$–	345-8250
Sheraton World Resort	1	★★★★	83	$$$–	352-1100
Sierra Suites Lake Buena Vista	2	★★★★	83	$$$	239-4300
Sierra Suites Pointe Orlando	1	★★★★	83	$$$	903-1500
Sunterra Resorts Cypress Pointe	3	★★★★	83	$$+	532-1000
Clarion Suites Resort World (suites)	3	★★★½	82	$$$	396-8300
Doubletree Guest Suites	WDW	★★★½	82	$$$	934-1000
Holiday Inn Family Suites Resort	1	★★★½	82	$$$–	387-5437
Sheraton Royal Safari	2	★★★½	82	$$$+	(800) 423-3297

		Room Star Rating	Room Quality Rating	Cost ($=$50)	Phone (A/C 407)
Hotel	**Location**				
Sheraton Studio City	1	★★★½	82	$$−	351-2100
Summerfield Suites	1	★★★½	82	$$$$+	352-2400
WDW Villas at the Disney Institute (bungalows)	WDW	★★★½	82	$$$$+	934-7639
Wyndham Palace	WDW	★★★½	82	$$$−	827-2727
Amerisuites Orlando Convention Center	1	★★★½	81	$$$−	370-4720
Buena Vista Suites	3	★★★½	81	$$$$−	239-8588
Clarion Plaza	1	★★★½	81	$$$$+	352-9700
Club Hotel by Doubletree	2	★★★½	81	$$	239-4646
Hawthorne Suites Orlando	1	★★★½	81	$$+	351-6600
Radisson Resort Parkway	3	★★★½	81	$$−	396-7000
Wyndham Orlando	1	★★★½	81	$$+	351-2420
Caribe Royale Resort Suites	3	★★★½	80	$$$+	238-8000
Holiday Inn Sun Spree Resort	2	★★★½	80	$$+	239-4500
Homewood Suites Maingate	3	★★★½	80	$$$−	396-2229
Omni Rosen Hotel	1	★★★½	80	$$$$	354-9840
Radisson Inn Lake Buena Vista	2	★★★½	80	$$$+	239-8400
Residence Inn Orlando	1	★★★½	80	$$$−	345-0117
Summerfield Suites Lake Buena Vista	2	★★★½	80	$$$$	238-0777

How the Hotels Compare (continued)

How the Hotels Compare *(continued)*

Hotel	Location	Room Star Rating	Room Quality Rating	Cost ($=$50)	Phone (A/C 407)
Homewood Suites Intl.	1	★★★½	79	$$	248-2232
WDW Fort Wilderness Resort	WDW	★★★½	79	$$$$–	934-7639
Country Inn & Suites (suites)	2	★★★½	78	$$–	239-1115
Courtyard	1	★★★½	76	$$$–	351-2244
Grosvenor Resort	WDW	★★★½	76	$$+	828-4444
Holiday Inn Hotel & Suites Maingate East (suites)	3	★★★½	76	$$–	396-4488
Radisson Barcelo Inn Intl.	1	★★★½	76	$$+	345-0505
WDW Caribbean Beach Resort	WDW	★★★½	76	$$$–	934-7639
Westgate Towers	3	★★★½	76	$$$$+	396-2500
Courtyard Disney Village	WDW	★★★½	75	$$	828-8888
Courtyard Maingate	3	★★★½	75	$$–	396-4000
Doubletree Orlando Suites & Villas	3	★★★	74	$$$+	397-0555
Holiday Inn Intl. Resort	1	★★★	74	$$$–	351-3500
Holiday Inn Universal Studios	1	★★★	74	$$$–	351-3333
Hyatt Orlando	3	★★★	74	$$$–	396-1234
Quality Suites Intl.	1	★★★	74	$$+	363-0332
RUI Orlando	2	★★★	74	$$$+	239-8500
Doubletree Resort & Conference Center	3	★★★	73	$$$–	396-1400
Holiday Inn Nikki Bird Resort	3	★★★	73	$$	396-7300

How the Hotels Compare *(continued)*

Hotel	Location	Room Star Rating	Room Quality Rating	Cost ($=$50)	Phone (A/C 407)
Quality Suites Maingate East	3	★★★	73	$$$–	396-8040
WDW All-Star Resort	WDW	★★★	73	$$	934-7639
Westgate Lakes	1	★★★	73	$$$$+	352-8051
Country Inn & Suites (rooms)	2	★★★	72	$+	239-1115
Days Suites Maingate East	3	★★★	72	$$$+	396-7900
La Quinta Inn Intl.	1	★★★	72	$$–	351-1660
Holiday Inn Hotel & Suites Maingate East (rooms)	3	★★★	71	$$–	396-4488
Ramada Plaza and Inn Gateway (tower rooms)	3	★★★	71	$$–	396-4400
Best Western Disney Village	WDW	★★★	70	$$+	828-2424
Holiday Inn Express	1	★★★	70	$+	351-4430
Comfort Suites Orlando	1	★★★	69	$$–	351-5050
Travelodge Suites Eastgate	3	★★★	69	$+	396-7666
Hampton Inn Universal Studios	1	★★★	68	$$–	351-6716
Hotel Royal Plaza	WDW	★★★	68	$$+	828-2828
Best Western Lake Cecile	3	★★★	67	$$–	396-2056
Clarion Universal	1	★★★	67	$$	351-5009
Courtyard	2	★★★	67	$$$+	239-6900
Enclave Suites	1	★★★	67	$$$	351-1155

How the Hotels Compare *(continued)*

Hotel	Location	Room Star Rating	Room Quality Rating	Cost ($=$50)	Phone (A/C 407)
Ramada Resort Florida Center	1	★★★	67	$$	351-4600
Sheraton Four Points Hotel by Lakeside	3	★★★	67	$$	396-2222
Wellesley Inn	1	★★★	67	$$$–	345-0026
Country Hearth Inn	1	★★★	66	$$$–	352-0008
Hampton Inn Maingate	3	★★★	66	$$–	396-8484
Hampton Inn Sandlake	1	★★★	66	$$–	363-7886
Red Roof Inn Kissimmee	3	★★★	66	$	396-0065
Holiday Inn Maingate West	3	★★★	65	$+	396-1100
Howard Johnson Plaza Resort	1	★★★	65	$$–	351-2000
Days Inn Eastgate	3	★★½	64	$$–	396-7700
Days Inn Maingate East	3	★★½	64	$$	396-7900
Delta Orlando Resort	1	★★½	64	$$$–	351-3340
Hampton Inn Intl.	1	★★½	64	$$–	345-1112
Howard Johnson Maingate West	3	★★½	64	$+	396-9300
Las Palmas Hotel	1	★★½	64	$+	351-3900
Quality Inn Lake Cecile	3	★★½	64	$+	396-4455
Howard Johnson Resort Hotel	3	★★½	63	$+	396-4343

How the Hotels Compare *(continued)*

Hotel	Location	Room Star Rating	Room Quality Rating	Cost ($=$50)	Phone (A/C 407)
Howard Johnson South Intl. Drive	1	★★½	63	$$	351-5100
MIC Lakefront Inn	1	★★½	63	$+	345-5340
Best Inn	1	★★½	62	$$−	351-4410
Best Western Plaza Intl.	1	★★½	62	$+	345-8195
Days Inn	3	★★½	62	$	(800) 544-5713
Days Inn Lake Buena Vista	2	★★½	62	$$$+	239-4441
Howard Johnson Express Inn and Suites (suites)	3	★★½	62	$$−	396-4762
Quality Inn Plaza	1	★★½	62	$+	345-8585
Ramada Inn Westgate	3	★★½	62	$$−	(941) 424-2621
Ramada Resort Maingate	3	★★½	62	$$−	396-4466
Days Inn Maingate West	3	★★½	61	$+	396-1000
Days Inn Universal Studios	1	★★½	61	$+	351-3800
Fairfield Inn Intl.	1	★★½	61	$+	363-1944
Best Inn Maingate	3	★★½	60	$+	396-7500
Clarion Suites Resort World (rooms)	3	★★½	60	$$$	396-8300
Comfort Inn at Lake Buena Vista	2	★★½	60	$$−	239-7300
Days Inn Orlando Lakeside	1	★★½	60	$+	351-1900
Days Inn Sea World/ Convention Center	1	★★½	60	$$+	352-8700

How the Hotels Compare *(continued)*

Hotel	Location	Room Star Rating	Room Quality Rating	Cost ($=$50)	Phone (A/C 407)
Diplomat Resort	3	★★½	60	$$	396-6000
Ramada Eastgate Fountain Park	3	★★½	60	$$+	396-1111
Travelodge Intl.	1	★★½	60	$+	(800) 327-0750
Travelodge Maingate East	3	★★½	60	$$–	396-4222
Best Western Maingate	3	★★½	59	$+	396-0100
Econo Lodge Maingate Hawaiian	3	★★½	59	$$–	396-2000
Howard Johnson Express Inn and Suites (rooms)	3	★★½	59	$+	396-4762
Magic Castle	3	★★½	59	$	396-2212
Quality Inn Intl.	1	★★½	59	$–	351-1600
Ramada Plaza and Inn Gateway (garden rooms)	3	★★½	59	$$–	396-4400
Wynfield Inn Westwood	1	★★½	59	$$–	(800) 346-1551
Days Inn Intl.	1	★★½	58	$$+	351-1200
Quality Inn Maingate West	3	★★½	58	$+	396-1828
Ramada Limited Universal Maingate	1	★★½	58	$+	354-3996
Red Roof Inn Orlando	1	★★½	58	$$–	352-1507
Super 8 Maingate	3	★★½	58	$+	396-8883
Best Western Eastgate	3	★★½	57	$$–	396-0707

		How the Hotels Compare *(continued)*			
Hotel	Location	Room Star Rating	Room Quality Rating	Cost ($=$50)	Phone (A/C 407)
Howard Johnson Inn Maingate East	3	★★½	57	$$	396-1748
Motel 6 Maingate East	3	★★½	57	$–	396-6333
Kissimmee Super 8	3	★★½	56	$	396-1144
Masters Inn Maingate	3	★★½	56	$+	396-7743
Riande Continental Plaza	1	★★½	56	$	352-8211
Super 8 Universal	1	★★½	56	$+	352-8383
Travelodge Suites	3	★★½	56	$$–	396-1780
Knights Inn Maingate	3	★★	55	$	396-4200
Larson's Inn Maingate	3	★★	55	$$–	396-6100
Masters Inn	3	★★	55	$$–	396-4020
Rodeway Inn Intl.	1	★★	55	$+	351-4444
Golden Link Motel	3	★★	54	$–	396-0555
Howard Johnson Lodge	1	★★	54	$+	351-2900
Wynfield Inn Maingate	3	★★	54	$$	(800) 346-1551
Park Inn Intl.	3	★★	53	$+	396-1376
Knights Inn Maingate East	3	★★	52	$–	396-8186
Motel 6 Maingate West	3	★★	52	$–	396-6427
Sleep Inn Maingate	3	★★	52	$+	396-1600
Traveler's Inn	3	★★	52	$+	396-1668
Universal Inn	1	★★	52	$$–	351-4100

How the Hotels Compare *(continued)*

Hotel	Location	Room Star Rating	Room Quality Rating	Cost ($=$50)	Phone (A/C 407)
Central Motel	3	★★	51	$–	396-2333
Motel 6 Intl.	1	★★	49	$	351-6500
Monte Carlo	3	★★	48	$–	396-4700
Red Carpet Inn East	3	★★	47	$–	396-1133
Sun Motel	3	★½	46	$–	396-2673

THE TOP 30 BEST DEALS

Now let's take a look at the best combinations of quality and value in a room. As before, rankings are made without consideration of location or availability of restaurant(s), recreational facilities, entertainment, and/or amenities. Each lodging is awarded a value rating on a 0–100 scale. The higher the rating, the better the value.

Value ratings aim to give you some sense of value received for dollars spent. A ★★½ room at $50 may have the same value rating as a ★★★★ room at $105, but that doesn't mean the rooms will be of comparable quality. Regardless of whether it's a good deal, a ★★½ room is still a ★★½ room.

Note the scarcity of Disney hotels on the best-deal list. This is because our ratings focus exclusively on the quality of the guest room, not on the amenities associated with Disney hotels. If you factor in these extras, the rates charged at Disney hotels appear to be a fair value for the money.

Listed below are the best room buys for the money, regardless of location or star classification, based on averaged rack rates. Note that a suite sometimes can cost less than a hotel room.

The Top 30 Best Deals					
Hotel	Location	Room Star Rating	Room Quality Rating	Cost ($=$50)	Phone (A/C 407)
1. Red Roof Inn Kissimmee	3	★★★	66	$	396-0065
2. Quality Inn Intl.	1	★★½	59	$–	351-1600
3. Radisson Resort Parkway	3	★★★½	81	$$–	396-7000
4. Country Inn & Suites (suites)	2	★★★½	78	$$–	239-1115
5. Motel 6 Maingate East	3	★★½	57	$–	396-6333
6. Sheraton Studio City	1	★★★½	82	$$–	351-2100
7. Travelodge Suites Eastgate	3	★★★	69	$+	396-7666
8. Country Inn & Suites (rooms)	2	★★★	72	$+	239-1115

The Top 30 Best Deals *(continued)*

Hotel	Location	Room Star Rating	Room Quality Rating	Cost ($=$50)	Phone (A/C 407)
9. Days Inn	3	★★½	62	$	(800)544-5713
10. Courtyard Maingate	3	★★★½	75	$$–	396-4000
11. Magic Castle	3	★★½	59	$	396-2212
12. Central Motel	3	★★	51	$–	396-2333
13. Sunterra Resorts Cypress Pointe	3	★★★★	83	$$+	532-1000
14. Doubletree Club	2	★★★½	81	$$	239-4646
15. Golden Link Motel	3	★★	54	$–	396-0555
16. The Castle Hotel (Doubletree)	1	★★★★	84	$$+	345-1511
17. Holiday Inn Express	1	★★★	70	$+	351-4430
18. Riande Continental Plaza	1	★★½	56	$	352-8211
19. Kissimmee Super 8	3	★★½	56	$	396-1144
20. Homewood Suites Intl.	1	★★★½	79	$$	248-2232
21. La Quinta Inn Intl.	1	★★★	72	$$–	351-1660
22. Best Inn Maingate	3	★★½	60	$+	396-7500
23. Holiday Inn Hotel & Suites Maingate East (rooms)	3	★★★	71	$$–	396-4488
24. Howard Johnson Express Inn and Suites (rooms)	3	★★½	59	$+	396-4762
25. MIC Lakefront Inn	1	★★½	63	$+	345-5340
26. Radisson Twin Towers	1	★★★★	86	$$$	(800)327-2110
27. Motel 6 Maingate West	3	★★	52	$–	396-6427

		Room Star Rating	Room Quality Rating	Cost ($=$50)	Phone (A/C 407)
Hotel	**Location**				
28. Courtyard Disney Village	WDW	★★★½	75	$$	828-8888
29. Marriott Orlando World Center	2	★★★★½	92	$$$+	239-4200
30. Renaissance Orlando Resort	1	★★★★½	92	$$$+	351-5555

The Top 30 Best Deals (continued)

Part Four

Walt Disney World with Kids

Considerations and Situations

Children and parents brighten at the prospect of visiting Disney World. But it's a big trip for both, and lack of planning may steal the magic from Walt's magic kingdoms. Here are some important considerations:

Age Disney entertainment is generally oriented to older children and adults. Kids need to be a fairly mature seven years old to *appreciate* the Magic Kingdom and the Animal Kingdom, and a year or two older to get much out of Epcot or Disney-MGM.

Time of Year to Visit Avoid the hot, crowded summer months, especially with preschoolers. Try to go in October, November (except Thanksgiving), early December, January, February, or May. If your school-age children are good students, take them out of school so you can visit during the off-season. Arrange study assignments relating to the educational aspects of Disney World. *Nothing* will enhance your Walt Disney World vacation as much as avoiding summer and holidays.

Building Naps and Rest into Your Itinerary Disney World is huge. Don't try to see everything in one day. At any season, tour in the early morning and return to your hotel around 11:30 a.m. for lunch, a swim, and a nap. Return to the park in late afternoon or early evening.

Where to Stay If you can afford to stay in Walt Disney World, do it and save time and hassle in commuting. In or out of the World, it's imperative that your young children have a midday rest break.

Your hotel should be within a 20-minute one-way commute

of the theme parks. If you're traveling with children ages 12 and younger, we recommend the Polynesian, Grand Floridian, or Wilderness Lodge Resorts (in that order) if they fit your budget. Less expensive are Dixie Landings, Port Orleans, or Caribbean Beach Resorts. Bargain accommodations are available at the All-Star Resorts. Trailers and prefab log cabins at Fort Wilderness Campground are also an economic option.

Least Common Denominators   Somebody in your group will run out of steam first, and the whole family will be affected. Pushing the tired or discontented beyond their capacity will spoil the day for them—and you.

Setting Limits and Making Plans   Avoid arguments and disappointment by establishing guidelines for each day, and get everybody committed in advance.

Be Flexible   Any day at Walt Disney World includes surprises; be prepared to adjust.

Overheating, Sunburn, and Dehydration   These are young children's most common problems at Disney World. Carry sunscreen, and use it generously, even on children in canopied strollers. Avoid overheating by taking periodic breaks in the shade or in an air-conditioned restaurant or show. Sodas and fountains aren't enough. Carry plastic water bottles, and push fluids.

Blisters   Wear comfortable, well-broken-in shoes and two pairs of thin socks (preferable to one pair of thick socks). Preschoolers may not know blisters are forming. Inspect their feet at least twice a day. Precut Moleskin bandages to use; they won't sweat off. Before a blister forms, air out the hot spot and protect it with Moleskin.

First Aid   Each theme park has a First Aid Center.

Things You Forgot or Things You Ran Out Of   Rain gear, diapers, diaper pins, formula, film, aspirin, topical sunburn treatments, and other sundries are sold at all the major theme and swimming parks. Rain gear is cheap; most other items aren't.

Caring for Infants at the Theme Parks   Centralized facilities for infant and toddler care provide everything necessary for changing diapers, preparing formula, and warming bottles. Food and baby supplies are sold. The Magic Kingdom's Baby Center is next to the Crystal Palace at the end of Main Street. At Epcot, Baby Services is near the Odyssey Center, to the right of the World of Motion in Future World. At Disney-MGM, Baby Care is in Guest Relations, left of the entrance. At the Animal Kingdom, Baby Changing/Nursing is in Safari Village.

Strollers   Bring your own or rent one for a modest daily fee at any major theme park. Disney has replaced the ancient blue clunkers at Epcot and the Magic Kingdom with brand new strollers. Obtain one for any child age six and younger that fits. If you rent a stroller at the Magic Kingdom and later go to Epcot or Disney-MGM, return your Magic Kingdom stroller and present your receipt at the next park. You'll be issued another stroller without additional charge. If you return to your hotel for a break, leave your stroller near an attraction by the park's entrance and reclaim it when you return.

Only collapsible strollers are permitted on Disney monorails and buses. When you enter a show or ride, you'll have to park your stroller, usually in an open, unprotected area. It's unlikely to be stolen, but it may be moved by Disney cast members "tidying up." Tie a scarf or ribbon on it for easy identification.

Rent a stroller to the right of the entrance at the Magic Kingdom, on the left side of the Entrance Plaza at Epcot, and at Oscar's Super Service just inside the entrance of Disney-MGM Studios. Stroller rentals at the Animal Kingdom are just inside the entrance and to the right.

DISNEY, KIDS, AND SCARY STUFF

Disney rides and shows are adventures. Though all of the endings are happy, the adventures may intimidate or frighten young children. Monsters and special effects at Disney-MGM are more real and sinister than those at other theme parks. Think twice about exposing a preschooler to machine-gun battles, earthquakes, and the creature from *Alien*.

Preschoolers should start with Dumbo and work up to the Jungle Cruise in late morning. Skip Pirates of the Caribbean.

See the Appendix, "Small Child Fright-Potential Chart," on page 296 for a quick reference to scary rides in each of the parks.

Waiting Line Strategy

Switching Off (The Baby Swap)   Since several attractions may frighten young children or have minimum height and/or age requirements, some couples bypass these, while others take turns riding. Skipping some of Disney's best rides or waiting twice in line is unnecessary.

Solve the problem with "switching off" (The Baby Swap). To switch off, there must be at least two adults. Everybody waits in line together. When you reach a Disney attendant, say you want to switch off. The greeter will allow everyone, including the children, to enter. When you reach the loading area, one adult will ride while the other stays with the kids. Upon completion of the ride, the riding adult disembarks and takes over the children while the other adult rides.

Attractions Where Switching Off Is Common	
Magic Kingdom	
Tomorrowland	Space Mountain
	Alien Encounter
Frontierland	Splash Mountain
	Big Thunder Mountain Railroad
Epcot	
Future World	Body Wars
	Test Track
Disney-MGM Studios	Star Tours
	The Twilight Zone Tower of Terror
	Rock 'n' Roller Coaster
Animal Kingdom	
DinoLand U.S.A.	Dinosaur
Asia	Kali River Rapids

Attractions That Eat Even Adults

Several attractions at Walt Disney World cause motion sickness or other problems for older children and adults. We refer to them as attractions that eat adults.

Attractions That Eat Adults	
Magic Kingdom	
Tomorrowland	Space Mountain
	Alien Encounter
Fantasyland	Mad Tea Party
Frontierland	Big Thunder Mountain Railroad
	Splash Mountain
Epcot	
Future World	Body Wars
	Test Track
Disney-MGM Studios	Star Tours
	The Twilight Zone Tower of Terror
	Rock 'n' Roller Coaster
Animal Kingdom	
DinoLand U.S.A.	Dinosaur
Asia	Kali River Rapids

THE DISNEY CHARACTERS

The large and friendly costumed versions of Mickey, Minnie, Donald, Goofy, and others—known as "Disney characters"—link Disney animated films and the theme parks. About 250 have been brought to life and mix with patrons or perform in shows or parades in the major theme parks and hotels.

Prepare your child to meet the characters. Almost all are quite large, and several are huge. All can intimidate a preschooler. Don't thrust your children at the characters; let them approach gradually. You may need to make the first contact to show your children that the characters are harmless.

Some costumes offer poor visibility, and children approaching on a character's blind side may not be seen or may be stepped on or bowled over. Children should approach from the front, and parents should stay with them, stepping back only to take photos.

If you want to *meet* the characters, get autographs, and take photos, consult the *Disney Character Greeting Location Guide* found in each park handout map.

At the Magic Kingdom, characters are encountered more frequently than anywhere else in Walt Disney World. There's almost always one next to City Hall on Main Street and usually one or more in Town Square or around the railroad station. If it's rainy, check the veranda of Tony's Restaurant or the Town Square Exposition Hall next to Tony's. Characters appear in all the "lands" but are more apt to be in Fantasyland and Mickey's Toontown Fair. At Toontown Fair, meet Mickey privately in his "Judge's Tent." Characters work shifts at the Toontown Hall of Fame next to Mickey's House. Line up to meet a selection of Mickey's Pals, Toon Pals, or Famous Friends (Goofy, Chip 'n' Dale, Pluto, Minnie, Donald), 100 Acre Wood Friends (mostly Winnie the Pooh characters), Villains (Captain Hook, Cruella DeVille), or Princesses (Sleeping Beauty, Snow White, Belle, Mary Poppins). Each group has its greeting area and (of course) line.

In Fantasyland, Cinderella greets diners at Cinderella's Royal Table in the Castle (priority seating required) and Ariel holds court in her own grotto. Nearby, check out the Fanatasyland Character Festival by the lagoon opposite Dumbo. Also, look for characters in the Central Hub and by Splash Mountain in Frontierland.

Characters arc featured in the afternoon and evening parades and play a major role in Castle Forecourt shows (entrance to the Castle on the moat side) and at the Galaxy Palace Theater in Tomorrowland.

At Epcot, in keeping with the park's theme, Goofy roams Future World in a metallic cape reminiscent of Buck Rogers, and Mickey, in a Ben Franklin costume, greets guests in front of the American Adventure.

Don't expect to encounter either the number or variety of characters at Epcot that you would in the Magic Kingdom, but your kids generally can interact more with them at Epcot. Two of Epcot's original characters, Dreamfinder and Figment, stay around the Imagination Institute pavilion in Future World, and assorted characters appear at the Showcase Plaza each morning. Characters also occasionally visit the American Adventure pavilion and the United Kingdom in World Showcase. Character shows are performed daily at the American Gardens Theater in World Showcase.

At Disney-MGM Studios, characters most frequently are in front of the Animation Building, along Mickey Avenue (leading to the soundstages), and at the end of New York Street on the backlot. Mickey and "his friends" pose for keepsake photos (about $10) on Hollywood and Sunset boulevards. Characters are also prominent in shows, with *Voyage of the Little Mermaid* running almost continuously, and an abbreviated version of *Beauty and the Beast* performed several times daily at the Theater of the Stars.

At the Animal Kingdom, a small land called Camp Minnie-Mickey is the gathering place for Disney characters. There are designated character greeting "trails" where you can meet Mickey, Minnie, and various characters from the *Jungle Book* and *The Lion King.* Also at Camp Minnie-Mickey are two stage shows featuring characters from *The Lion King* and from *Pocahontas.*

Each theme park has information about characters on its handout map. The map lists where and when characters will be available and provides information on character dining.

BABY-SITTING

Childcare Centers   Childcare isn't available inside the theme parks, but each hotel connected by the monorail and Epcot resorts (BoardWalk Inn and Villas, Yacht and Beach Club Resorts) offers childcare for potty-trained children older than age three. Generally, children can be left between 4 p.m. and midnight. Snacks, blankets, and pillows are provided. Play is supervised but not organized, and toys, videos, and games are plentiful. Guests at any Disney resort or campground may use the service.

The most elaborate childcare "club" or "camp" is the Neverland Club at the Polynesian Resort. This and one at Wilderness Lodge and Villas include a buffet dinner. At other locations, you can arrange for room service to deliver your children's meals. At Camp Dolphin in the Dolphin hotel, children may eat at the Coral Cafe or the Soda Shop next door.

Readers invariably praise the Neverland Club. Cost is $8 per child, with a three-hour minimum. Call (407) WDW-DINE.

If you aren't staying at a Disney resort offering a childcare club, and you *do not* have a car, use in-room baby-sitting.

Kinder-Care Learning Centers also operate childcare facilities at Walt Disney World. Originally developed for use by Disney

Childcare Clubs *			
Hotel	Name of Program	Ages	Phone
Wyndham Palace	All About Kids	All	(407) 812-9300
BoardWalk Inn & Villas	Harbor Club	4–12	(407) 939-6301
Contemporary Resort	Mouseketeer Clubhouse	4–12	(407) 824-3038
Grand Floridian Beach Resort	Mouseketeer Club	4–12	(407) 824-2985
The Hilton	Vacation Station	4–12	(407) 827-3820
Polynesian Resort	Neverland Club	4–12	(407) 824-2000 ext. 2184
Wilderness Lodge	Cub's Den	4–12	(407) 824-1083
Yacht and Beach Clubs	Sandcastle Club	4–12	(407) 934-3750

* Clubs operate afternoons and evenings. Reservations required.

employees, Kinder-Care also accepts guests' children on a space-available basis. Kinder-Care provides services similar to hotels' clubs, except that their daytime *Learning While Playing Development Program* is more structured and educational. Children ages one (provided they're walking and can eat table food) through 12 are eligible. Open Monday–Friday, 6 a.m.–9 p.m. and Saturday and Sunday, 6 a.m.–6 p.m. For reservations call (407) 827-5437 or (407) 824-3290.

In-Room Baby-sitting   In-room baby-sitting is available through Kinder-Care (phone (407) 827-5444), the Fairy Godmother service, or All About Kids.

Fairy Godmother is on call 24 hours a day and provides the area's most flexible and diversified service. Godmothers will come to any hotel at any hour, and they'll take your children to the theme parks. There's no age limit for the Godmothers, who also tend the elderly. All sitters are female nonsmokers. Cost is $10 an hour for up to three children in the same family ($2 more for each additional child in the same family), with a four-hour minimum and a $10 travel fee. Godmothers will sit a group of children from different families for $7 an hour per family. For reservations call (407) 277-3724 or (407) 275-7326.

All About Kids (phone (407) 812-9300) offers in-room service to all Buena Vista–area hotels. Sitters range in age from college students to grandparents and are licensed, bonded, and insured. Base rates are $10 an hour (add $1 an hour for each additional child), with a four-hour minimum and a $6 travel fee. For jobs that start after 9 p.m., add $2 an hour. They will even take your child to the theme parks if you pay the sitter's admission.

Part Five

Special Tips
for Special People

Walt Disney World for Couples

So many couples marry or honeymoon at Walt Disney World that a department has been formed to meet their needs. *Disney's Fairy Tale Weddings & Honeymoons* offers a range of wedding venues and services, as well as honeymoon packages. They're all expensive. Contact:

Disney's Fairy Tale Weddings & Honeymoons
P.O. Box 10000
Lake Buena Vista, FL 32830-0020
(800) 370-6009
www.disneyworld.com

Romantic Getaways

Walt Disney World is a favorite getaway for honeymooners and other couples. But not all Disney hotels are equally romantic. We recommend these Disney lodgings for romantics:

1. Animal Kingdom Lodge
2. Polynesian Resort
3. Wilderness Lodge
4. Grand Floridian Beach Resort
5. BoardWalk Inn & Villas
6. Yacht and Beach Club Resorts

Romantic Dining

Quiet, romantic restaurants with good food are rare in the theme parks. Only the Coral Reef, the terrace at the Rose & Crown, and the San Angel Inn at Epcot satisfy both requirements. Portobello Yacht Club and Fulton's Crab House at Pleasure Island offer waterfront dining, as do Narcoossee's at the Grand Floridian and Cap'n Jack's Oyster Bar in Downtown Disney Marketplace. The California Grill atop the Contemporary Resort offers the best view at Walt Disney World. If window tables are unavailable, ask to be served in the adjoining lounge. Victoria & Albert's is the World's showcase gourmet restaurant, but it's expensive. Other romantic choices include Shula's Steak House and Kimonos at the Swan and Dolphin Resorts, 'Ohana at the Polynesian Resort, and Spoodles and the Flying Fish Cafe at the BoardWalk.

Eat later in the evening and choose among the restaurants listed, but always expect to encounter children—well-behaved or otherwise.

Romantic Stuff to Do

1. *Lounges.* There's a nice but pricey lounge atop the Contemporary Resort that's great for watching sunsets or evening fireworks. If you want just the view, access an outside promenade through the glass doors at the end of the lounge. Another wonderful getaway with a view is Mizner's Lounge on the Alcazar level of the Grand Floridian. Each evening, a dance band plays '20s and '30s music on the adjacent landing.

2. *The Floating Electrical Pageant.* One of Disney's most romantic entertainments, the parade of spectacularly lighted barges starts after dark. Watch from the pier or beach at the Polynesian Resort, or from the Wilderness Lodge, the Grand Floridian, or Fort Wilderness.

3. *Take a boat ride.* Small launches shuttle guests to and from the Grand Floridian, Polynesian, Magic Kingdom, Wilderness Lodge, and Fort Wilderness Campground well into the night. Disney launches also cruise the canal connecting Disney-MGM and Epcot.

   During daytime at the Fort Wilderness dock, rent boats for exploring Bay Lake and the Seven Seas Lagoon. The adjacent campground is honeycombed with footpaths for lovely walks in early morning or evening.

   If you enjoy hiking and boating, visit Juniper Springs

Recreation Area in the Ocala National Forest. About an hour and a half north of Disney World, the forest is extraordinarily beautiful. For information, call (352) 625-2808.

4. *Picnic* during temperate months on the beaches of Bay Lake and the Seven Seas Lagoon or at Fort Wilderness Campground. Room service at resorts can prepare your lunch. Drinks, including wine and beer, are less expensive in hotel convenience shops.

5. *Dine and dance on the BoardWalk,* which offers nice restaurants and an upscale dance club.

6. *Rent bikes* at Wilderness Lodge and explore Fort Wilderness Campground. Maps are available at the rental shed.

Walt Disney World for Singles

Safe, clean, and low-pressure, Disney World is great for singles. They can relax and only rarely be hit on. Fewer single men vacation in Disney World than single women, making romance unlikely. And, most singles at Disney World are employed there.

Between Disney's BoardWalk and Downtown Disney, nightlife options abound. Parking lots everywhere in the World are well lighted and patrolled.

Walt Disney World for Seniors

Most seniors enjoy Disney World much more when they tour with folks their own age. Personal tastes rule; there are no attractions we categorically advise against. But there are some considerations seniors should weigh before they go.

Magic Kingdom

Space Mountain   This roller coaster in the dark vibrates a lot. Put your glasses in your fanny pack. (We can't guarantee they'll stay in your pocket.)

Big Thunder Mountain Railroad   Although sedate compared with Space Mountain, this ride is very jarring, especially the side-to-side shaking.

Splash Mountain   This ride combines Disney whimsy with the thrill of a log flume. There's one big drop near the end and a bit of a splash.

The Swiss Family Treehouse   This isn't a thrill ride, but it involves lots of stair climbing and an unsteady pontoon bridge.

Mad Tea Party   An adaptation of a carnival ride: big teacups spin until you're nauseous.

Epcot

Body Wars   This ride jolts more than Star Tours at Disney-MGM and is more apt to cause motion sickness than the Mad Hatter's teacups.

Test Track   This newest thrill ride in Future World simulates test-driving a race car. Both fast and bumpy, Test Track whizzes around hairpin turns, over rough road, down straightaways, and up and down steep inclines.

Disney-MGM Studios

Star Tours   If you're prone to motion sickness, this flight simulation will affect you.

Tower of Terror   Although most thrills are visual, the Tower features a gut-wrenching simulation of an elevator in free fall.

Rock 'n' Roller Coaster   This is arguably Disney's wildest coaster. If you thought Space Mountain was rough, stay away from this one.

Animal Kingdom

Dinosaur   The show consists primarily of visual effects, but the ride is pretty jerky.

Kali River Rapids   This ride simulates a whitewater raft trip. It's not all that rough, but it's very wet.

Getting Around

A seven-hour visit to one of the theme parks normally includes four to eight miles on foot. If you aren't up for that much walking, let an athletic member of your party push you in a rented wheelchair.

The theme parks also offer electric carts. Your rental receipt is good for a replacement wheelchair in any park during the same day.

Lodging

If you can afford it, stay in Walt Disney World. The rooms are some of the area's nicest, always clean and well maintained. And transportation is always available, at no extra cost, to any destination in Disney World.

Disney hotels assign rooms closer to restaurants and transportation to guests of any age who can't tolerate much walking. They will also transport guests to and from their rooms in golf carts.

Seniors intending to spend more time at Epcot and Disney-MGM than at the Magic Kingdom should consider the Yacht and Beach Club Resorts, the Swan, the Dolphin, or the BoardWalk Inn.

The Contemporary Resort is excellent for seniors who want to be on the monorail system, as are the Grand Floridian and Polynesian Resorts. The latter two, however, occupy many acres and may entail considerable walking. For a restful, rustic feeling, choose the Wilderness Lodge. If you want a kitchen and the comforts of home, book the Old Key West Resort or BoardWalk Villas. For those who enjoy watching birds and animals, try the Animal Kingdom Lodge.

RVers will like Fort Wilderness Campground. Also, within 20 minutes of Disney World are several KOA campgrounds. None offer the wilderness setting or amenities that Disney does, but they cost less.

Something Extra

We think at least one behind-the-scenes tour should be part of every senior's visit. Most are at Epcot and offer in-depth looks at Disney World operations. Especially worthwhile are Hidden Treasures and Gardens of the World. If you don't have time for these lengthy tours, join the shorter Greenhouse Tour at The Land pavilion, also in Epcot. Backstage Magic visits behind-the-scenes locations at several theme parks, while Keys to the Kingdom reveals the history and hidden operations of the Magic Kingdom.

Ranging in duration from one to seven hours and in price from $5 to $160 per person, all tours require a lot of walking and standing.

Walt Disney World for Disabled Guests

Wholly or Partially Nonambulatory Guests may rent wheelchairs. Most rides, shows, attractions, rest rooms, and restaurants accommodate the nonambulatory disabled. For specific inquiries or problems, call (407) 939-7807 (voice) or (407) 939-7670 (TDD). If you're in a park and need assistance, go to Guest Relations.

Close parking for the disabled is available at all Disney World lots. Request directions when you pay.

An information booklet for disabled guests is available at all wheelchair rental locations. Theme park maps distributed free to each guest pinpoint wheelchair-accessible attractions.

Even if an attraction doesn't accommodate wheelchairs, nonambulatory guests may still ride if they can transfer from their wheelchair to the ride's vehicle. Disney staff members aren't trained or permitted to assist in these transfers.

Because most queuing areas won't accommodate wheelchairs, nonambulatory guests and their parties should request boarding instructions from an attendant as soon as they arrive at an attraction. The group usually gets priority entry.

Visitors with Dietary Restrictions   Visitors on special or restricted diets, including those requiring kosher meals, can be assisted at Guest Relations in the parks.

Sight- and/or Hearing-Impaired Guests   Complimentary cassettes and portable tape players are available at Guest Relations for sight-impaired guests. A $25 refundable deposit is required. TDD telephones for the hearing-impaired are at Guest Relations in the theme parks. Braille guide maps are also available from Guest Relations at all theme parks. To reserve an interpreter for live theater shows call (407) 824-4321 or (407) 939-8255.

Part Six

Arriving and Getting Around

Getting There

DIRECTIONS

Motorists can reach any Walt Disney World destination via World Drive, off US 192, or via Epcot Drive, off I-4 (see map, pages 4–5).

From I-10   Take I-10 east across Florida to I-75 southbound. Exit I-75 onto the Florida Turnpike. Exit at Clermont and take US 27 south. Turn onto US 192 and follow the signs to Disney World.

From I-75 southbound   Follow I-75 south to the Florida Turnpike. Exit at Clermont and take US 27 south. Turn onto US 192. Follow the signs.

From I-95 southbound   Follow I-95 south to I-4. Go west on I-4, passing through Orlando. Take Exit 26 (Epcot/Disney Village) and follow the signs.

From Daytona or Orlando   Go west on I-4 through Orlando. Take Exit 26 (Epcot/Disney Village) and follow the signs.

From the Orlando International Airport   Go southwest on the Central Florida Greenway toll road (FL 417). Keep left at the intersection with FL 536. FL 536 crosses over I-4 and becomes Epcot Drive. From there, follow the signs. An alternate route is to take FL 528 (Beeline Highway toll road) west from the airport for about 12 miles to the intersection with I-4. Go west on I-4 to Exit 26 (Epcot/Disney Village) and follow the signs.

From Miami, Fort Lauderdale, and southeastern Florida   Go north on the Florida Turnpike to I-4 westbound. Take Exit 26 (Epcot/Disney Village) and follow the signs.

From Tampa and southwestern Florida   Take I-75 northbound to I-4. Go east on I-4. Take Exit 25 onto US 192 westbound. Follow the signs.

   The entrance to Walt Disney World Village is separate from entrances to the theme parks. To reach it, take the FL 535 exit off I-4. Go north. Follow the signs.

GETTING TO WALT DISNEY WORLD
FROM THE AIRPORT

There are three basic options for getting to Walt Disney World from the airport:

Taxi   Taxis carry four to eight passengers. Rates vary according to distance. If your hotel is in Walt Disney World, your fare will be about $32, not including tip. For the US 192 area, your fare will be about $40. If you're going to International Drive or downtown Orlando, expect to pay about $27.

Shuttle Service   Mears Motor Transportation Service (phone (407) 423-5566) and Transtar (phone (407) 856-7777) operate from Orlando International Airport. Mears and Transtar charge the same *per-person* rates (children under age 4 ride free). Both one-way and round-trip services are available.

From the Airport to:	One-Way	Round Trip
International Drive	$13	$23
DowntownOrlando (Mears Only)	$13	$23
Walt Disney World/ Lake Buena Vista	$15	$27
US 192 "Main Gate" Area	$15	$27

   You may have to wait a while at the airport for a vehicle to fill to capacity. Once underway, it's probable your shuttle will make several stops to disembark other passengers before it reaches your hotel. Transtar has an edge over Mears because they do not use buses. Obviously, it takes less time to fill and unload a van than a bus. On your return to the airport, since shuttle services pick up folks at different hotels, you'll need to be ready for pick-up much earlier than you would if you were taking a cab or returning a rental car.

Rental Car   Rental cars are available for short- and long-term rentals. Most companies allow you to drop a rental car at certain hotels or one of their subsidiary locations in the Walt Disney World area if you do not want the car for your entire stay. Likewise, you can pick up a car at any time during your stay at the same hotels and locations without trekking to the airport.

Dollars and Sense

The number of people in your party and the value you attach to your time will determine which option is the best deal. If you have only one or two in your party and won't need a rental car, the shuttle service is your least expensive bet. A cab for two people will cost about $4 per person more than a shuttle. A one-day car rental will cost $34–70, plus you'll have to trouble yourself with completing paperwork, retrieving the vehicle, and filling the tank before you return the car. If there are more than two of you, a cab will be more economical than the shuttle. Likewise with the rental car.

Getting Oriented

WHERE IN THE WORLD?

The Walt Disney World Property Map is available from Guest Relations at any of the theme parks or Disney hotels.

FINDING YOUR WAY AROUND

To avoid getting lost in sprawling Disney World, think of the complex as five major areas, or clusters:

1. The first encompasses all hotels and theme parks around Seven Seas Lagoon. This includes the Magic Kingdom, hotels connected by monorail, Shades of Green resort, and three golf courses.
2. The second includes developments on and around Bay Lake: Wilderness Lodge, Fort Wilderness Campground, Discovery Island, River Country, and two golf courses.
3. Epcot, Disney-MGM Studios, Disney's BoardWalk, Disney's Wide World of Sports, the Epcot resorts, and the Caribbean Beach Resort make up the third cluster.

4. The fourth encompasses Walt Disney World Village; the Disney Institute; Downtown Disney (including Downtown Disney Marketplace, Pleasure Island, and Disney's West Side); Typhoon Lagoon; another golf course; the Disney Village Hotel Plaza; and the Port Orleans, Dixie Landings, and Old Key West Resorts.

5. The fifth and newest contains the Animal Kingdom; Blizzard Beach; and the All-Star, Coronado Springs, and Animal Kingdom Lodge Resorts.

How to Travel around the World

TRANSPORTATION TRADE-OFFS FOR GUESTS LODGING OUTSIDE WALT DISNEY WORLD

Disney World day-guests not staying in the complex can use the monorail system, most of the bus system, and some of the boat system. Make sure your car is parked in the lot of the theme park (or other Disney destination) where you plan to finish your day. This is critical if you stay at a park until closing.

Driving to the Magic Kingdom

Most Magic Kingdom day-guests park in the Transportation and Ticket Center (TTC) parking lot. Its sections are named for Disney characters. On the reverse of your parking receipt are aisle numbers and section names. Mark where you have parked. You'll probably need this reminder to find your car later.

After parking, walk to a loading station and catch a tram to the TTC, where you can buy theme park admissions. If you want to go to the Magic Kingdom, ride the ferry across Seven Seas Lagoon or catch the monorail. If the monorail line is long, take the ferry. The monorail trip takes about 3½ to 5 minutes. The ferry takes 6½ minutes.

If you drive to another theme park on the same day, show your earlier parking receipt and park free.

Going to Epcot from the Magic Kingdom   In the morning, take the monorail to the TTC and transfer to the Epcot monorail. In the afternoon, take the ferry to the TTC. If you plan to spend the remainder of the day at Epcot and your car is in the TTC lot, drive your car to Epcot. If you plan to return to the Magic Kingdom or don't have a car at the TTC, commute via the Epcot monorail.

Going to Disney-MGM from the Magic Kingdom   Either take a Disney bus or drive. If you plan to conclude your day at the Studios, drive. If you intend to return to the Magic Kingdom, take the bus. The Studios bus loads to the immediate left of the Magic Kingdom exit. You don't have to return to the TTC.

Going to the Animal Kingdom from the Magic Kingdom   Drive or take the bus. If you intend to finish your day at the Animal Kingdom, drive. If you plan to return to the Magic Kingdom, take the bus.

Leaving the Magic Kingdom at Day's End   If you conclude your day at the Magic Kingdom and need to return to the TTC, first try the ferry. If it's mobbed, take either the "express" or "local" (stops at hotels) monorail, whichever has the shortest line.

Driving to Epcot

Park in the Epcot lot unless you plan to conclude your day at the Magic Kingdom. Sections are named for pavilions in the park's Future World area. Access to Epcot is direct from the tram.

Going to the Magic Kingdom from Epcot   Take the monorail to the TTC and transfer to the Magic Kingdom express monorail. If you don't plan to return to Epcot and have a car in the Epcot lot, drive to the TTC and take the ferry or monorail.

Going to Disney-MGM Studios from Epcot   If you plan to finish the day at the Studios, drive. If you plan to return to Epcot, leave the park through the main entrance and take the bus to the Studios. Or leave through the International Gateway in World Showcase and catch a boat at the nearby Yacht and Beach Club Resorts. The latter option is best if you're returning to Epcot for dinner at a World Showcase restaurant.

Going to the Animal Kingdom from Epcot   Drive or take the bus. If you plan to return to Epcot, take the bus. If you intend to finish your day at the Animal Kingdom, drive.

At all Disney parks, if you leave and intend to return to that park or visit another on the same day, have your hand stamped for free re-entry.

Driving to Disney-MGM

Going to the Magic Kingdom from Disney-MGM Regardless of where you intend to conclude the day, it's easier to take the bus to the Magic Kingdom. Because the bus unloads at the park's entrance instead of the TTC, you avoid reparking, taking the tram to the TTC, and catching the monorail or ferry. It's the same when you return to the Studios.

Going to Epcot from Disney-MGM Drive to the Epcot parking lot if you don't intend to return to the Studios. If you plan to return, take a bus or boat to Epcot. Take the bus if you want to start at Epcot's main entrance, the boat if you're headed for World Showcase.

Going to the Animal Kingdom from Disney-MGM Drive or take the bus. If you plan to return to the Studios, take the bus. If you intend to end your day at the Animal Kingdom, drive.

Driving to the Animal Kingdom

The new park is accessed only by road and has its own pay parking lot. Drive your car unless you intend to return to the Animal Kingdom from the Magic Kingdom. If returning, use the bus.

Taking a Shuttle from Your Out-of-the-World Hotel

Many lodgings near Disney World provide trams and buses. They save parking fees and drop you near theme park entrances, but they may not get you there as early as you want or be available when you want to return. Also, most don't add vehicles at peak hours (you might have to stand), and some stop at other hotels before arriving at Disney World. Check particulars at your hotel.

If you're depending on hotel shuttles, leave the park at least 45 minutes before closing. If you stay until closing and are tired, hail a cab at stands near the Bus Information buildings at the Animal Kingdom, Epcot, Disney-MGM Studios, and the TTC. If cabs aren't available, the staff at Bus Information will call one. If you're at the Magic Kingdom at closing, take the monorail to a resort and get a cab there.

TRANSPORTATION TRADE-OFFS FOR GUESTS AT WALT DISNEY WORLD RESORTS AND CAMPGROUND

The Walt Disney World transportation system is large, diversified, and generally efficient, but it can be overwhelmed during peak traffic, especially at park opening and closing times, and it's difficult to figure out how bus, boat, and monorail systems interconnect.

If a resort offers boat or monorail service, its bus service will be limited. This means you'll have to transfer at the TTC for many Disney World destinations. If you're staying at a Magic Kingdom resort served by monorail (Polynesian, Contemporary, Grand Floridian), you'll commute efficiently to the Magic Kingdom by monorail. If you want to visit Epcot, however, you must take the monorail to the TTC and transfer to the Epcot monorail. (Guests at the Polynesian can eliminate the transfer by walking about ten minutes to the TTC and catching the direct monorail to Epcot.)

If you're staying at an Epcot resort, walk or commute by boat to the International Gateway at Epcot. Although direct buses link Epcot resorts to the Magic Kingdom and the Animal Kingdom, there's no direct bus service to Epcot's main entrance or to Disney-MGM Studios. To reach the Studios from the Epcot resorts, take a boat.

Caribbean Beach, Dixie Landings, Wilderness Lodge and Villas, Port Orleans, Coronado Springs, Old Key West, Animal Kingdom Lodge, and All-Star Resorts, plus the Villas at the Disney Institute, offer direct buses to all theme parks. The rub is that guests sometimes must walk a long way to catch a bus that makes numerous stops en route to the parks. Morning riders may have to stand. Evening riders may be put on indirect routes that add many minutes to the commute.

Since Disney Village Hotel Plaza terminated its contract with Disney Transportation Operations and hired another carrier, shuttle service has become a problem for guests. Before booking a Plaza hotel, check the nature and frequency of its shuttle.

Walt Disney World Bus Service

Buses in the Disney World system have illuminated panels above the front windshield that flash the bus's destination. At theme parks, waiting areas are labeled by destination. At resorts, go to any bus stop and wait for the bus with your destination displayed.

Service from the resorts to the theme parks is fairly direct. You may have intermediate stops, but you won't have to transfer. Service to the water parks and other Disney hotels may require transfers.

Buses to parks run about every 20 minutes, beginning about 7 a.m. on days when the parks' opening is 9 a.m. Buses to Disney-MGM Studios or Epcot go to the park entrance. Until one hour before the park opens, buses to the Magic Kingdom deliver early riders to the TTC, where they must transfer. Buses go directly to the park on early-entry mornings.

If you're commuting to an early-entry theme park, count on its opening to eligible guests an hour to an hour and a half before the official time. Buses to the early-entry park begin running about two hours before opening.

For your return bus in the evening, leave the park 40 minutes to one hour before closing. If you get caught in the exodus, don't worry. Buses, boats, and monorails operate for two hours after the parks close.

Note: Avoid using Downtown Disney as a transfer point. Since each bus makes three stops within the Downtown Disney complex, it takes 16–25 minutes just to get out of Downtown Disney!

Walt Disney World Monorail Service

Picture the monorail system as three loops. Loop A is an express route running counterclockwise that connects the Magic Kingdom with the TTC. Loop B runs clockwise alongside Loop A, making all stops, with service to (in this order) the TTC, Polynesian Resort, Grand Floridian Beach Resort, Magic Kingdom, and Contemporary Resort. The long Loop C dips southeast, connecting the TTC with Epcot. The hub for all loops is the TTC, where you usually park when visiting the Magic Kingdom.

Monorail service to Magic Kingdom resorts usually starts two hours before official opening time on early-entry days and an hour and a half before opening on other days. If you're staying at a Magic Kingdom resort and want to be among the first in the Magic Kingdom on a non-early-entry morning when the official opening is 9 a.m., board the monorail at these times:

From Contemporary Resort   7:45–8 a.m.

From Polynesian Resort   7:50–8:05 a.m.

From Grand Floridian   8–8:10 a.m.

On an early-entry morning (when the opening is 9 a.m.), go 45–60 minutes earlier. If the official opening is 8 a.m., bounce everything up another hour.

If you're a day-guest (no early-entry privileges), you'll be allowed on the monorail at the TTC between 8:15 and 8:30 a.m. when the official opening is 9 a.m. If you want to board earlier, take the walkway from the TTC to the Polynesian Resort and board there.

The monorail loop connecting Epcot with the TTC opens at 7:30 a.m. when Epcot's official opening is 9 a.m. To be at Epcot when it opens, catch the Epcot monorail at the TTC no later than 8:05 a.m.

You can't go directly from the Magic Kingdom to Epcot. You must catch the express monorail (Loop A) to the TTC and transfer to Loop C. If lines are short, the trip takes 25–35 minutes. In late afternoon, the wait to board Loop A may be a half hour or more. The total commute then is 45–55 minutes.

Monorails usually run two hours after closing. If the monorail is too crowded or has quit running for the day, catch a bus.

If you want to ride in front with the conductor, ask.

Major Tip!

Using the Disney Transportation System, you can often eliminate a double transfer by commuting to the theme park closest to your destination and transferring there. DTS works from park opening until an hour after park closing.

Part Seven

Bare Necessities

Credit Cards and Money

Credit Cards

MasterCard, VISA, and American Express are accepted for theme park admission and at Disney shops, full-service restaurants, counter-service restaurants, and resorts.

Financial Matters

Cash   Branches of Sun Bank are across the street from Downtown Disney Marketplace and at 1675 Buena Vista Drive. Service at the theme parks is limited to automated teller machines.

A License to Print Money

One of Disney's more sublime ploys for separating you from your money is the printing and issuing of Disney Dollars. Available in denominations of $5 (Goofy Greenbacks), $10 (Minnie Money or Simba Sawbucks), and $20 (Mickey Moolah), the colorful cash can be used for purchases at Disney World, Disneyland, and Disney Stores nationwide. Disney Dollars also can be exchanged dollar-for-dollar for U.S. currency. Disney money is available all over Disney World.

Unspent dollars usually end up in a drawer *at home* which is what Disney accountants hoped would happen.

Problems and Unusual Situations

Attractions Closed for Repairs

Check in advance to learn what attractions may be closed during your visit. Major attractions may be unavailable, but ticket prices will be unchanged.

Car Trouble

Security or tow-truck patrols will help if you lock the keys in your car or return to a dead battery. The nearest auto repair center is Maingate Exxon, US 192 west of I-4 (phone (407) 396-2721). Disney security will help you contact them.

Lost and Found

If you lose or find something in the Magic Kingdom, City Hall handles it. At Epcot, Lost and Found is in the entrance plaza. At Disney-MGM Studios and the Animal Kingdom, it's at Guest Relations. If you discover your loss later, call (407) 824-4245.

Medical Matters

If You Need a Doctor   Main Street Physicians provides 24-hour service. Doctors are available for house-calls to all hotels and camp-grounds (Disney and non-Disney). Cost is $165 per visit. Or you can go (walk-ins only) to the clinic, at 2901 Parkway Boulevard, Suite 3-A, in Kissimmee. Minimum charge is $80. Hours are Monday–Friday 8 a.m.–8 p.m.; Saturday and Sunday 8 a.m.–5 p.m. Call Mediclinic at (407) 396-1195.

Also available is the Centra Care Walk-In Clinic, with two locations on Apopka-Vineland Road. Hours vary, but one location is open until midnight on weekdays; the other is open until 10 p.m. on weekends. They operate a total of four locations in the Disney area. Call (407) 239-7777 for fees and details. For information about 24-hour house-call service, phone (407) 238-2000.

Prescription Medicine   The closest pharmacy is Walgreen's Lake Buena Vista (phone (407) 238-0600). For $5 extra, Turner Drugs (phone (407) 828-8125) will deliver to your hotel. The fee is charged to your hotel account. This service is available to Disney resort guests and guests at nearby non-Disney hotels.

Rain

Weather bad? Go to the parks anyway. Crowds are lighter, and most attractions are covered. Showers, especially during warmer months, are short. Rain gear is a bargain. Ponchos cost about $6; umbrellas, about $12.

Services and Shopping

Cameras and Film

Camera Centers at the parks sell disposable cameras (about $10; $19 with flash). Film is widely available. Developing is provided by most Disney hotel gift shops and the Camera Centers. Outlets displaying the Photo Express sign offer two-hour developing. Only the Express centers at the Magic Kingdom are consistently on time.

Disney Souvenirs

The greatest variety and best deals in Disney souvenirs are at World of Disney, a 50,000-square-foot character superstore at Downtown Disney Marketplace. Less crowded than shops in the theme parks, it's accessible by bus or boat.

There are stuffed toys of Disney characters, Disney books and records, character hats, and items that are hard if not impossible to find outside Disney shops.

T-shirts, the most popular souvenir, are sold areawide. Those in Disney World are expensive ($19–40) but high-quality, 100% cotton. Shirts outside the World ($7–18) are usually of a lower quality, 50/50 cotton and polyester.

The only retailer selling discounted items from Walt Disney World is Character Warehouse (phone (407) 345-5285) in Mall Two of the Belz Factory Outlet World at the north end of International Drive. Prices are good, but selection generally is limited to closeouts.

A good selection of cotton/poly shirts and other character merchandise is available at Bargain World (phone (407) 345-8772) at 6454 International Drive, 8102 International Drive, and 8520 International Drive.

Pet Care

Pets aren't allowed in the major or minor theme parks. But *never* leave an animal in a hot car while you tour; the pet will die. Kennels and holding facilities are provided near the TTC, to the left of the entrance plaza at Epcot and Disney-MGM Studios; at the outer entrance of the Animal Kingdom; and at Fort Wilderness Campground. You must provide escape-proof cages for small pets.

Kennels open one hour before the park and close 30 minutes to one hour after. They're staffed 24 hours a day. Disney resort guests may board a pet for $9 per pet, per night. Other guests are charged $11 per pet, per night. Day care for all is $6. Multiday boarding isn't available. Owners must exercise their pets. For more information on pet care in the World, call the Magic Kingdom Kennel at (407) 824-6568.

Excuse Me, But Where Can I Find ...

Someplace to Put These Packages?   Lockers are on the ground floor of the Main Street railroad station in the Magic Kingdom, to the right of Spaceship Earth in Epcot, to the right of the Disney-MGM Studios entrance at Oscar's Super Service, inside the main entrance to the left at the Animal Kingdom, and on the east and west ends of the TTC.

Package Pick-up is available at all theme parks. Ask the salesperson to send your purchases to Package Pick-up. When you leave the park, they'll be waiting for you. Epcot has two exits and two Package Pick-ups—specify which you want.

A Mixed Drink or Beer?   Alcoholic beverages aren't sold in the Magic Kingdom, but they're available at other Disney theme parks and resorts.

A Grocery Store?   Gooding's Supermarket in Crossroads Shopping Center is a large, designer grocery. If you want gourmet foods or a good wine selection, it's your best bet. If you just want staples, try Publix Supermarket on the corner of FL 535 and US 192. There are also supermarkets on US 192, north of Walt Disney World's "main gate."

Sunscreen?   This and other sundries are sold in the Emporium on Main Street in the Magic Kingdom, in most shops at Disney-MGM Studios and the Animal Kingdom, and in many shops in Epcot's Future World and World Showcase.

A Smoke?   Cigarettes are sold throughout the theme parks, but smoking is prohibited in all attractions, waiting areas, and shops.

Feminine Hygiene Products?   They're available in women's rest rooms throughout Disney World.

Part Eight

Dining in
Walt Disney World

Exploring Dining Options

Food and beverage offerings are defined by service, price, and convenience.

Full-Service Restaurants   More than five dozen full-service restaurants operate in Disney World, with the quality and variety of food improving every year. Sit-down dining is offered in all Disney resorts (except the All-Star Resorts), all major theme parks, Downtown Disney Marketplace, Pleasure Island, and Disney's West Side. Disney operates the restaurants in the theme parks and in its hotels. Contractors or franchisees operate the restaurants in the hotels of Disney Village Hotel Plaza, the Swan and Dolphin, Pleasure Island, Disney's West Side, and some in Downtown Disney Marketplace. Priority seating is recommended for all full-service restaurants except those in Disney Village Hotel Plaza. Most major credit cards are accepted.

Buffets   Buffets have multiplied in Disney World in recent years. Many feature Disney characters, and most have children's menus. Several restaurants serve an all-you-can-eat, fixed-price, family-style meal (platters of food are brought to your table). Priority seating is required for character buffets and recommended for all other buffets and family-style restaurants. Most major credit cards are accepted.

Counter Service   Counter-service fast food is available in all the theme parks and at Downtown Disney Marketplace, Pleasure Island, Disney's BoardWalk, and Disney's West Side. The food compares in quality with McDonald's, Captain D's, or Taco Bell, but it is often served in larger portions and is more expensive. Most major credit cards are accepted.

Cafeterias and Food Courts   In all the major theme parks, cafeterias offer a middle ground between full-service and counter-service dining. Food courts, with a collection of counter-service eateries under one roof, are in the theme parks and at moderate (Coronado Springs, Caribbean Beach, Dixie Landings, Port Orleans) and budget (All-Star) Disney resorts. Priority seating isn't required. Most major credit cards are accepted.

Vendor Food   Vendors abound at the theme parks, Disney Marketplace, Pleasure Island, Disney's West Side, and Disney's BoardWalk. Offerings include popcorn, ice cream bars, churros (Mexican pastry), soft drinks, bottled water, and fresh fruit. Cash only.

The Cost of Counter-Service Food

To help you develop your dining budget, here are prices of common counter-service items. Sales tax isn't included.

Food	Cost
Barbecue Platter	$8
Brownie	$1.50
Cake or Pie	$2.25–2.50
Cheeseburger	$3.50–6 (double)
Chicken Breast Sandwich (grilled)	$4.55–6.95
Children's Meal	$3.25
Chips	$1.50
Cookies	$1–1.50
Deli Sandwich	$4.95–6.50
Fish Basket (fried)	$5.60
French Fries	$1.55
Fried Chicken Nuggets	$6.25
Fruit (whole piece)	$1
Fruit Cup/Fruit Salad	$2.40–5
Ham & Cheese, Turkey, or Tuna Sub	$4.65–6.50
Hot Dog	$3.10–4.75
Ice Cream Bar	$2–2.60

The Cost of Counter-Service Food (continued)		
Food	**Cost**	
Nachos with Cheese	$4.25	
Pasta Salad	$1.35–5.85	
Pizza (per slice)	$3.50–5.35	
Pizza (individual)	$5.30–6	
Popcorn	$2.15–3	
Salad (entree)	$5.40–6.95	
Salad (side)	$1.95–4	
Smoked Turkey Leg	$4.50	
Soup/Chili	$2–3.25	
Taco	$4.55 for two	
Taco Salad	$5	
Drinks	**Small**	**Large**
Beer	$3.75	$4.25
(not available in the Magic Kingdom)		
Bottled Water	N/A	$2.50
Cappuccino/Espresso	$2.95	N/A
Coffee	$1.25	$1.50
Fruit Juice	$1.50	N/A
Lemonade	$2	N/A
Milk	$1	N/A
Soft Drink (Coke, etc.)	$1.70	$2.25
Tea	$1.25	N/A

WHEN TO EAT

All theme park restaurants are busiest between 11:30 a.m. and
2:15 p.m. for lunch, and 6 –9 p.m. for dinner. For shorter lines
and faster service, avoid eating during these hours.

FAST FOOD PARK BY PARK

Magic Kingdom   The Magic Kingdom is a wonder and a marvel, but for all its beauty, imagination, and wholesomeness, it's
hard to get a good meal. Of the fast-food eateries, Aunt Polly's
Dockside Inn, Columbia Harbour House, El Pirata y el Perico,
The Diamond Horseshoe Saloon Revue, and the Plaza Pavilion are
the better of the lot.

Epcot   We've been reviewing Epcot's food service since the park opened in 1982 and have seen many changes, most of them for the better. The best fast food can be found at Pasta Piazza Ristorante and Pure and Simple in Future World, Kringla Bakeri og Kafé in Norway, Sommerfest in Germany, and Yakitori House in Japan.

Disney-MGM Studios   Dining at Disney-MGM Studios is more interesting than in the Magic Kingdom and less ethnic than at Epcot. We suggest Sunset Market Ranch, ABC Commissary, and Toy Story Pizza Planet.

Animal Kingdom   The best counter-service food is at Flame Tree Barbecue across from the Tree of Life in Safari Village and the rotisserie chicken at Tuskers in Africa at Harambe.

FULL-SERVICE RESTAURANTS AND PRIORITY SEATINGS

They're overpriced, but if you want to eat in full-service restaurants, arrange priority seatings in advance at (407) 939-3463. These aren't firm reservations; they only mean you'll be seated ahead of walk-ins. Book lunch at full-service restaurants; the menus are largely the same as at dinner, but prices are lower.

If you haven't made priority seatings before you leave home:

1. If you're driving, make priority seating arrangements at Ocala Disney Information Center off I-75 in Ocala, Florida.
2. If you're lodging outside Walt Disney World or at a hotel in the Disney Village Hotel Plaza, call 939-3463 for advance priority seating.
3. If you're a Disney resort or campground guest, dial the preprogrammed dining button on your room's phone for same-day priority seating and 56 for advance priority seating. Or call 939-3463.
4. In the theme parks, same-day priority seating can be arranged in the morning at the door of the restaurant. While the restaurants don't begin serving food until 11 a.m., their front desks are staffed as of the park's opening.

At Epcot, arrive at the entrance, admission in hand, 45 minutes before the park opens. On entering, go quickly to the priority-seating service at Guest Relations (to the left of the geosphere).

Lunch and dinner priority seatings can be made at the same time. World Showcase restaurants are popular; be ready with alternatives both for restaurants and seatings.

At Disney-MGM Studios, make priority seatings at Guest Relations left of the main entrance.

At the Animal Kingdom, there is only one full-service restaurant, the Rainforest Cafe. No priority seatings are accepted.

At the Magic Kingdom, restaurants have no central priority seating service. If you want same-day priority seating, go immediately to the restaurant's door after entering the park, or at a public phone dial *88 and then WDW-DINE (toll free).

THE FULL-SERVICE RESTAURANTS OF WALT DISNEY WORLD

Star Rating   The star rating represents the entire dining experience: style, service, ambience, presentation, and quality of food. Five stars is the highest rating and indicates that the restaurant offers the best of everything. Four-star restaurants are above average, and three-star restaurants offer meals that are good, but not necessarily memorable. Two-star restaurants serve mediocre fare, and one-star restaurants are below average.

Cost   We include a main dish with vegetable or side dish and a choice of soup or salad. Appetizers, desserts, drinks, and tips aren't included. Cost is rated inexpensive, moderate, or expensive.

Inexpensive	=	$12 or less per person
Moderate	=	$13–23 per person
Expensive	=	More than $23 per person

Quality Rating   If you want the best food, and cost isn't an issue, look no further than the quality ratings. They're based on a scale of 0 to 100, with 100 as the best and zero (0) as the worst. The rating is based on preparation, presentation, taste, freshness, and creativity of the food served.

Value Rating   If you're looking for both quality and a good deal, check the value rating. They range from A to F, as follows:

A	=	Exceptional value, a real bargain
B	=	Good value
C	=	Fair value, you get exactly what you pay for
D	=	Somewhat overpriced
F	=	Extremely overpriced

Walt Disney World Restaurants by Cuisine

Type of Restaurant	Location	Overall Rating	Price	Quality Rating	Value Rating
American					
California Grill	Contemporary	★★★★½	Exp	96	C+
Artist Point	Wilderness Lodge	★★★½	Mod	87	C
Planet Hollywood	Pleasure Island	★★★½	Mod	86	C
The Hollywood Brown Derby	Disney-MGM	★★★	Exp	84	C
Kona Cafe	Polynesian	★★★	Mod	84	B
Seasons Dining Room	Disney Institute	★★★	Mod	84	C
Wild Horse Saloon	Pleasure Island	★★★	Mod	84	C
Olivia's Cafe	Old Key West	★★★	Mod	81	C
Yacht Club Galley	Yacht Club	★★★	Mod	81	C
House of Blues	West Side	★★★	Mod	80	C
Wolfgang Puck Cafe	West Side	★★★	Exp	78	C
The Garden Grill Restaurant	Epcot	★★½	Mod	79	C
Whispering Canyon Cafe	Wilderness Lodge	★★½	Mod	79	B
Hollywood & Vine	Disney-MGM	★★½	Inexp	74	C
Liberty Tree Tavern	Magic Kingdom	★★½	Mod	74	C
Boatwright's Dining Hall	Dixie Landings	★★½	Mod	73	D
Cinderella's Royal Table	Magic Kingdom	★★½	Mod	73	D
Rainforest Cafe	Marketplace/ Animal Kingdom	★★½	Mod	73	D
ESPN Club	BoardWalk	★★	Mod	73	C
Baskervilles	Grosvenor Resort	★★	Mod	71	C
Big River Grille & Brewing Works	BoardWalk	★★	Mod	71	D

Walt Disney World Restaurants by Cuisine *(continued)*

Type of Restaurant	Location	Overall Rating	Price	Quality Rating	Value Rating
American (continued)					
50's Prime Time Cafe	Disney-MGM	★★	Mod	69	D
Grand Floridian Cafe	Grand Floridian	★★	Mod	68	D
Pleasure Island Jazz Company	Pleasure Island	★★	Mod	68	C
Coral Cafe	Dolphin	★★	Mod	67	D
Gulliver's Grill at Garden Grove	Swan	★★	Exp	67	D
Sci-fi Dine-In Theater Restaurant	Disney-MGM	★★	Mod	67	D
Buffet					
Cape May Cafe	Beach Club	★★★½	Mod	89	B
Restaurant Akershus	Epcot	★★★½	Mod	89	B
Crystal Palace	Magic Kingdom	★★½	Mod	79	C
1900 Park Fair	Grand Floridian	★★½	Mod	79	C
Biergarten	Epcot	★★½	Mod	75	C
Hollywood & Vine	Disney-MGM	★★½	Inexp	74	C
Chef Mickey's	Contemporary	★★	Mod	67	C
Trail's End	Fort Wilderness	★★	Mod	66	C
Chinese					
Nine Dragons Restaurant	Epcot	★★½	Exp	74	F
Cuban					
Bongos Cuban Cafe	West Side	★★	Mod	74	D

Walt Disney World Restaurants by Cuisine *(continued)*

Type of Restaurant	Location	Overall Rating	Price	Quality Rating	Value Rating
English					
Rose & Crown Dining Room	Epcot	★★★	Mod	81	C
French					
Chefs de France	Epcot	★★★★	Mod	90	C
Bistro de Paris	Epcot	★★★	Exp	81	D
German					
Biergarten	Epcot	★★½	Mod	75	C
Gourmet					
Victoria & Albert's	Grand Floridian	★★★★½	Exp	96	D
Arthur's 27	Wyndham Palace	★★★★	Exp	87	C
Italian					
Portobello Yacht Club	Pleasure Island	★★★½	Exp	88	D
Palio	Swan	★★★	Exp	81	C
Tony's Town Square Restaurant	Magic Kingdom	★★½	Mod	78	D
L'Originale Alfredo di Roma Ristorante	Epcot	★★½	Exp	74	D
Mama Melrose's Ristorante Italiano	Disney-MGM	★★½	Exp	74	D
Japanese					
Kimonos	Swan	★★★★	Mod	90	C
Teppanyaki Dining Room	Epcot	★★★½	Exp	85	C
Tempura Kiku	Epcot	★★★	Mod	83	C
Benihana—The Japanese Steakhouse	Hilton	★★½	Mod	75	C

Walt Disney World Restaurants by Cuisine *(continued)*

Type of Restaurant	Location	Overall Rating	Price	Quality Rating	Value Rating
Mediterranean					
Citricos	Grand Floridian	★★★★	Exp	91	C
Spoodles	BoardWalk	★★★½	Mod	87	C
Mexican					
San Angel Inn Restaurante	Epcot	★★★	Exp	84	D
Juan & Only's Bar and Jail	Dolphin	★★★	Mod	80	B
Maya Grill	Coronado	★★	Exp	66	D
Moroccan					
Restaurant Marrakesh	Epcot	★★★	Mod	81	C
Norwegian					
Restaurant Akershus	Epcot	★★★½	Mod	89	B
Polynesian					
'Ohana	Polynesian	★★★	Mod	79	C
Seafood					
Flying Fish Cafe	BoardWalk	★★★★	Exp	94	C
Narcoossee's	Grand Floridian	★★★½	Exp	88	D
Artist Point	Wilderness Lodge	★★★½	Mod	87	C
Cap'n Jack's Oyster Bar	Village Marketplace	★★★	Mod	84	D
Bonfamille's Cafe	Port Orleans	★★★	Mod	80	C
Coral Reef	Epcot	★★½	Exp	79	D
Fulton's Crab House	Pleasure Island	★★½	Exp	79	D
Captain's Tavern	Caribbean Beach	★★	Mod	67	C
Finn's Grill	Hilton	★	Mod	55	D
Steak					
Shula's Steak House	Dolphin	★★★½	Exp	86	C–

Walt Disney World Restaurants by Cuisine (continued)

Type of Restaurant	Location	Overall Rating	Price	Quality Rating	Value Rating
Yachtsman Steakhouse	Yacht Club	★★★	Exp	80	D
Concourse Steakhouse	Contemporary	★★½	Mod	72	D
Le Cellier Steakhouse	Epcot	★★	Mod	67	C
The Outback	Wyndham Palace	★★	Exp	67	D

Part Nine

The Magic Kingdom

EARLY ENTRY

The Magic Kingdom/Transportation and Ticket Center parking lot opens about two hours before the park's official opening. After paying a fee and parking, guests are transported to the TTC by tram. From there, they take a monorail or ferry to the park's entrance.

Guests at the Contemporary, Polynesian, or Grand Floridian Resorts can commute directly to the Magic Kingdom by monorail (for guests at the Contemporary, it's quicker to walk). From Wilderness Lodge or Fort Wilderness Campground, access is by boat. Guests of other Disney resorts can reach the park by bus. All Disney guests, regardless of how they arrive, are taken directly to the park entrance, bypassing the commute from the TTC.

On specified days each week, the Magic Kingdom opens an hour early to Disney World hotel and campground guests (excluding those at Disney Village Hotel Plaza). If you aren't a Disney resort guest, avoid the Magic Kingdom on those days. Crowds balloon with resort guests exercising early-entry privileges, and congestion is nearly unmanageable by 10 a.m., especially during summer or holiday periods.

If you're a Disney resort guest, arrive at the park for early entry one hour and 40 minutes before official opening time via Disney transportation. Do not drive your own car. When you're admitted, you'll be allowed into all Fantasyland attractions except *Legend of the Lion King* and all Tomorrowland attractions except *The Timekeeper* and *Carousel of Progress*. Sometimes Space Mountain opens a half hour behind the other Tomorrowland attractions.

Early-entry guests should be aboard a bus to the park two hours before official opening. Take advantage of early entry, then leave the midmorning crowding and go to another park for the remainder of the day.

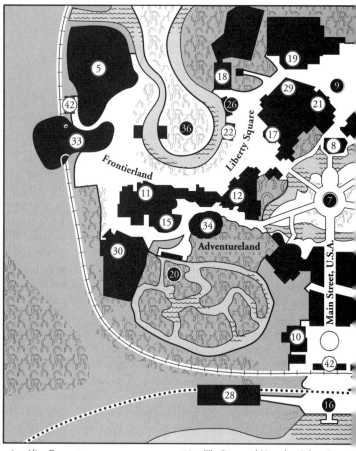

1. *Alien Encounter*
2. Ariel's Grotto
3. Astro Orbiter
4. Barnstormer
5. Big Thunder Mountain Railroad
6. Buzz Lightyear's Space Ranger Spin
7. Central hub
8. Cinderella Castle
9. Cinderella's Golden Carrousel
10. City Hall
11. *Country Bear Jamboree*

12. *The Diamond Horseshoe Saloon Revue*
13. Donald's Boat
14. Dumbo the Flying Elephant
15. *Enchanted Tiki Birds*
16. Ferry dock
17. *The Hall of Presidents*
18. The Haunted Mansion
19. It's a Small World
20. Jungle Cruise
21. *Legend of the Lion King*
22. *Liberty Belle* Riverboat
23. Mad Tea Party

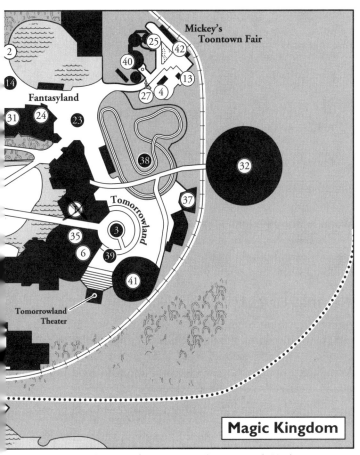

Magic Kingdom

Not to Be Missed at the Magic Kingdom	
Adventureland	Pirates of the Caribbean
Frontierland	Big Thunder Mountain Railroad
	Splash Mountain
Liberty Square	The Haunted Mansion
Tomorrowland	Space Mountain
	The Timekeeper
Special Events	Evening Parade

The early-entry schedule changes often. Call Walt Disney World Information (phone (407) 824-4321) in advance to verify which days will be early entry during your stay. Guests seeking early entry must show their identification card (issued upon check-in) when they present their admission pass.

GETTING ORIENTED

At the Magic Kingdom, stroller and wheelchair rentals are to the right of the train station; lockers (cleaned out nightly) are on the ground floor of the station. City Hall, on your left as you enter Main Street, serves as the center for information, lost and found, guided tours, and entertainment schedules.

A guidemap to the park is available at City Hall. It lists all attractions, shops, and eating places; pinpoints first aid, baby care, and assistance for the handicapped; and gives photography tips. It also lists times for special events, live entertainment, other activities that day, and when and where to find Disney characters.

Main Street ends at a central hub, from which branch the entrances to five other sections of the Magic Kingdom: Adventureland, Frontierland, Liberty Square, Fantasyland, and Tomorrowland. Mickey's Toontown Fair is wedged between Fantasyland and Tomorrowland and doesn't connect to the central hub.

STARTING THE TOUR

Be open-minded and adventuresome about Magic Kingdom attractions. Don't dismiss one until *after* you have tried it.

Take advantage of what Disney does best: the fantasy adventures of Splash Mountain and The Haunted Mansion, and the

audio-animatronic (talking robots) attractio
Hall of Presidents and Pirates of the Caribbea

Don't burn daylight shopping unless you pla..
imum of two and a half days at the Magic Kingdom, a...
then wait until midday or later. Limit your time on carnival-type
rides; you probably have something similar near your hometown.
(Don't, however, mistake Space Mountain and Big Thunder
Mountain Railroad for amusement park rides. They may be roller
coasters, but they're pure Disney genius.) Eat a good breakfast
early and avoid lines at eateries. Snack on vendor foods during
the day.

FASTPASS AT THE MAGIC KINGDOM

The Magic Kingdom offers five FASTPASS attractions, the most
in any Disney park. Strategies for using FASTPASS at the Magic
Kingdom have been integrated into our touring plans(see p. 20
for details). The Magic Kingdom FASTPASS attractions are:

Tomorrowland	Space Mountain
	Buzz Lightyear's Space Ranger Spin
Adventureland	Jungle Cruise
Frontierland	Splash Mountain
Fantasyland	Winnie the Pooh

Main Street, U.S.A.

Begin and end your Magic Kingdom visit on Main Street, which
opens a half hour before and closes a half hour to an hour after
the rest of the park. The Walt Disney World Railroad stops at the
Main Street Station; board here for a grand tour of the park or a
ride to Frontierland or Mickey's Toontown Fair.

Main Street is a sanitized version of a turn-of-the-century,
small-town American street. Its buildings are real. All interiors,
furnishings, and fixtures are true to the period. Along the street
are shops and eateries, City Hall, and a fire station. Horse-drawn
trolleys, double-decker buses, fire engines, and horseless carriages
transport visitors along Main Street to the central hub.

The following attraction ratings are based on a scale of zero to
five stars. Five stars is the best rating.

Main Street Services	
Most park services are centered on Main Street, including:	
Wheelchair & Stroller Rental	Right of the main entrance before passing under the railroad station
Banking Services	ATMs are underneath the Main Street railroad station
Storage Lockers	Ground floor of the railroad station at the end of Main Street; all lockers are cleaned out each night
Lost & Found	City Hall at the railroad station end of Main Street
Live Entertainment and Parade Info	City Hall at the railroad station end of Main Street
Lost Persons	City Hall
Local Attraction Information	City Hall
First Aid	Next to The Crystal Palace, left around the central hub (toward Adventureland)
Baby Center/ Baby-Care Needs	Next to The Crystal Palace, left around the central hub (toward Adventureland)

Walt Disney World Railroad

What It Is: Scenic railroad ride around theme park's perimeter; also transportation to Frontierland and Mickey's Toontown Fair

Scope & Scale: Minor attraction

When to Go: Anytime

Special Comments: Main Street is usually the least congested station

Author's Rating: Plenty to see; ★★½
Appeal by Age Group:

Pre-school	Grade School	Teens	Young Adults	Over 30	Senior Citizens
★★★★	★★★	★★	★★½	★★★	★★★

Duration of Ride: About 19 minutes for a complete circuit
Avg. Wait in Line per 100 People ahead of You: 8 minutes
Assumes: 2 or more trains operating
Loading Speed: Fast

Description and Comments A transportation ride blending sights and experiences with an energy-saving way to get around the park. The train provides glimpses of all lands except Adventureland.

Touring Tips Save the train until after you have seen the featured attractions or need transportation. On busy days, lines form at the Frontierland Station, but rarely at Main Street and Mickey's Toontown Fair Stations. Strollers aren't allowed on the train, but you can obtain a replacement stroller at your destination. Just take your personal belongings, stroller name card, and rental receipt with you on the train. Wheelchair access is only available at Frontierland and Mickey's Toontown Fair stations.

Main Street Eateries and Shops

Description and Comments This is the place to find some of the Magic Kingdom's better food and specialty/souvenir shopping in a nostalgic, happy setting. The Emporium offers the park's best selection of Disney souvenirs.

Touring Tips If seeing the attractions is your goal, save Main Street until day's end. If you want to shop, avoid noon, parade times, and closing time, when stores are most crowded.

The Crystal Palace, at the central hub end of Main Street, has a character buffet often overlooked by lunch (but not dinner) crowds.

Adventureland

Adventureland is the first land to the left of Main Street. It combines African safari and New Orleans/Caribbean themes.

Swiss Family Treehouse

What It Is: Outdoor walk-through treehouse
Scope & Scale: Minor attraction
When to Go: Before 11:30 a.m. and after 5 p.m.
Special Comments: Requires climbing a lot of stairs
Author's Rating: A visual delight; ★★★
Appeal by Age Group:

Pre-school	Grade School	Teens	Young Adults	Over 30	Senior Citizens
★★★	★★★½	★★★	★★★	★★★	★★★

Duration of Tour: 10–15 minutes
Avg. Wait in Line per 100 People ahead of You: 7 minutes
Assumes: Normal staffing

Description and Comments   An immense replica of the ship-wrecked family's treehouse home will delight your children. It's the king of all treehouses.

Touring Tips   A self-guided tour involves many stairs but no ropes or ladders. Tourists who stop for extra-long looks or to rest may create bottlenecks. Visit in late afternoon or early evening if you're on a one-day tour schedule, or in the morning of your second day.

Jungle Cruise (FASTPASS)

What It Is: Outdoor safari-themed boat-ride adventure
Scope & Scale: Major attraction
When to Go: Before 10 a.m. or two hours before closing
Author's Rating: An enduring Disney masterpiece; ★★★
Appeal by Age Group:

Pre-school	Grade School	Teens	Young Adults	Over 30	Senior Citizens
★★★½	★★★½	★★½	★★★	★★★	★★★

Duration of Ride: 8–9 minutes
Avg. Wait in Line per 100 People ahead of You: 3½ minutes
Assumes: 10 boats operating
Loading Speed: Moderate

Description and Comments   An outdoor cruise through jungle waterways. Passengers encounter animatronic elephants, lions, hostile natives, and a menacing hippo. Boatman's spiel adds to the fun. The ride's technology is now dated and worn.

Touring Tips Among the park's oldest attractions and one that occupies a good third of Adventureland. A convoluted queuing area makes it very difficult to estimate the length of wait for the Jungle Cruise. It's usually longer than it looks. Fortunately, the Jungle Cruise is a FASTPASS attraction (see page 20). Pick up your FASTPASS *before* enjoying other Adventureland and Frontierland attractions.

Pirates of the Caribbean

What It Is: Indoor pirate-themed adventure boat ride
Scope & Scale: Headliner
When to Go: Before noon or after 5 p.m.
Special Comments: Frightens some children
Author's Rating: Disney Audio-Animatronics at its best; not to be missed; ★★★★★
Appeal by Age Group:

Pre-school	Grade School	Teens	Young Adults	Over 30	Senior Citizens
★★★	★★★★★	★★★★	★★★★	★★★★½	★★★★½

Duration of Ride: About 7½ minutes
Avg. Wait in Line per 100 People ahead of You: 1½ minutes
Assumes: Both waiting lines operating
Loading Speed: Fast

Description and Comments Scenes along an indoor boat's course depict a pirate raid on an island settlement, from bombardment of the fortress to debauchery after the victory.

Touring Tips One of the park's most elaborate and imaginative attractions. It's engineered to move large crowds fast and has two lines, both covered.

Enchanted Tiki Birds

What It Is: Audio-animatronic Pacific Island musical theater show
Scope & Scale: Minor attraction
When to Go: Before 11 a.m. and after 3:30 p.m.

Special Comments: Frightens some preschoolers
Author's Rating: Very, very unusual; ★★★½
Appeal by Age Group:

Pre-school	Grade School	Teens	Young Adults	Over 30	Senior Citizens
★★★★	★★★½	★★★	★★★	★★★	★★★

Duration of Presentation: 15½ minutes
Preshow Entertainment: Talking birds
Probable Waiting Time: 15 minutes

Description and Comments   Upgraded in 1998, this theater presentation now features two of Disney's most beloved bird characters, Iago from *Aladdin* and Zazu from *The Lion King.* A new song, "Friend Like Me," and a revamped plotline add some much needed zip, but the production remains (pardon the pun) a feather-weight in the Disney galaxy of attractions.

Touring Tips   Usually not too crowded. In late afternoon, you'll appreciate a break with air conditioning.

Adventureland Eateries and Shops

Description and Comments   Restaurants less crowded during lunch than elsewhere in the park.

Touring Tips   El Pirata y el Perico, serving Mexican fast food and hot dogs, is often overlooked.

Frontierland

Frontierland adjoins Adventureland as you tour clockwise. Focus is on the Old West, with stockade-type structures and pioneer trappings.

Splash Mountain (FASTPASS)

What It Is: Indoor/outdoor water-flume adventure boat ride
Scope & Scale: Super headliner
When to Go: At park opening time or just before closing
Special Comments: Children must be 40" tall; younger than 7 must ride with an adult. Switching off option provided (page 54)
Author's Rating: A wet winner; not to be missed; ★★★★★

Appeal by Age Group:

Pre-school	Grade School	Teens	Young Adults	Over 30	Senior Citizens
†	★★★★★	★★★★★	★★★★★	★★★★★	★★★½

† Many preschoolers are too short to ride; others are intimidated by watching from the waiting line. Those who ride generally give it high marks (3–5 stars).

Duration of Ride: About 10 minutes

Avg. Wait in Line per 100 People ahead of You: 3½ minutes

Assumes: Operation at full capacity

Loading Speed: Moderate

Description and Comments   Amusement-park flume ride, Disney-style. Highly imaginative. Splash Mountain combines steep chutes with excellent special effects. The ride covers more than half a mile, splashing through swamps, caves, and backwoods bayous before climaxing in a five-story plunge and Brer Rabbit's triumphant return home. More than 100 audio-animatronic characters regale riders with songs, including "Zip-a-Dee-Doo-Dah."

Touring Tips   This happy, exciting, and adventuresome ride vies with Space Mountain as the park's most popular one. Crowds build fast in the morning, and two-hour waits can be expected once the park fills. Get in line first thing, no later than 45 minutes after opening. If you miss Splash Mountain in the morning, lines are shorter during afternoon or evening parades, or just before the park closes.

If you have only one day to see the Magic Kingdom, ride Space Mountain first, then see *Alien Encounter* (also in Tomorrowland), then hot-foot it over to Splash Mountain. If the line isn't too long, go ahead and ride. Otherwise, obtain a FASTPASS. FASTPASS strategies have been incorporated into the Magic Kingdom One-Day touring plans (see page 20).

At Splash Mountain, if you ride in the front seat, you will almost certainly get wet. Riders elsewhere get splashed. Since you don't know what seat you'll be assigned, be prepared. On a cool day, carry a plastic garbage bag. Tear holes in the bottom and sides to make a water-resistant sack dress. Tuck the bag in under your bottom. Leave your camera with a nonriding member of your group or wrap it in plastic.

The scariest part of this ride is the steep chute you see when standing in line, but the drop looks worse than it really is. Despite reassurances, however, many children wig out after watching it. One reader's kids tried to hold their breath throughout the ride, thinking they would be going underwater.

Big Thunder Mountain Railroad

What It Is: Tame, western-mining-themed roller coaster
Scope & Scale: Headliner
When to Go: Before 10 a.m., during parades, or in the hour before closing
Special Comments: Children must be 40" tall; younger than age 7 must ride with an adult. Switching off option provided (page 54)
Author's Rating: Great effects, relatively tame ride; not to be missed; ★★★★
Appeal by Age Group:

Pre-school	Grade School	Teens	Young Adults	Over 30	Senior Citizens
★★★	★★★★	★★★★	★★★★	★★★★	★★★

Duration of Ride: Almost 3½ minutes
Avg. Wait in Line per 100 People ahead of You: 2½ minutes
Assumes: 5 trains operating
Loading Speed: Moderate to fast

Description and Comments   Roller coaster through and around a "mountain." The idea is that you're on a runaway mine train during Gold Rush. This roller coaster is about 5 on a "scary scale" of 10. First-rate examples of Disney creativity are showcased: realistic mining town, falling rocks, and an earthquake. People who don't like roller coasters and some seniors and preschoolers won't enjoy this ride.

Touring Tips   Emphasis is placed on the sights instead of the roller-coaster thrill.

Nearby Splash Mountain affects the traffic flow to Big Thunder Mountain Railroad. Adventuresome guests ride Splash Mountain first, then go next door to Big Thunder. This means large crowds in Frontierland all day and long waits for Big Thunder. The best way to experience Magic Kingdom "mountains" is to ride Space Mountain when the park opens, Big Thunder Mountain Railroad immediately afterward, and then Splash Mountain.

Country Bear Jamboree

What It Is: Audio-animatronic country-hoedown theater show

Scope & Scale: Major attraction

When to Go: Before 11:30 a.m., during the two hours before closing, or right before a parade

Special Comments: Shows change at Christmas and during summer

Author's Rating: A Disney classic; ★★★

Appeal by Age Group:

Pre-school	Grade School	Teens	Young Adults	Over 30	Senior Citizens
★★★½	★★★	★★½	★★★	★★★	★★★

Duration of Presentation: 15 minutes

Preshow Entertainment: None

Probable Waiting Time: This attraction is very popular but has a relatively small capacity. Waiting time on a busy day between noon and 5:30 p.m. averages 30–50 minutes.

Description and Comments   A cast of charming robotic bears sing and stomp through a western-style hoedown. Repeat visitors find that the humorous and upbeat show hasn't been revised for many moons; some are disappointed.

Touring Tips   The *Jamboree* is very popular and draws large crowds even early in the day.

Tom Sawyer Island and Fort Sam Clemens

What It Is: Outdoor walk-through exhibit / rustic playground

Scope & Scale: Minor attraction

When to Go: Midmorning through late afternoon

Special Comments: Closes at dusk

Author's Rating: The place for rambunctious kids; ★★★

Appeal by Age Group:

Pre-school	Grade School	Teens	Young Adults	Over 30	Senior Citizens
★★★★★	★★★★★	★★	★★	★★	★★

Description and Comments   Tom Sawyer Island is a getaway within the park, with hills, a cave, a windmill, a tipsy barrel bridge, and paths to explore. It delights and relaxes adults while providing harmless, closely supervised freedom for children. There's even a "secret" escape tunnel.

Touring Tips   Tom Sawyer Island isn't a top attraction, but it's one of the park's better conceived ones. Attention to detail is excellent. It's a must for families with children ages 5–15. If your group is adults, visit on your second day or stop by on your first after you've seen the attractions you most wanted to see.

Although kids could spend a whole day there, plan at least 20 minutes. Access is by raft from Frontierland; two operate simultaneously, and the trip is efficient. Our favorite Magic Kingdom restaurant for lunch is Aunt Polly's Dockside Inn on Tom Sawyer Island. The menu is limited: cold fried chicken served with potato salad and a biscuit, and ham-and-cheese and peanut butter sandwiches. However, prices are reasonable, and the river view is fine.

The Diamond Horseshoe Saloon Revue

What It Is: Live western song-and-dance show

Scope & Scale: Minor attraction

When to Go: Check the daily entertainment schedule

Special Comments: No Disney characters in this show

Author's Rating: Fast-paced and funny; ★★★

Appeal by Age Group:

Pre-school	Grade School	Teens	Young Adults	Over 30	Senior Citizens
★★	★★★	★★	★★★½	★★★½	★★★½

Duration of Show: About 40 minutes

Avg. Wait in Line per 100 People ahead of You: No wait

Description and Comments   The Diamond Horseshoe Saloon Revue is a PG-rated cattle-town saloon show, with comedy, song, and can-can dancing. Audience members are conscripted to join the cast.

Touring Tips   Reservations aren't required; walk in and have a seat. If you don't want to be in the show, sit upstairs. Sandwiches, chips, cookies, and soft drinks are sold at the bar. Lunch crowds overlook the *Diamond Horseshoe,* especially between shows. The best times to see the show are over lunch and after the afternoon parade.

Frontierland Eateries and Shops

Description and Comments   Coonskin caps and western-theme shopping. Fast-food eateries are usually very crowded between 11:30 a.m. and 2 p.m. An exception is the relaxing Aunt Polly's Dockside Inn outdoors on Tom Sawyer Island.

Touring Tips   Don't waste time shopping unless that's what you came for. Skip Aunt Polly's if the wait to board the raft is long. A great timesaver is to eat at the *Diamond Horseshoe* just a few minutes after a show has concluded.

Liberty Square

Liberty Square re-creates colonial America at the time of the American Revolution. Architecture is federal or colonial. A real, 130-year-old live oak (dubbed the "Liberty Tree") lends dignity and grace to the setting.

The Hall of Presidents

What It Is: Audio-animatronic historical theater presentation
Scope & Scale: Major attraction
When to Go: Anytime
Author's Rating: Impressive and moving; ★★★
Appeal by Age Group:

Pre-school	Grade School	Teens	Young Adults	Over 30	Senior Citizens
★	★★½	★★★	★★★½	★★★★	★★★★

Duration of Presentation: Almost 23 minutes
Preshow Entertainment: None
Probable Waiting Time: Lines look awesome but usually are swallowed up when the show in progress lets out. Even during busiest times, waits rarely exceed 40 minutes.

Description and Comments   A 20-minute, strongly inspirational and patriotic program highlights milestones in American history. The performance climaxes with a roll call of presidents, with words of encouragement from President Lincoln. A very moving show coupled with one of Disney's best and most ambitious robotic efforts. The narration is by Maya Angelou.

Touring Tips   Detail and costumes are masterful. If your children fidget during the show, notice that the presidents do, too. The attraction is one of the park's most popular, especially among seniors, drawing large crowds between 11 a.m. and about 5 p.m. Don't be put off by lines; the theater holds more than 700 people. On less busy days, you'll probably have no wait to enter the lobby.

Liberty Belle Riverboat

What It Is: Outdoor scenic boat ride

Scope & Scale: Major attraction

When to Go: Anytime

Author's Rating: Slow, relaxing, and scenic; ★★½

Appeal by Age Group:

Pre-school	Grade School	Teens	Young Adults	Over 30	Senior Citizens
★★★½	★★★	★★½	★★★	★★★	★★★

Duration of Ride: About 16 minutes

Avg. Wait to Board: 10–14 minutes

Assumes: Normal operations

Description and Comments   Large-capacity paddle wheeler that cruises around Tom Sawyer Island and Fort Sam Clemens. This beautiful riverboat provides a lofty perspective of Frontierland and Liberty Square.

Touring Tips   One of two boat rides on the same waters. The Mike Fink Keelboats are slower in loading; ride the riverboat.

The Haunted Mansion

What It Is: Haunted-house dark ride

Scope & Scale: Major attraction

When to Go: Before 11:30 a.m. or after 8 p.m.

Special Comments: Frightens some very young children

Author's Rating: Some of Disney World's best special effects; not to be missed; ★★★★

Appeal by Age Group:

Pre-school	Grade School	Teens	Young Adults	Over 30	Senior Citizens
(Varies)	★★★★★	★★★★	★★★★	★★★★	★★★★

Duration of Ride: 7-minute ride plus a 1½-minute preshow

Avg. Wait in Line per 100 People ahead of You: 2½ minutes

Assumes: Both "stretch rooms" operating

Loading Speed: Fast

Description and Comments   More fun than scary. Some children become anxious about what they think they'll see. Almost nobody is scared by the actual sights.

Touring Tips   Lines ebb and flow more than at other Magic Kingdom high spots because the mansion is near *The Hall of Presidents* and *Liberty Belle* Riverboat. Those attractions disgorge 750 and 450 people, respectively, when each show or ride ends, and many of those folks head straight for the mansion. Slip in between crowds.

Mike Fink Keelboats

What It Is: Outdoor scenic boat ride

Scope & Scale: Minor attraction

When to Go: Before 11:30 a.m. or after 5 p.m.

Special Comments: Don't ride if the lines are long; closes at dusk

Author's Rating: ★★

Appeal by Age Group:

Pre-school	Grade School	Teens	Young Adults	Over 30	Senior Citizens
★★★	★★★	★★½	★★½	★★½	★★½

Duration of Ride: 9½ minutes

Avg. Wait in Line per 100 People ahead of You: 15 minutes

Assumes: 2 boats operating

Loading Speed: Slow

Description and Comments   Small keelboats that circle Tom Sawyer Island and Fort Sam Clemens on the same route as the *Liberty Belle* Riverboat. The riverboat is fastest. Keelboat's top deck is exposed to the elements.

Liberty Square Eateries and Shops

Description and Comments   American crafts and souvenirs in shops. There's one restaurant, the Liberty Tree Tavern; it's often overlooked by lunch crowds.

Touring Tips   Liberty Tree Tavern offers character lunches and dinners with a fixed menu served family-style. Characters aside, the food is rivaled only by the Crystal Palace buffet as the Magic Kingdom's best. Priority seatings are required.

Fantasyland

Fantasyland is the heart of the Magic Kingdom, an enchanting place spread gracefully like a miniature alpine village beneath the steepled towers of Cinderella Castle.

It's a Small World

What It Is: Indoor boat ride with world-brotherhood theme

Scope & Scale: Major attraction

When to Go: Anytime

Author's Rating: Exponentially "cute"; ★★★

Appeal by Age Group:

Pre-school	Grade School	Teens	Young Adults	Over 30	Senior Citizens
★★★½	★★★	★★½	★★½	★★½	★★★

Duration of Ride: About 11 minutes

Avg. Wait in Line per 100 People ahead of You: 10 minutes

Assumes: Busy conditions with 30 or more boats operating

Loading Speed: Fast

Description and Comments   Happy, upbeat, indoor attraction with a catchy tune you won't soon forget. Small boats carry visitors on a tour around the world, with singing and dancing dolls showcasing dress and culture of each nation. Almost everyone enjoys It's a Small World (at least the first time). It stands, however, along with *Enchanted Tiki Birds,* in the "What Kind of Drugs Were They on When They Thought This Up?" category.

Touring Tips   Cool off here during the heat of the day. Lines are shortest from 11 a.m. to 5 p.m. If you wear a hearing aid, turn it off.

Peter Pan's Flight

What It Is: Indoor track ride

Scope & Scale: Minor attraction

When to Go: Before 10 a.m. or after 6 p.m.

Author's Rating: Happy, mellow, and well done; ★★★★

Appeal by Age Group:

Pre-school	Grade School	Teens	Young Adults	Over 30	Senior Citizens
★★★½	★★★½	★★★½	★★★½	★★★½	★★★½

Duration of Ride: A little over 3 minutes

Avg. Wait in Line per 100 People ahead of You: 5½ minutes

Assumes: Normal operation

Loading Speed: Moderate to slow

Description and Comments Peter Pan's Flight is superbly designed and absolutely delightful, with a happy theme uniting some favorite Disney characters, beautiful effects, and charming music. Unlike Snow White's Adventures, there's nothing here that will jump out at you or frighten young children.

Touring Tips Lines are long all day. Try before 10 a.m., during a parade, or just before the park closes.

Legend of the Lion King

What It Is: Live mixed-media and puppet theater show

Scope & Scale: Major attraction

When to Go: Before 11 a.m. and during parades

Author's Rating: Uplifting and fun; ★★★

Appeal by Age Group:

Pre-school	Grade School	Teens	Young Adults	Over 30	Senior Citizens
★★★	★★★½	★★★	★★★	★★★	★★★

Duration of Presentation: About 16 minutes

Preshow Entertainment: 7-minute preshow

Probable Waiting Time: 12 minutes

Description and Comments It's a close cousin to *Voyage of the Little Mermaid* at Disney-MGM Studios. The story is poignant and engaging, with some dark moments, ending on a happy and triumphant note. Imaginative puppetry, animation, and special effects create an effective collage.

Touring Tips Budget a 30- to 40-minute wait and go at about 10 a.m. or during live events. The theater holds about 500 people, swallowing most of the line each time one show ends and another begins.

Cinderella's Golden Carrousel

What It Is: Merry-go-round

Scope & Scale: Minor attraction

When to Go: Before 11 a.m. or after 8 p.m.

Special Comments: Adults enjoy the beauty and nostalgia of this ride

Author's Rating: A beautiful children's ride; ★★★

Appeal by Age Group:

Pre-school	Grade School	Teens	Young Adults	Over 30	Senior Citizens
★★★★	★★½	—	—	—	—

Duration of Ride: About 2 minutes

Avg. Wait in Line per 100 People ahead of You: 5 minutes

Assumes: Normal staffing

Loading Speed: Slow

Description and Comments   One of the most elaborate and lovely merry-go-rounds anywhere, especially with the lights on.

Touring Tips   Watch from the sidelines unless your group includes young children.

The Many Adventures of Winnie the Pooh (FASTPASS)

What It Is: Indoor track ride

Scope & Scale: Minor attraction

When to Go: Before 10 a.m. or in the 2 hours before closing

Author's Rating: Fantasyland's newest attraction; ★★★½

Appeal by Age Group:

Pre-school	Grade School	Teens	Young Adults	Over 30	Senior Citizens
★★★½	★★★½	★★★	★★★	★★★	★★★

Duration of Ride: About 4 minutes

Avg. Wait in Line per 100 People ahead of You: 4 minutes

Assumes: Normal operation

Loading Speed: Moderate

Description and Comments   This newest addition to Fantasyland replaces Mr. Toad's Wild Ride. Pooh is sunny, upbeat, and fun— more in the image of Peter Pan's Flight or Splash Mountain. You encounter Pooh and his friends as they contend with a blustery day.

Touring Tips   Because Pooh is new, expect larger-than-average crowds for a while or use FASTPASS. Beware that the daily allocation of FASTPASSES for Winnie the Pooh is often distributed by noon or 1 p.m., and your scheduled return might be hours away. You also can't obtain a FASTPASS for another attraction until you use your FASTPASS to Pooh. Thus, holding a Pooh FASTPASS for half the day will keep you from using FASTPASS on Space Mountain, Splash Mountain, Jungle Cruise, and Buzz Lightyear.

Snow White's Adventures

What It Is: Indoor track ride

Scope & Scale: Minor attraction

When to Go: Before 11 a.m. and after 6 p.m.

Special Comments: Terrifying to many young children

Author's Rating: Worthwhile if wait isn't long; ★★½

Appeal by Age Group:

Pre- school	Grade School	Teens	Young Adults	Over 30	Senior Citizens
★	★★½	★★	★★½	★★½	★★½

Duration of Ride: Almost 2½ minutes

Avg. Wait in Line per 100 People ahead of You: 6¼ minutes

Assumes: Normal operation

Loading Speed: Moderate to slow

Description and Comments   Mine cars travel through a spook house showing Snow White as she narrowly escapes harm at the hands of the wicked witch. Action and effects are not as good as Peter Pan's Flight or Winnie the Pooh.

Touring Tips   We get more mail about this ride than any other Disney attraction. It terrifies many kids age six and younger. After a 1995 upgrade of the ride, Snow White plays a greater role, but the relentless and ubiquitous witch continues to be the focal character. Many readers say their young children won't ride any attraction that operates in the dark after experiencing Snow White's Adventures. One mother wrote that preschoolers expect forest animals and dwarfs but get a terrifying witch—and lots of her.

Experience Snow White if lines aren't long, or on a second day at the park.

Ariel's Grotto

What It Is: Interactive fountain and character-greeting area

Scope & Scale: Minor attraction

When to Go: Before 10 a.m. and after 9 p.m.

Author's Rating: One of the most elaborate character-greeting
venues; ★★★

Appeal by Age Group:

Pre-school	Grade School	Teens	Young Adults	Over 30	Senior Citizens
★★★★★	★★★★	★★	★	★	★

Avg. Wait in Line per 100 People ahead of You: 30 minutes

Description and Comments   Ariel's Grotto is on the lagoon side
of Dumbo, where the 20,000 Leagues Under the Sea submarines
were until their removal in 1997. Ariel's Grotto consists of a small
children's play area with an interactive fountain and a rock grotto
where Ariel, the Little Mermaid, poses for photos and signs autographs. If "interactive fountain" is new for you, it means an opportunity for your children to get ten times wetter than a trout. Can
you say "hy-po-ther-mi-a"?

Touring Tips   The Grotto is small and the wait to meet Ariel
is usually long. Because kids in line are fresh from the fountain,
the experience is "like being packed in a pen with wet cocker
spaniels," as one reader said. Except before 10 a.m., count on a
20–40 minute wait.

   Then there's the fountain. Allow your children to disrobe to
the legal limit. (Forget umbrellas or ponchos; water squirts up
from below.)

Dumbo the Flying Elephant

What It Is: Disneyfied midway ride

Scope & Scale: Minor attraction

When to Go: Before 10 a.m. and after 9 p.m.

Author's Rating: An attractive children's ride; ★★★

Appeal by Age Group:

Pre-school	Grade School	Teens	Young Adults	Over 30	Senior Citizens
★★★★★	★★★★	★½	★½	★½	★½

Duration of Ride: 1½ minutes
Avg. Wait in Line per 100 People ahead of You: 20 minutes
Assumes: Normal staffing
Loading Speed: Slow

Description and Comments Tame, happy children's ride based on the lovable flying elephant. Despite being similar to rides at state fairs and amusement parks, Dumbo is the favorite Magic Kingdom attraction of many younger children. They'll wait patiently for more than an hour to take the one and a half minute ride.

Touring Tips If Dumbo is critical to your child's happiness, make it your first stop, preferably within 15 minutes of park opening.

Mad Tea Party

What It Is: Midway-type spinning ride
Scope & Scale: Minor attraction
When to Go: Before 11 a.m. and after 5 p.m.
Special Comments: Make your teacup spin faster by turning the wheel in the center
Author's Rating: Fun, but not worth the wait; ★★
Appeal by Age Group:

Pre-school	Grade School	Teens	Young Adults	Over 30	Senior Citizens
★★★★	★★★★	★★★★	★★★	★★	★★

Duration of Ride: 1½ minutes
Avg. Wait in Line per 100 People ahead of You: 7½ minutes
Assumes: Normal staffing
Loading Speed: Slow

Description and Comments Riders whirl feverishly in big teacups. Teenagers like to lure adults onto the teacups, then turn the wheel in the middle, making the cups spin faster, until the adults are on the verge of throwing up.

Touring Tips This ride, well-done but not unique, is notoriously slow in loading. Skip it on a busy schedule—if the kids will let you. Ride the morning of your second day if your schedule is more relaxed.

Fantasyland Eateries and Shops

Description and Comments   Many Magic Kingdom visitors want to know, "What's in Cinderella Castle?" The answer is: You can't see it all, but you can inspect a fair-sized chunk if you eat at Cinderella's Royal Table. Priority seating is required.

However, you don't have to eat at her Royal Table to see Cinderella, who greets diners in the restaurant's waiting area. Enter through the left door by the hostess's stand. She can tell you when Cinderella will appear.

Fantasyland shops offer abundant specialty and souvenir shopping.

Touring Tips   We don't recommend Cinderella's Royal Table if you're in a hurry or mind paying fancy prices for ho-hum food. If you do plan to go, make priority seating arrangements 60 days in advance to ensure a table. Call (407) 939-3463.

Mickey's Toontown Fair

Mickey's Toontown Fair is the first new "land" to be added to the Magic Kingdom since its opening and the only land that doesn't connect to the central hub. Attractions include meeting Mickey Mouse, touring Mickey's house and Minnie Mouse's house, and riding a child-size roller coaster.

Mickey's Toontown Fair is sandwiched on three acres between Fantasyland and Tomorrowland. It's by far the smallest "land" and is more like an attraction. Though you can enter from Fantasyland or a totally obscure path from Tomorrowland, Mickey's Toontown Fair generally receives guests arriving by Walt Disney World Railroad.

This land is the Magic Kingdom's greeting headquarters for Disney characters, who are available on a reliable schedule.

In general, Mickey's Toontown Fair doesn't handle crowds very well. We recommend touring first thing in the morning. If you only have one day to visit the Magic Kingdom and hitting the child-oriented attractions is a priority, head first to Fantasyland and ride Dumbo, Pooh, and Peter Pan, then split for Toontown. In Toontown, ride Goofy's Barnstormer first, then tour Mickey's and Minnie's houses. Go next to the Toontown Hall of Fame for character pics and autographs.

Mickey's Country House & Judge's Tent

What It Is: Walk-through tour of Mickey's House and a meeting with Mickey

Scope & Scale: Minor attraction

When to Go: Before 11:30 a.m. and after 4:30 p.m.

Author's Rating: Well done; ★★★

Appeal by Age Group:

Pre-school	Grade School	Teens	Young Adults	Over 30	Senior Citizens
★★★½	★★★	★★½	★★½	★★½	★★½

Duration of Attraction: 15–30 minutes (depending on the crowd)

Avg. Wait in Line per 100 People ahead of You: 20 minutes

Assumes: Normal staffing

Touring Speed: Slow

Description and Comments   Mickey's House is the start of a self-guided tour through the famous mouse's house, into his backyard, and past Pluto's doghouse. If you want to tour Mickey's house, but skip meeting Mickey, you'll find an exit just before entering his tent.

Touring Tips   Discerning observers will see immediately that Mickey's House & Judge's Tent is a cleverly devised queuing area for visitors to Mickey's office for the Mouse Encounter. It also heightens anticipation and displays a lot of Disney memorabilia.

   If meeting Mickey is your child's priority, take the railroad from Main Street to the Mickey's Toontown Fair station as soon as you enter the park.

Minnie's Country House

What It Is: Walk-through exhibit

Scope & Scale: Minor attraction

When to Go: Before 11:30 a.m. and after 4:30 p.m.

Author's Rating: Great detail; ★★

Appeal by Age Group:

Pre-school	Grade School	Teens	Young Adults	Over 30	Senior Citizens
★★★	★★★	★★½	★★½	★★½	★★½

Duration of Tour: 10 minutes
Avg. Wait in Line per 100 People ahead of You: 12 minutes
Touring Speed: Slow

Description and Comments Minnie's Country House offers a self-guided tour through the rooms and backyard of Mickey's main squeeze. Similar to Mickey's Country House, only more feminine, Minnie's also showcases Disney memorabilia. Among its highlights are the fanciful appliances in Minnie's kitchen.

Touring Tips The main difference between Mickey's and Minnie's houses is that Mickey is at home to receive guests. Minnie was never home during our visits.

Toontown Hall of Fame

What It Is: Character-greeting venue
Scope & Scale: Minor attraction
When to Go: Before 10:30 a.m. and after 5:30 p.m.
Author's Rating: You want characters? We got 'em! ★★
Appeal by Age Group:

Pre-school	Grade School	Teens	Young Adults	Over 30	Senior Citizens
★★★★	★★★★	★★★	★★★	★★★	★★★

Duration of Greeting: About 7–10 minutes
Avg. Wait in Line per 100 People ahead of You: 35 minutes
Touring Speed: Slow

Description and Comments Toontown Hall of Fame offers Disney World's largest and most dependably available collection of characters. It's at the end of a small plaza between Mickey's and Minnie's houses. Just inside to the right are entrances to three queuing areas. Signs over each suggest, somewhat ambiguously, which characters you will meet. Character assortments in each greeting area change, as do the names of the assortments themselves. On a given day you will find two or three groupings available: Famous Friends (also called Toon Pals and sometimes Minnie's Famous Pals) include Minnie, Goofy, Donald, Pluto, and sometimes Uncle Scrooge, Chip 'n' Dale, Roger Rabbit, and Daisy. 100 Acre Wood Pals are mostly Winnie the Pooh characters, but may include any character that fits the forest theme. Fairy

Tale Friends are Snow White, various dwarfs, Belle, the Beast, Sleeping Beauty, Prince Charming, etc. Other categories include Mickey's Pals, Disney Princesses, Disney Villains, and so on.

Each category occupies a room where 15–20 guests are admitted for seven to ten minutes, long enough for a photo, autograph, and hug with each character.

Touring Tips   To visit all categories, you must queue up three times. Each line is slow moving. Famous Friends (aka Toon Pals and Minnie's Famous Pals) are slightly more popular than the other categories, but the longest wait is usually for groupings that include face characters who are allowed to talk with children, prolonging the visit.

All characters work in 25-minute shifts, with breaks on the hour and half hour. Because characters change frequently, it's possible to see many if you recirculate. Ask the Disney greeter or departing guests who's on duty.

In early morning, you can meet all categories in less than an hour.

The Barnstormer at Goofy's Wiseacres Farm

What It Is: Small roller coaster

Scope & Scale: Minor attraction

When to Go: Before 10:30 a.m., during the parades and *Fantasmic!* in the evening, and just before the park closes

Author's Rating: Great for little ones, but not worth the wait for adults; ★★

Appeal by Age Group:

Pre-school	Grade School	Teens	Young Adults	Over 30	Senior Citizens
★★★★	★★★	★★½	★★½	★★½	★★

Duration of Ride: About 50 seconds

Avg. Wait in Line per 100 People ahead of You: 10 minutes

Assumes: Normal staffing

Loading Speed: Slow

Description and Comments   Goofy's Barnstormer is a small roller coaster. The ride is zippy, but supershort. In fact, 32 of the 53 seconds the ride is in motion are consumed in exiting the loading area, being ratcheted up the first hill, and braking into the off-loading area. Riders spend just 21 seconds careening around the track.

Touring Tips   The cars of this dinky coaster are too small for most adults. Unfortunately, the ride is visually appealing. All kids want to ride, subjecting the whole family to glacially moving lines. If you don't have kids with you, skip Goofy's Barnstormer. If you decide to ride, try to go before 9:30 a.m.

Donald's Boat

What It Is: Interactive fountain and playground
Scope & Scale: Diversion
When to Go: Anytime
Special Comments: Kids will get wet
Author's Rating: Spontaneous, yeah! ★★½
Appeal by Age Group:

Pre-school	Grade School	Teens	Young Adults	Over 30	Senior Citizens
★★★★	★★½	★	★½	★½	★½

Description and Comments   Spurts of water erupt randomly from tiny holes in the side of Donald's Boat, which purportedly is springing leaks. Children walk around on deck, plugging holes with their hands and feet and trying to guess where the water will squirt next.

Touring Tips   Young children love this attraction and will play in the fountains until they're drenched. Strip your munchkins to the legal limit and turn them loose. If you want to plan ahead, bring extra underwear and a towel.

Tomorrowland

Tomorrowland is a mix of rides and experiences relating to the technological development of humankind and what life will be in the future. If this sounds like Epcot's theme, it's because Tomorrowland was a breeding ground for ideas that spawned Epcot. Yet Tomorrowland and Epcot are very different in more than scale. Epcot is educational. Tomorrowland is more for fun, depicting the future as envisioned in science fiction.

Exhaustive renovation of Tomorrowland was completed in 1995. The new design is ageless, reflecting a nostalgic vision of the future imagined by dreamers and scientists in the 1920s and '30s, with fanciful mechanical rockets and metallic cities. Disney calls the renovated Tomorrowland the "Future That Never Was." *Newsweek* dubbed it "retro-future."

Space Mountain (FASTPASS)

What It Is: Roller coaster in the dark

Scope & Scale: Super headliner

When to Go: First thing when the park opens, during the hour before closing, or between 6 and 7 p.m.

Special Comments: Great fun and action, much wilder than Big Thunder Mountain Railroad. Children must be 44" tall to ride and, if younger than age 7, must be accompanied by an adult. Switching off is available (page 54).

Author's Rating: A great roller coaster with excellent special effects; not to be missed; ★★★★

Appeal by Age Group:

Pre-school	Grade School	Teens	Young Adults	Over 30	Senior Citizens
†	★★★★★	★★★★★	★★★★½	★★★★	†

† Some preschoolers loved Space Mountain; others were frightened. Our sample of senior riders was too small to develop an accurate rating.

Duration of Ride: Almost 3 minutes

Avg. Wait in Line per 100 People ahead of You: 3 minutes

Assumes: 2 tracks operating at 21-second dispatch intervals

Loading Speed: Moderate to fast

Description and Comments   Totally enclosed in a mammoth futuristic structure, Space Mountain has always been the Magic Kingdom's most popular attraction. The theme is a space flight through dark recesses of the galaxy. Effects are superb, and the ride is the fastest and wildest in the Magic Kingdom. Space Mountain is much more thrilling than Big Thunder Mountain Railroad but much tamer than the Rock 'n' Roller Coaster at the studios.

   Space Mountain is a designer version of The Wild Mouse, a carnival midway ride that's been around for at least 40 years. There are no long drops or swooping hills like on a traditional roller coaster— only quick, unexpected turns and small drops. Disney improves upon The Wild Mouse by adding a space theme and putting it in the dark. Indeed, this does make the mouse seem wilder.

Touring Tips   Ride only if you can handle a fairly wild roller coaster. What sets Space Mountain apart is that the cars plummet through darkness, with only occasional lighting. Half the fun is not knowing where the car will go next.

Each rider has his own seat. Parents can't sit next to their child.

Space Mountain is the favorite attraction of many visitors. Each morning before the park opens, particularly during summer and holiday periods, several hundred SM "junkies" crowd rope barriers at the central hub awaiting the signal to head to the ride.

To get ahead of the competition, be one of the first in the park (easy if you have early-entry privileges), go to the end of Main Street, and wait at the entrance to Tomorrowland.

If you don't catch Space Mountain in early morning, use FAST-PASS or try again during the hour before closing, when would-be riders are often held in line outside the entrance until all those previously in line have ridden, thus emptying the attraction. The appearance from outside is that the line is enormous, when, in fact, the only people waiting are those visible. This crowd-control technique, known as stacking, discourages visitors from getting in line and ensures the ride will be able to close on schedule.

Splash Mountain siphons off some guests who would have made Space Mountain their first stop. Even so, a mob rushes to Space Mountain as soon as the park opens. If you especially like thrill attractions and have only one day, ride Space Mountain first in the morning, followed by *Alien Encounter*, Splash Mountain, and Big Thunder Mountain Railroad.

If you're an early-entry guest and Big Thunder and Splash Mountains are high on your list, see *Alien Encounter* and ride Space Mountain (as well as Fantasyland attractions) until 10–15 minutes before the general public is admitted. At that time, go to the boundary between Fantasyland and Liberty Square and wait for the park to open. When it does, move quickly along the Liberty Square and Frontierland waterfronts to Big Thunder and Splash Mountains.

If you aren't eligible for early entry, visit the Magic Kingdom on a day when early entry isn't in effect and make Space Mountain and *Alien Encounter* your first two attractions. If you aren't eligible for early entry but your schedule requires you to visit on an early-entry day, ride Splash Mountain and Big Thunder Mountain Railroad first, then obtain a FASTPASS for Space Mountain and see *Alien Encounter* while you wait for your FASTPASS time slot.

Tomorrowland Speedway

What It Is: Drive-'em-yourself miniature cars

Scope & Scale: Major attraction

When to Go: Before 11 a.m. and after 5 p.m.

Special Comments: Must be 52" tall to drive

Author's Rating: Boring for adults (★); great for preschoolers

Appeal by Age Group:

Pre-school	Grade School	Teens	Young Adults	Over 30	Senior Citizens
★★★★	★★★	★	½	½	½

Duration of Ride: About 4¼ minutes

Avg. Wait in Line per 100 People ahead of You: 4½ minutes

Assumes: 285-car turnover every 20 minutes

Loading Speed: Slow

Description and Comments An elaborate miniature raceway with gasoline-powered cars that travel up to seven miles per hour. The raceway, with sleek cars and racing noises, is alluring. Unfortunately, the cars poke along on a track. Ho-hum for most adults and teens. The height requirement often excludes young children who would enjoy the ride.

Because cars jam up at the end, it can take as long to get off as to get on.

Touring Tips This ride is appealing visually but definitely one adults can skip. Preschoolers, however, love it. If your preschooler is too short to drive, ride along and allow your child to steer the car on its guiderail while you work the gas pedal. Go as slowly as possible to prolong the ride.

The line for the Speedway is routed across a pedestrian bridge that leads to the loading areas. For a shorter wait, turn right off the bridge to the first loading area.

Astro Orbiter

What It Is: Buck Rogers–style rockets revolving around a central axis

Scope & Scale: Minor attraction

When to Go: Before 11 a.m. or after 5 p.m.

Special Comments: This attraction is not as innocuous as it
   appears

Author's Rating: Not worth the wait; ★★

Appeal by Age Group:

Pre-school	Grade School	Teens	Young Adults	Over 30	Senior Citizens
★★★★	★★★	★★½	★★½	★★	★

Duration of Ride: 1½ minutes

Avg. Wait in Line per 100 People ahead of You: 13½ minutes

Assumes: Normal staffing

Loading Speed: Slow

Description and Comments   Though recently upgraded and visu-
ally appealing, Astro Orbiter is still a slow-loading carnival ride.
The fat little rockets simply fly in circles. The best thing about
Astro Orbiter is the view aloft.

Touring Tips   If you ride with preschoolers, seat them first, then
board. The Astro Orbiter flies higher and faster than Dumbo and
frightens some children. It also can turn adults green.

Tomorrowland Transit Authority

What It Is: Scenic tour of Tomorrowland

Scope & Scale: Minor attraction

When to Go: During the hot, crowded period of the day
   (11:30 a.m.–4:30 p.m.)

Special Comments: A good way to check out the crowd at Space
   Mountain

Author's Rating: Scenic, relaxing, informative; ★★★

Appeal by Age Group:

Pre-school	Grade School	Teens	Young Adults	Over 30	Senior Citizens
★★★½	★★★	★★½	★★½	★★½	★★★

Duration of Ride: 10 minutes

Avg. Wait in Line per 100 People ahead of You: 1½ minutes

Assumes: 39 trains operating

Loading Speed: Fast

Description and Comments   A once-unique prototype of a linear induction–powered mass-transit system, the people mover's tram cars carry riders on a leisurely tour of Tomorrowland that includes a peek inside Space Mountain.

Touring Tips　A relaxing ride where lines move quickly. It's good to take during busier times of day, when the kids need a short nap, or when mom needs to nurse the baby. Ride repeatedly without disembarking.

Walt Disney's Carousel of Progress

What It Is:　Audio-animatronic theater production
Scope & Scale:　Major attraction
When to Go:　Anytime
Author's Rating:　Nostalgic, warm, and happy; ★★★
Appeal by Age Group:

Pre-school	Grade School	Teens	Young Adults	Over 30	Senior Citizens
★★	★★½	★★½	★★★	★★★	★★★½

Duration of Presentation:　18 minutes
Preshow Entertainment:　Documentary on the attraction's long history
Probable Waiting Time:　Less than 10 minutes

Description and Comments　Updated and improved during the Tomorrowland renovation, *Carousel of Progress* cheerfully looks at how technology and electricity have changed the lives of an audio-animatronic family over several generations. It's thoroughly delightful, showcasing a likable family and a happy tune that bridges the generations.

Touring Tips　This attraction is a great favorite of repeat visitors and is included on all of our one-day touring plans. *Carousel of Progress* handles big crowds effectively and is a good choice during busier times of day.

Buzz Lightyear's Space Ranger Spin (FASTPASS)

What It Is:　Whimsical space travel–theme indoor ride
Scope & Scale:　Minor attraction
When to Go:　Anytime
Author's Rating:　A real winner! ★★★★

Appeal by Age Group:

Pre-school	Grade School	Teens	Young Adults	Over 30	Senior Citizens
★★★★	★★★★★	★★★★½	★★★★	★★★★	★★★★

Duration of Ride: About 4½ minutes

Avg. Wait in Line per 100 People ahead of You: 3 minutes

Assumes: Normal operation

Loading Speed: Fast

Description and Comments   This attraction, based on the space-commando character of Buzz Lightyear from the film *Toy Story,* replaces the Take Flight attraction as the final installment of Tomorrowland's four-year makeover. The marginal storyline has you and Buzz Lightyear trying to save the universe from the evil Emperor Zurg. The indoor ride is interactive to the extent that you can spin your car and shoot simulated "laser cannons" at Zurg and his minions.

Tourings Tips   Each car is equipped with two laser cannons and a score-keeping display. A joystick allows you to spin the car to line up the various targets. On the first ride, most people are occupied with learning how to use the equipment and figuring out how the targets work. The next ride you'll surprise yourself by how much better you do. Because Buzz Lightyear is an exceedingly fast-loading attraction, we're somewhat surprised that it's in the FASTPASS lineup. Even though Buzz Lightyear can handle crowds without FASTPASS, because it's there waits for anyone in the regular line will be prolonged. On really crowded days you might have to resort to FASTPASS in self-defense. If the expected wait in the regular line is 20 minutes or less, forget FASTPASS.

The Timekeeper

What It Is: Time-travel movie adventure

Scope & Scale: Major attraction

When to Go: Anytime

Special Comments: Audience must stand throughout presentation

Author's Rating: Outstanding; not to be missed; ★★★★

Appeal by Age Group:

Pre- school	Grade School	Teens	Young Adults	Over 30	Senior Citizens
★★	★★★½	★★★½	★★★½	★★★★	★★★★

Duration of Presentation: About 20 minutes

Preshow Entertainment: Robots, lasers, and movies

Probable Waiting Time: 8–15 minutes

Description and Comments Developed as *Le Visionarium* for Disneyland Paris, *The Timekeeper* adds audio-animatronic characters and a storyline to the long-successful Circle-Vision 360 technology. The preshow introduces Timekeeper (a humanoid) and 9-Eye (a time-traveling robot with nine cameras that serve as eyes). Then the audience enters the main theater, where Timekeeper places 9-Eye into a time machine and dispatches her on a crazed journey into the past and future. What 9-Eye sees on her odyssey is projected onto huge screens surrounding the audience. The robot travels back to prehistoric Europe and then forward to meet French author and visionary Jules Verne, who hitches a ride into the future. Circle-Vision film technology, Audio-Animatronics, and high-tech special effects establish *The Timekeeper* as one of Tomorrowland's premier attractions.

Touring Tips *The Timekeeper* draws large crowds from mid-morning on. Because the theater accommodates more than 1,000 guests per showing, there's never much of a wait.

Alien Encounter

What It Is: Theater-in-the-round science-fiction horror show

Scope & Scale: Major attraction

When to Go: Before 10 a.m. or after 6 p.m.

Special Comments: Frightens children of all ages; 44" minimum height

Author's Rating: ★★★

Appeal by Age Group:

Pre- school	Grade School	Teens	Young Adults	Over 30	Senior Citizens
—	★★★½	★★★★	★★★★	★★★★	★★★

Duration of Presentation: About 12 minutes
Preshow Entertainment: About 6 minutes
Probable Waiting Time: 12–40 minutes

Description and Comments Heralded as the showpiece of the "new" Tomorrowland, *Alien Encounter* is staged in the former home of *Mission to Mars.* Guests witness "interplanetary teleportation," a technique that converts travelers into electrons for transmission to distant locations. In this case, the demonstration goes awry (of course), and an extremely unsavory alien arrives in the theater. Mayhem ensues.

Alien Encounter is the antithesis of most Disney attractions: There is no uplifting message and no happy ending. There is death in *Alien Encounter,* and its tone is dark and foreboding. While *The Twilight Zone* Tower of Terror at Disney-MGM Studios is suspenseful and subtle, *Alien Encounter* is uncomfortable and gross. The discomfort begins at the preshow, where in a teleportation experiment, a cuddly audio-animatronic character is hideously fried and deformed, then vomited screaming into outer space.

Alien Encounter has its advocates, but we think it's mean and twisted. The coup de grâce is the hawking of T-shirts in the adjacent gift shop bearing the image of the little creature that was tortured and maimed.

Touring Tips Though reader reaction is mixed, almost everyone agrees *Alien Encounter* isn't for young children. It stays busy all day.

Tomorrowland Eateries and Shops

Description and Comments Cosmic Ray's Starlight Cafe is the largest and most efficient Magic Kingdom fast-food restaurant. The Plaza Pavilion, however, serves better food.

Touring Tips Forget shopping until your second day unless it's your top priority.

Live Entertainment in the Magic Kingdom

Daily live entertainment—bands, character appearances, parades, singing, dancing, and ceremonies—further enliven the Magic Kingdom. For events on the day you visit, check the schedule in your handout map. If you don't receive one as you enter, get one at City Hall. Remember: If you're on a tight schedule, it's impossible to see featured attractions *and* the live performances. Our one-day touring plans exclude the live shows because some parades and performances siphon crowds away from popular rides, shortening lines.

Here's an incomplete list of events scheduled with some regularity for which reservations aren't required.

Sword in the Stone   A ceremony with audience participation based on the Disney animated feature of the same name. Merlin the Magician selects youngsters to test their strength by removing Excalibur from the stone. Staged several times daily behind Cinderella Castle.

Bay Lake and Seven Seas Lagoon Electrical Pageant   This is one of our favorites among the Disney floating extras, but you have to leave the Magic Kingdom to see it. The pageant is a stunning electric light show afloat on small barges and accompanied by electronic music. It's performed at nightfall on World Showcase Lagoon and Bay Lake. Exit the Magic Kingdom and take the monorail to the Polynesian Resort. Get a drink and walk to the end of the pier. The show begins about 9 p.m. during summer.

Fantasy in the Sky   A stellar fireworks display after dark on nights the park is open late. Watch from the terrace of The Plaza Pavilion restaurant in Tomorrowland.

Disney Character Shows and Appearances   On most days, a character poses for photos from 9 a.m. until 10 p.m. next to City Hall. Mickey and two or three assortments of other characters are available most of the day at Mickey's Toontown Fair. Daily shows at Castle Forecourt Stage and Tomorrowland Galaxy Palace Theater feature characters. They also roam the park throughout the day but almost always can be found in Fantasyland. For daily whereabouts of characters, obtain a *Character Greeting Guide* printed on the inside of the handout park maps.

PARADES

Parades are spectaculars with dozens of Disney characters and amazing special effects. In late 1991, the beloved Main Street Electrical Parade was unplugged, and the afternoon parade was replaced by an eye-popping celebration of carnivals worldwide. The new parades are larger, more colorful, and more elaborate. The afternoon parade is outstanding; the evening parade is not to be missed.

Parades disrupt traffic in the park. It's nearly impossible, for example, to get to Adventureland from Tomorrowland, or vice versa, during a parade.

Afternoon Parade

Usually at 3 p.m., this production includes bands, floats, and marching characters.

Evening Parade(s)

After trying myriad experiments with electroluminescent and fiber-optic technologies, light-spreading thermoplastics, and clouds of underlit liquid-nitrogen smoke (I swear we're not making this up), Disney has caved in to popular sentiment and brought back the venerable Main Street Electrical Parade. With umpteen-billion teeny, twinkling lights, jazzy fiber-optics, and a bouncy synthesizer musical score, the parade is still pretty high-tech, but at least you won't need a gas mask or an asbestos suit to watch. It's staged once or twice depending on how late the park is open.

During slower times of year, the evening parade is held only on weekends, and sometimes not then. Call (407) 824-4321 if you want to confirm it's on.

Parade Route and Vantage Points

Magic Kingdom parades circle Town Square, head down Main Street, go around the central hub, and cross the bridge to Liberty Square, where they follow the waterfront, ending in Frontierland. Sometimes they begin in Frontierland, run the route in the opposite direction, and end in Town Square.

Most guests watch from the central hub or from Main Street. One of the best and most popular vantage points is the upper platform of the Walt Disney World Railroad station at the Town Square end of Main Street. This also is a good place for watching Fantasy in the Sky fireworks. The problem is, you have to stake out your position 30–45 minutes before show time.

To avoid the largest crowds, watch parades from Liberty Square or Frontierland. Great vantage points are:

1. Sleepy Hollow snack shop, on your right as you cross the bridge into Liberty Square but only when the parade begins on Main Street.

2. Anywhere along the pathway on the Liberty Square side of the moat from the Sleepy Hollow sandwich shop to Cinderella Castle. Once again, this spot works only for parades coming from Main Street.
3. The elevated, covered walkway connecting the Liberty Tree Tavern and *The Diamond Horseshoe Saloon Revue.*
4. Elevated wooden platforms in front of the Frontierland Shootin' Arcade, Frontier Trading Post, and the building labeled FRONTIER MERCHANDISE. Be there 10–12 minutes before parade time.
5. Benches along the perimeter of the central hub, between the entrances to Liberty Square and Adventureland. The view is unobstructed, but somewhat removed. What you lose in proximity, however, you make up for in comfort.

Assuming it starts on Main Street, the parade takes 16–20 minutes to reach Liberty Square or Frontierland.

Shopping in the Magic Kingdom

Shops add realism and atmosphere to the theme settings and offer extensive souvenirs, clothing, novelties, and decorator items. Many goods, with the exception of trademark souvenirs, are available elsewhere for less, but there's also a lot of stuff we've never seen *anywhere* else. One-day visitors should bypass the shops. Those with more time should browse in early afternoon when rides are crowded. Main Street shops open earlier and close later than the rest of the park. Stow your purchases in lockers at Main Street Station or have the shop forward your packages to Package Pick-up for retrieval when you leave. Purchases by Disney resort guests can be delivered to their rooms.

Most trademark merchandise sold at Disney World is available from Walt Disney Attractions Mail Order Department at (407) 363-6200 or from the catalog department at (800) 237-5751.

Magic Kingdom Touring Plans

Our step-by-step Magic Kingdom touring plans are field-tested for seeing *as much as possible* in one day with a minimum of time in lines. They're designed to avoid crowds and bottlenecks on days of moderate to heavy attendance. But there's more to see in the Magic Kingdom than can be experienced in one day.

On days of lighter attendance, touring plans will still save time but won't be as critical to successful touring. Don't worry that other people will be following the same plan. Fewer than 1 in 500 people in the park will have been exposed to it.

Choosing the Right Touring Plan

We offer four Magic Kingdom touring plans:

- Author's Selective Magic Kingdom One-Day Touring Plan for Adults
- Magic Kingdom One-Day Touring Plan for Parents with Young Children
- Magic Kingdom Dumbo-or-Die-in-a-Day Touring Plan for Parents with Young Children
- Magic Kingdom Two-Day Touring Plan

If you have two days (or even two mornings) at the Magic Kingdom, the Two-Day Touring Plan is *by far* the most relaxed and efficient. This plan takes advantage of early morning, when lines are short and the park hasn't filled. It works well all year and eliminates much of the extra walking required by the one-day plans. No matter when the park closes, our two-day plan guarantees the most efficient touring and the least time in line. It's perfect for guests who wish to sample both the attractions and the atmosphere, including parades and fireworks.

If you have only one day, use the Author's Selective One-Day Touring Plan. It features only the best in the park.

If you have children younger than age eight, adopt the One-Day Touring Plan for Parents with Young Children. It's a compromise, integrating preferences of younger children with those of older siblings and adults. The plan includes many children's rides in Fantasyland but omits roller-coaster rides and attractions that are frightening or barred by height requirements. An alternative would be the One-Day Touring Plan for Adults or the Author's Selective One-Day Touring Plan, taking advantage of switching off (page 54).

The Dumbo-or-Die-in-a-Day Touring Plan for Parents with Young Children is designed for parents who will spare no sacrifice for their children. On Dumbo-or-Die, adults generally stand around, sweat, wipe noses, pay for stuff, and watch the children enjoy themselves.

Two-Day Touring Plans for Families with Young Children

If you have young children and are looking for a two-day itinerary, combine the Magic Kingdom One-Day Touring Plan for Parents with Young Children and the second day of the Magic Kingdom Two-Day Touring Plan.

The Single-Day Touring Conundrum

Touring the Magic Kingdom in a day is complicated by the fact that the premier attractions are at opposite ends of the park: Splash Mountain and Big Thunder Mountain Railroad in Frontierland, and Space Mountain and *Alien Encounter* in Tomorrowland. It's virtually impossible to ride all without encountering lines at one or another. It doesn't matter which you ride first.

The best way to ride all four without long waits is to tour the Magic Kingdom over two mornings: Ride Space Mountain and experience *Alien Encounter* first thing one morning, then ride Splash Mountain and Big Thunder Mountain first thing on the other. If you only have one day, be present at opening time on a non-early-entry day. Speed immediately to Space Mountain, then take in *Alien Encounter*. After *Alien Encounter* rush to Frontierland and scope out the situation at Splash Mountain. If the posted wait time is 30 minutes or less, go ahead and hop in line. If the wait exceeds 30 minutes, get a FASTPASS for Splash Mountain, then ride Big Thunder Mountain.

Magic Kingdom Attractions Crowded in Early Morning	
Tomorrowland	Space Mountain *Alien Encounter*
Frontierland	Splash Mountain Big Thunder Mountain Railroad
Fantasyland	Dumbo the Flying Elephant The Many Adventures of Winnie the Pooh
Adventureland	Jungle Cruise

Combining Early Entry with the Touring Plans

1. Adults touring without children should arrive when the turnstiles open and experience *Alien Encounter,* then go directly to Space Mountain, which sometimes opens a half hour later. If the mountain isn't open when you arrive, wait (ten minutes or less). After riding Space Mountain, quiet your nerves on Peter Pan and Snow White in Fantasyland.

Guests ineligible for early entry generally will be admitted 30 minutes before official opening. When they join the early-entry throng, the park becomes stuffed. If you want to ride Splash Mountain and Big Thunder Mountain Railroad without horrendous waits, position yourself on the border of Fantasyland and Liberty Square and hustle to the mountains the second the rest of the park opens. Pick up your touring plan after you've finished at Big Thunder and Splash mountains, skipping attractions you experienced during early entry.

2. Adults touring with children should arrive as early as possible and enjoy attractions in Fantasyland and the Tomorrowland Speedway. Interrupt your touring ten minutes before day guests are admitted and position yourself to rush to either Frontierland or Adventureland. When the rest of the park opens, ride Splash Mountain if your kids are at least 40" tall. Otherwise, ride the Jungle Cruise in Adventureland. Afterward, return to Fantasyland and see *Legend of the Lion King.* Pick up your touring plan after *Legend of the Lion King,* bypassing attractions you've already seen.

E-Ride Night

In 2000 Disney offered a new program called E-Ride Night. As with early-entry, only Disney resort guests with multi-day passports (and annual and seasonal pass holders) are eligible. For $10 you can purchase a pass that allows you to remain in the Magic Kingdom for three hours after the official closing time and enjoy the following attractions:

Space Mountain	Splash Mountain	Big Thunder Mountain
Alien Encounter	Astro Orbiter	Pirates of the Caribbean
The Timekeeper	Haunted Mansion	*Country Bear Jamboree*

E-Ride Night is not good for admission to the park by itself. It must be used with a multiday admission used at any of the major theme parks on the day in question. Now for the bad news. Thus far, Disney has operated this program only during the slower times of year when the Magic Kingdom closes relatively early (7 or 8 p.m.), and even then on just one day each week. As with all things Disney, this program is subject to change or cancellation at any time.

If You Are Not a Disney Resort Guest

If you aren't eligible for early entry, avoid the Magic Kingdom on early-entry days, regardless of time of year.

Note: During holiday periods, the parks frequently open 90 minutes early for everyone.

Preliminary Instructions for All Magic Kingdom Touring Plans

On days of moderate to heavy attendance, follow your chosen touring plan exactly, deviating only:

1. *When you aren't interested in an attraction it lists.*

2. *When you encounter a very long line at an attraction it calls for.* It's possible that this is a temporary situation caused by hundreds of people arriving from a recently concluded theater performance. Move to the plan's next step and return to the attraction later.

What to Do If You Get Off Track

If you experience an unexpected interruption that throws off the touring plan, consult the "When to Go" information in the individual attraction profiles.

Before You Go

1. Call (407) 824-4321 a day ahead for the official opening time. Ask where early entry will be in effect.
2. Buy your admission.

Author's Selective Magic Kingdom
One-Day Touring Plan for Adults

For: Adults touring without young children
Assumes: Willingness to experience all major rides and shows

This plan includes only those attractions the author thinks are the best in the Kingdom. It requires considerable walking and some backtracking to avoid long lines. You likely won't complete the tour. How far you get depends on how quickly you move among rides, how many times you rest or eat, how quickly the park fills, and what time the park closes.

1. If you're a Disney hotel guest, use Disney transportation to commute to the park, arriving 100 minutes before official opening on *early-entry days* and 40 minutes before official opening on *non-early-entry days.*

    If you're a day guest, arrive at the parking lot 50 minutes before the Magic Kingdom's stated opening time on *non-early-entry days.* Arrive 90 minutes earlier if it's a holiday period. Add 15 minutes if you must buy your admission. Take the tram to the Transportation and Ticket Center. At the TTC, transfer to the monorail or ferry to reach the park's entrance. If the line is short, take the monorail; otherwise, catch the ferry.

2. At the park, proceed through the turnstiles and have one person go to City Hall for park guidemaps containing the daily entertainment schedule.

3. Regroup and move quickly down Main Street to the central hub. Because the Magic Kingdom uses two opening procedures, you'll probably encounter one of the following:

    a. The entire park will be open. In this case, proceed quickly to Space Mountain in Tomorrowland.

    b. Only Main Street will be open. In this case, proceed to the central hub and position yourself at the entrance to Tomorrowland. When the rope drops, head to Space Mountain.

4. Exit Space Mountain and hurry to *Alien Encounter*.

5. Turn left upon exiting *Alien Encounter* and proceed to Fantasyland (passing through Tomorrowland, keeping the

Tomorrowland Indy Speedway on your right). Swing left at the Mad Tea Party and proceed to The Many Adventures of Winnie the Pooh. Ride.

6. Exit Winnie the Pooh to the left and cross Fantasyland to Peter Pan's Flight.

7. Exit Peter Pan left and depart Fantasyland for Liberty Square. On entering Liberty Square turn right and experience The Haunted Mansion.

8. After leaving The Haunted Mansion, turn right and continue along the waterfront into Frontierland and on to Splash Mountain. At Splash Mountain, get in line if the posted wait is less than 30 minutes. Otherwise, obtain a FASTPASS for each member of your party.

9. After obtaining your Splash Mountain FASTPASS (or riding), go next door to Big Thunder Mountain and ride.

10. Proceed to adjacent Adventureland. Ride Pirates of the Caribbean.

11. By this time you should be coming up on your FASTPASS time slot to return and ride Splash Mountain. If you are already in your Splash Mountain time slot, try to obtain a FASTPASS to the Jungle Cruise (a second FASTPASS can usually be obtained once you are in the return time slot of your first FASTPASS). If you are not within your Splash Mountain return window, continue the touring plan. Don't attempt to get your Jungle Cruise FASTPASS until you are in your Splash Mountain return window. If you continue to enjoy other attractions before returning to ride Splash Mountain, don't cut it too close. Head back to Splash Mountain with at least 15 minutes to spare.

12. Feel free to have lunch or enjoy a live show at any time after you ride Splash Mountain. If you were not able to get a FASTPASS for the Jungle Cruise earlier, obtain one immediately after riding Splash Mountain.

13. In Adventureland try *Enchanted Tiki Birds*.

14. Check your watch to see if you are coming up on your Jungle Cruise FASTPASS return window. Continue with the Touring Plan, breaking off to ride the Jungle Cruise with at least 15 minutes to spare.

15. In Liberty Square, experience the *Liberty Belle* Riverboat and *The Hall of Presidents*. Begin with whichever gets underway first, followed by the other.

16. After riding the Jungle Cruise with your FASTPASS, see any of the attractions in Steps 9–15 that you missed in order to keep a FASTPASS appointment.
17. Return via the central hub to Tomorrowland.
18. In Tomorrowland check out the wait for Buzz Lightyear. If the wait is 25 minutes or less, get in line. Otherwise obtain FASTPASSES for everyone in your party. If the wait for Buzz Lightyear is tolerable, consider picking up FASTPASSES for Space Mountain if you want to ride a second time.
19. In Tomorrowland, see *The Timekeeper*.
20. Also in Tomorrowland, try the *Carousel of Progress*.
21. Return with your FASTPASS to ride Buzz Lightyear.
22. Return to Fantasyland by way of the central hub and ride It's a Small World.
23. Also in Fantasyland, see *Legend of the Lion King*.
24. Depart Fantasyland and walk through Mickey's Toontown Fair. There's not much here for adults, though you might find Mickey's House and Minnie's House amusing.
25. Take the Walt Disney World Railroad for a round trip from the Toontown Station.
26. If you have time left before the park closes, backtrack to attractions you may have missed or bypassed. See parades, fireworks, or live performances that interest you. Grab a bite to eat.
27. Browse Main Street after the rest of the park has closed.

Magic Kingdom One-Day Touring Plan for Parents with Young Children

For: Parents with children younger than age eight
Assumes: Periodic stops for rest, toilets, and refreshment

This plan represents a compromise between the observed tastes of adults and those of younger children. It includes rides that children may be able to experience at local fairs and amusement parks. Consider omitting these rides. The following cycle-loading rides often have long lines:

Cinderella's Golden Carrousel	Mad Tea Party
Dumbo the Flying Elephant	Astro Orbiter

**To Convert This One-Day Touring Plan
into a Two-Day Touring Plan**

Skip steps 11, 12, and 17–19 on the first day. On the second day, arrive 30 minutes prior to opening and take the Walt Disney World Railroad from Main Street to Mickey's Toontown Fair. See Mickey's Toontown Fair in its entirety and then move on to Tomorrowland.

Instead of this touring plan, try either of the one-day plans for adults and take advantage of switching off (page 54).

Before entering the park, decide whether you will return to your hotel midday for a rest. You won't see as much if you do, but everyone will be more relaxed.

This plan requires considerable walking and some backtracking to avoid long lines. You may not complete the tour. How far you get depends on how quickly you move among rides, how many times you rest or eat, how quickly the park fills, and what time the park closes.

1. If you're a Disney resort guest, use Disney transportation to commute to the park, arriving 100 minutes before official opening on *early-entry days* and 40 minutes before official opening on *non-early-entry days.*

   If you're a day guest, arrive at the parking lot 50 minutes before the Magic Kingdom's stated opening on a *non-early-entry day.* Arrive 90 minutes earlier if it's a holiday period. Add 15 minutes if you must buy your admission. Take the tram to the Transportation and Ticket Center. At the TTC, transfer to the monorail or ferry to reach the park's entrance. If the line is short, take the monorail; otherwise, catch the ferry.

2. At the Magic Kingdom, proceed through the turnstiles and have one person go to City Hall for park guidemaps containing the daily entertainment schedule.

3. Rent strollers if necessary.

4. Move quickly to the end of Main Street. If the entire park is open, proceed briskly to Fantasyland. Otherwise, stand by the rope barrier at the central hub. When the barrier drops, go through the main door of the Castle and ride Dumbo the Flying Elephant.

5. Enjoy The Many Adventures of Winnie the Pooh.

6. Ride Peter Pan's Flight.

7. See *Legend of the Lion King.*

8. Exit left from *Legend of the Lion King* and go to Liberty Square. Turn right at the waterfront and go to The Haunted Mansion. Ride.

9. Enter Frontierland. See the *Country Bear Jamboree.*

10. Go to Adventureland via the passageway between the Frontierland Shootin' Arcade and the woodcarving shop. Ride Pirates of the Caribbean.

11. Turn left out of Pirates, then right into Frontierland. At the Frontierland station, catch a train to Mickey's Toontown Fair. Pick up a replacement stroller at Mickey's Toontown Fair.

12. At Mickey's Toontown Fair, visit the characters, explore the maze, and enjoy Donald's Boat. Ride the roller coaster if the line isn't prohibitive.

13. Return to Main Street by foot or train and leave the park for lunch and a rest at your hotel. Have your hand stamped for re-entry and keep your parking receipt so you won't have to repay when you return, refreshed, between 3:30 and 5 p.m. Once inside, proceed to Adventureland and obtain FASTPASSES for your entire party at the Jungle Cruise. Then continue on to Frontierland.

14. Take the raft to Tom Sawyer Island. Set time limits based on the park's closing, your energy level, and how many more attractions you want to experience. If you stayed in the park instead of taking a break, consider having lunch at Aunt Polly's Dockside Inn on the island.

15. Return to Adventureland via the castle and central hub. Try the Jungle Cruise.

16. Return to Fantasyland. Ride It's a Small World.

17. Go to Tomorrowland via the castle and central hub. Ride Buzz Lightyear's Space Ranger Spin. Use FASTPASS if the wait is not tolerable.

18. Ride the Tomorrowland Transit Authority.

19. Head back toward the central hub entrance to Tomorrowland and see *The Timekeeper.*

20. If time remains before the park closes, check the entertainment schedule for live performances, parades, fireworks,

and other special events. Grab a bite, or see attractions you
might have missed.

21. Browse Main Street after the rest of the park has closed.

Magic Kingdom Dumbo-or-Die-in-a-Day Touring Plan for Parents with Young Children

For: Adults compelled to devote every waking
moment to the pleasure and entertainment of their
young children, or rich people paying someone
else to take their children to the park
Prerequisite: This touring plan is designed for days when
the Magic Kingdom closes at 9 p.m. or later
Assumes: Frequent stops for rest, toilets, and refreshments

Note: Name aside, this itinerary is not a joke. It will provide
a young child with about as perfect a day as is possible at the
Magic Kingdom.

This plan addresses the preferences, needs, and desires of young
children to the virtual exclusion of those of adults or older siblings. It's wonderful if you're paying a sitter, nanny, or chauffeur
to take your children to the Magic Kingdom.

1. If you're a Disney resort guest, use Disney transportation
   to commute to the park, arriving 100 minutes before
   official opening on *early-entry days* and 40 minutes before
   official opening on *non-early-entry days.*

   If you're a day-guest, arrive at the parking lot 50 minutes before the Magic Kingdom's stated opening time on
   a *non-early-entry day.* Arrive 90 minutes earlier if it's a holiday period. Add 15 minutes if you must buy your admission. Take the tram to the Transportation and Ticket Center. At the TTC, transfer to the monorail or ferry to reach
   the park's entrance. If the line is short, take the monorail;
   otherwise, catch the ferry.

2. At the Magic Kingdom, proceed through the turnstiles
   and have one person go to City Hall for park guidemaps
   containing the daily entertainment schedule.

3. Rent a stroller (if needed).

4. Move quickly to the end of Main Street. If the entire park is open, proceed briskly to Fantasyland. Otherwise, stand by the rope barrier at the central hub. When the barrier drops, go through the main door of the Castle to Cinderella's Royal Table.

5. At Cinderella's Royal Table (on your right as you enter Cinderella Castle), make a priority seating for 7 p.m. This will give your kids a chance to see the inside of the Castle and meet Cinderella.

6. Ride Dumbo the Flying Elephant.

7. If your child wants, ride again. To avoid two waits in line, one adult should ride with the child while the other lines up behind another two-dozen riders.

8. Ride The Many Adventures of Winnie the Pooh, near Dumbo.

9. Ride Peter Pan's Flight.

10. Ride Cinderella's Golden Carrousel.

11. See *Legend of the Lion King.*

12. Ride the Tomorrowland Speedway. Let your child "steer" (cars are on guiderails) while you work the gas pedal.

13. Ride the Astro Orbiter. For safety, seat your children before you get in.

14. Ride Buzz Lightyear's Space Ranger Spin, near the Astro Orbiter.

15. Return to Main Street via the central hub. Leave the park for a rest break at your hotel. Have your hand stamped for re-entry and keep your parking receipt so you won't have to pay again when you return, refreshed, about 4 or 4:30 p.m. If you stay in the park, skip to Step 17.

16. Back from break, take the train to Frontierland.

17. Go by raft to Tom Sawyer Island. Stay as long as the kids want. If you're hungry, eat at Aunt Polly's Dockside Inn.

18. Leave the island and see the *Country Bear Jamboree* in Frontierland.

19. Take the train from Frontierland Station to Mickey's Toontown Fair.

20. Walk through Mickey's Country House and Minnie's Country House and play on Donald's Boat. Meet the characters at the Toontown Hall of Fame.

> ### To Convert This One-Day Touring Plan into a Two-Day Touring Plan
>
> Skip steps 20 and 21 on the first day. On the second day, arrive 30 minutes prior to opening and take the Walt Disney World Railroad from Main Street to Mickey's Toontown Fair. See Mickey's Toontown Fair in its entirety.

21. Check your watch. You should be within an hour of your dinner priority seating at Cinderella's Royal Table. Take the direct path from Mickey's Toontown Fair to Fantasyland. If you have 20 minutes or more before your Royal Table seating, ride It's a Small World.

22. After dinner, leave Fantasyland and go to Liberty Square. If your children want, see The Haunted Mansion. If not, skip to Step 23.

23. Evening parades are excellent. If you're interested, adjust the remaining touring plan to allow you to take a viewing position about ten minutes before the early parade starts (about 8 or 9 p.m.). If you aren't interested, enjoy attractions in Adventureland during the parade.

24. Go to Adventureland by way of Liberty Square, Frontierland, or the central hub. Take the Jungle Cruise if lines are reasonable. If they're long, obtain FASTPASSES and see *Enchanted Tiki Birds* and the Swiss Family Treehouse. If your children can stand a few skeletons, also see Pirates of the Caribbean.

25. After the birds, treehouse, and pirates, return with your fastpass to ride the Jungle Cruise.

26. If time remains before the park closes, repeat attractions the kids especially liked, or try ones you might have missed.

Magic Kingdom Two-Day Touring Plan

For: Parties wishing to spread their Magic Kingdom visit over two days

Assumes: Willingness to experience all major rides (including roller coasters) and shows

Timing: This two-day touring plan takes advantage of early-morning touring. Each day, you should complete the structured part of the plan by about 4 p.m. This leaves plenty of time for live entertainment. If the park is open late (after 8 p.m.), consider returning to your hotel at midday for a swim and a nap. Eat an early dinner outside Walt Disney World and return refreshed to enjoy the park's nighttime festivities.

Day One

1. If you're a Disney hotel guest, use Disney transportation to commute to the park, arriving 100 minutes before official opening time on *early-entry days* and 40 minutes before official opening on *non-early-entry days.*

    If you're a day-guest, arrive at the parking lot 50 minutes before the Magic Kingdom's official opening on a *non-early-entry day.* Arrive 90 minutes earlier than official opening if it's a holiday period. Add 15 minutes to the above if you must purchase your admission. These arrivals will give you time to park and catch the tram to the Transportation and Ticket Center. At the TTC, transfer to the monorail or ferry to reach the park's entrance. If the line for the monorail is short, take the monorail; otherwise, catch the ferry.

2. At the park, proceed through the turnstiles and have one person go to City Hall for guidemaps containing the daily entertainment schedule.

3. Move as fast as you can down Main Street to the central hub. Because the Magic Kingdom uses two procedures for opening, you probably will encounter one of the following:

    a. The entire park will be open. In this case, proceed quickly to Space Mountain in Tomorrowland.

    b. Only Main Street will be open. In this case, position yourself in the central hub at the entrance to Tomorrowland. When the park opens and the rope barrier drops, walk as fast as possible to Space Mountain.

4. After exiting Space Mountain, backtrack to *Alien Encounter.*

5. Exit *Alien Encounter*, bear left past the Tomorrowland Speedway, and go to Fantasyland. Experience The Many Adventures of Winnie the Pooh.

6. Exit Pooh to the left and ride Peter Pan's Flight.

7. Exit Peter Pan to the right and turn the corner. See *Legend of the Lion King*.

8. Exit *Lion King* to the left, cross the courtyard, and ride It's A Small World.

9. Exit Small World to the right and go to Liberty Square. Experience The Haunted Mansion.

10. See *The Hall of Presidents.*

11. If you're hungry, eat. Fast-food eateries that generally are less crowded include the Columbia Harbour House in Liberty Square, Aunt Polly's Dockside Inn on Tom Sawyer Island in Frontierland, El Pirata y el Perico in Adventureland, and The Crystal Palace at the central hub end of Main Street. As a lunchtime alternative, check your guidemap for the next performance of *The Diamond Horseshoe Saloon Revue.* If the timing is right, eat a sandwich while watching the show.

12. After lunch, ride the *Liberty Belle* Riverboat.

Note: At this point, check the entertainment schedule to see if any parades or live performances interest you. Note the times and alter the touring plan accordingly. Since you already have seen all the attractions that cause bottlenecks and have big lines, interrupting the touring plan here won't cause any problems. Simply pick up where you left off before the parade or show.

13. In Frontierland, take a raft to Tom Sawyer Island. Explore.

14. Return from the island and see the *Country Bear Jamboree.*

15. This concludes the touring plan for the day. Enjoy the shops, see some of the live entertainment, or revisit your favorite attractions until you're ready to leave.

Day Two

1. If you're a Disney hotel guest, use Disney transportation to commute to the park, arriving 100 minutes before official opening time on *early-entry days* and 40 minutes before official opening on *non-early-entry days*.

If you're a day-guest, arrive at the parking lot 50 minutes before the Magic Kingdom's official opening time on a *non-early-entry day.* Arrive 90 minutes earlier than official opening if it's a holiday period. Add 15 minutes to the above if you must purchase your admission. These arrivals will give you time to park and catch the tram to the Transportation and Ticket Center. At the TTC, transfer to the monorail or ferry to reach the park's entrance. If the line for the monorail is short, take the monorail; otherwise, catch the ferry.

2. At the park, proceed through the turnstiles. Stop at City Hall for guidemaps containing the day's entertainment schedule.

Note: If you're a Disney resort guest and enter the park on an early-entry day, revisit your favorite Fantasyland and Tomorrowland attractions. As the time approaches for the park to open to the public, position yourself in Fantasyland at the boundary between Fantasyland and Liberty Square. When the other lands open, head for the Liberty Square waterfront and from there to Splash Mountain. After Splash Mountain, pick up the touring plan at Big Thunder Mountain Railroad (Step 4, below), skipping steps that direct you to attractions you experienced during your early-entry hour.

3. Proceed to the end of Main Street. If the entire park is open, go immediately to Splash Mountain in Frontierland. Otherwise, turn left past Casey's Corner and position yourself in front of The Crystal Palace, facing the walkway bridge to Adventureland. When the park opens and the rope barrier drops, cross the bridge and turn left into Adventureland. Cut through Adventureland into Frontierland. Go straight to Splash Mountain and ride.

4. Ride Big Thunder Mountain Railroad, next to Splash Mountain.

5. Return to Adventureland. Ride the Jungle Cruise. If the wait seems prohibitive use FASTPASS.

6. Across the street, see the *Enchanted Tiki Birds.*

7. Walk through the Swiss Family Treehouse.

8. Exit the Treehouse to the left. Enjoy Pirates of the Caribbean.

Note: At this point, check the daily entertainment schedule to see if any parades or live performances interest you. Note the times, and alter the touring plan accordingly. Since you already have seen all the attractions that cause bottlenecks and have big lines, interrupting the touring plan here won't cause any problems. Simply pick up where you left off before the parade or show.

9. If you're hungry, eat. Fast-food eateries that generally are less crowded include the Columbia Harbour House in Liberty Square, Aunt Polly's on Tom Sawyer Island, El Pirata y el Perico in Adventureland, and The Crystal Palace at the central hub end of Main Street.

10. Exit Adventureland and go to the Frontierland train station between Splash and Big Thunder Mountains. Catch the Walt Disney World Railroad. Disembark at Mickey's Toontown Fair (first stop).

11. Tour the Fair and meet the Disney characters.

12. Exit the Fair via the path to Tomorrowland.

13. In Tomorrowland, if you haven't eaten, try Cosmic Ray's Starlight Cafe (okay) or The Plaza Pavilion (better).

14. Ride the Tomorrowland Transit Authority.

15. See *Carousel of Progress.*

16. Ride Buzz Lightyear's Space Ranger Spin. If there's a long wait, use FASTPASS.

17. Proceed toward the central hub entrance of Tomorrowland and experience *The Timekeeper.*

18. This concludes the touring plan. Enjoy the shops, see live entertainment, or revisit your favorite attractions until you are ready to leave.

Part Ten

Epcot

Not to Be Missed at Epcot	
World Showcase	*The American Adventure*
	IllumiNations
Future World	Spaceship Earth
	Living with the Land
	Honey, I Shrunk the Audience
	Test Track Ride
	Body Wars
	Cranium Command

OVERVIEW

Fantasy isn't the focus at Epcot; education and inspiration are. The park has only two theme areas: Future World and World Showcase. Still, it's more than twice as big as the Magic Kingdom or Disney-MGM Studios and requires considerably more walking among the sights. Lines are equally long.

Epcot's size means you can't see it in a day without skipping attractions or giving some areas a cursory glance. Fortunately, some attractions can be savored slowly or skimmed, depending on personal interests. For example, the first section of Test Track is a thrill ride, the second a collection of walk-through exhibits and mini-theaters. Nearly everyone takes the ride, but many people bypass the exhibits.

Epcot is the most "adult" of the Disney theme parks. What it gains in taking a futuristic and technological look at the world, it loses in warmth, happiness, and charm.

Operating Hours

Future World always opens before World Showcase in the morning and usually closes before World Showcase in the evening. Most of the year, World Showcase opens two hours later than Future World. For exact times, call (407) 824-4321.

Future World Services	
Wheelchair & Stroller Rental	To the left inside the main entrance, toward the rear of the Entrance Plaza
Banking Services	ATMs are outside the main entrance near the kennels on the Future World Bridge and at the Germany pavilion in World Showcase
Storage Lockers	Right at Spaceship Earth (all lockers cleaned out every night)
Lost & Found	At the main entrance, at the gift shop
Live Entertainment Information	Guest Relations, to the left of Spaceship Earth
Lost Persons	At Guest Relations and at Baby Center on World Showcase side of Odyssey Center
Dining Priority Seating	Guest Relations
Walt Disney World & Local Attraction Information	Guest Relations
First Aid	Next to the Baby Center on World Showcase side of Odyssey Center
Baby Center/ Baby-Care Needs	On World Showcase side of Odyssey Center

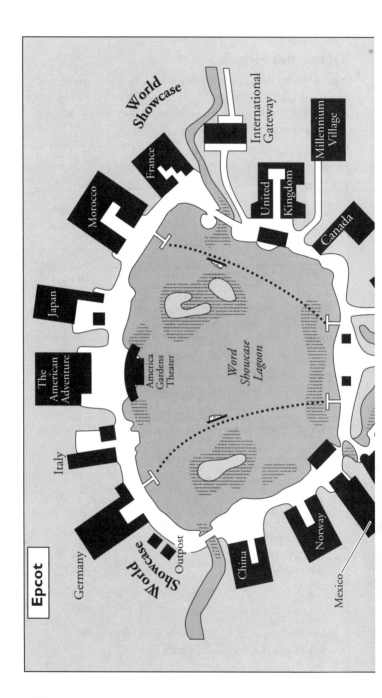

Epcot

World Showcase

International Gateway

Millennium Village

United Kingdom

Canada

France

Morocco

Japan

The American Adventure

America Gardens Theater

Word Showcase Lagoon

Italy

Germany

World Showcase

Outpost

China

Norway

Mexico

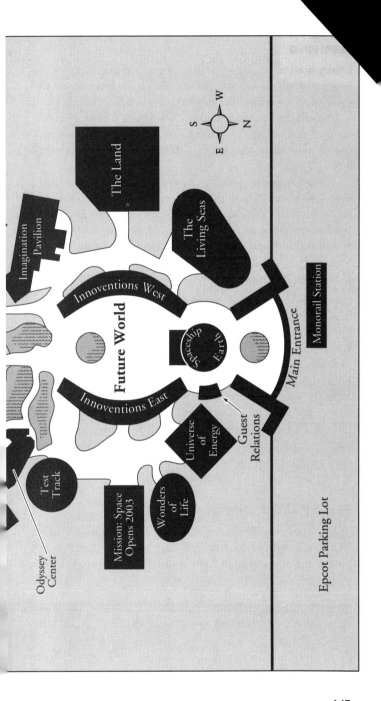

The Land

Imagination Pavilion

The Living Seas

Innoventions West

Future World

Spaceship Earth

Innoventions East

Guest Relations

Test Track

Universe of Energy

Mission: Space Opens 2003

Wonders of Life

Odyssey Center

Main Entrance

Monorail Station

Epcot Parking Lot

N W S E

...d campground guests are invited to enter Epcot one hour and a half early on specified days each week. If you have early-entry privileges, arrive about two hours before official opening.

Those lodging outside Disney World should avoid Epcot on early-entry days, which pack the park. Regardless, arrive 40–50 minutes before official opening. To verify early-entry days, call (407) 824-4321.

Epcot has its own parking lot, and there's no need to take a monorail or ferry to reach the entrance. Trams serve the lot, or you can walk to the front gate. Monorail service connects Epcot with the Transportation and Ticket Center, Magic Kingdom (transfer required), and Magic Kingdom resorts (transfer required).

GETTING ORIENTED

Epcot's themed sections are distinctly different. Future World combines Disney creativity and corporations' technological resources to examine where humankind has come from and is going. World Showcase features landmarks, cuisine, and culture of 11 nations—a sort of permanent World's Fair.

Navigating the park is fairly simple. Its focal point, Spaceship Earth, is visible from almost everywhere in Epcot. But the 180-foot geosphere is in a busy location, making it a poor meeting place. It's better to regroup at any national pavilion, but be specific. Each pavilion is a mini-town with buildings, monuments, gardens, and plazas. In Japan, for example, pinpoint a spot such as the sidewalk side of the pagoda.

FASTPASS AT EPCOT

Epcot offers two FASTPASS attractions. Strategies for using FASTPASS at the Magic Kingdom have been integrated into our touring plans. Epcot FASTPASS attractions are:

| Future World | *Honey, I Shrunk the Audience* |
| | Test Track Ride |

For a complete explanation about how FASTPASS works, refer to page 20.

EPCOT'S MILLENNIUM CELEBRATION

Epcot is Millennium headquarters for Walt Disney World, so expect larger-than-average crowds throughout the 15-month celebration that ends January 1, 2001. You can't miss the giant magic wand–wielding Mickey hand appended to Spaceship Earth. The 116-foot-long, star-tipped wand reflects light on billboard-size "2,000" numerals. The overall effect, though suggestive of an exponentially bloated Mr. Potato Head, is actually pretty festive.

For the most part, the big-deal Millennium attractions and events are found in the World Showcase section of Epcot— Millennium Village, Tapestry of Nations, and a special edition of *IllumiNations* called *Illuminations 2000: Reflections of Earth* to name a few. A more detailed description of Millennium Village, Tapestry of Nations, and *IllumiNations 2000* can be found later in this chapter.

Future World

Gleaming, futuristic structures define this theme area at Epcot's main entrance. Broad thoroughfares are punctuated with billowing fountains—all reflected in space-age facades. Everything is sparkling clean and seems bigger than life. Pavilions dedicated to humankind's past, present, and future technological accomplishments form the perimeter of Future World. Central is Spaceship Earth, flanked by Innoventions East and West.

Most services are concentrated in Future World's Entrance Plaza, near the main gate. Guest Relations, to the left of the sphere, is the park headquarters and information center. Staffed information booths and WorldKey Information Satellites are outside.

Touring Tips   Make priority seatings for sit-down restaurants through a WorldKey attendant instead of going to the restaurant itself.

Spaceship Earth

What It Is: Educational dark ride through past, present, and future

Scope & Scale: Headliner

When to Go: Before 10 a.m. or after 4 p.m.

Special Comments: If lines are long, try again after 4 p.m.

Author's Rating: One of Epcot's best. Not to be missed; ★★★★

Appeal by Age Group:

Pre-school	Grade School	Teens	Young Adults	Over 30	Senior Citizens
★★★	★★★★	★★★½	★★★★	★★★★	★★★★

Duration of Ride: About 16 minutes

Avg. Wait in Line per 100 People ahead of You: 3 minutes

Assumes: Normal operation

Loading Speed: Fast

Description and Comments   This AT&T ride spirals through the 18-story interior of Epcot's premier landmark, taking visitors past audio-animatronic scenes depicting mankind's developments in communications. The ride is compelling and well done.

Touring Tips   Because it's near Epcot's main entrance, Spaceship Earth is packed all morning. If you're interested in riding Test Track, wait to ride Spaceship Earth until after 4 p.m.

   If the line runs only along the right side of the sphere, you'll board in less than 15 minutes.

INNOVENTIONS

What It Is: Static and hands-on exhibits relating to products and technologies of the near future

Scope & Scale: Major diversion

When to Go: Second day at Epcot or after you've seen all major attractions

Special Comments: Most exhibits demand time and participation; not much gained here by a quick walk-through

Author's Rating: Vastly improved; ★★★½

Appeal by Age Group:

Pre-school	Grade School	Teens	Young Adults	Over 30	Senior Citizens
★½	★★★½	★★★★	★★★½	★★★	★★★

Description and Comments   Innoventions consists of two huge, crescent-shaped, glass-walled structures separated by a central plaza. Formerly called CommuniCore, the complex was designed to be Epcot's communications and community hub. But during Epcot's first 12 years, it was a staid museum of science and industry.

The changes of 1994 aimed to return it to its original concept. The result is a busy collection of industry-sponsored walk-through and hands-on exhibits. Dynamic, interactive, and forward-looking, Innoventions previews consumer and industrial goods of the near future. Electronics, communications, and entertainment technology are prominent. Exhibits, many changed each year, emphasize the product's or technology's effect on daily life. The most popular attraction is an arcade of video and simulator games. Frequently overlooked is the well-done tour of a Disney Imagineering studio. Innoventions also houses restaurants and shops.

Touring Tips   Innoventions can be crowded. Readers tell us that young children may not be able to get near some attractions and that noise is awesome. A few complain about exhibits' commercialism. Nonetheless, some exhibits are intriguing. Spend time here on your second day at Epcot. If you have only one day, visit during the evening, but be aware that many exhibits are technical and can't be enjoyed or understood if you're too weary.

THE LIVING SEAS

What It Is: Ride beneath a huge saltwater aquarium, plus
   exhibits on oceanography, ocean ecology, and sea life
Scope & Scale: Major attraction
When to Go: Before 10 a.m. or after 3 p.m.
Special Comments: The ride is only a small component of this
   attraction
Author's Rating: An excellent marine exhibit; ★★★½
Appeal by Age Group:

Pre-school	Grade School	Teens	Young Adults	Over 30	Senior Citizens
★★★	★★★	★★★	★★★★	★★★★	★★★★

Duration of Ride: 3 minutes
Avg. Wait in Line per 100 People ahead of You: 3½ minutes
Assumes: All elevators in operation
Loading Speed: Fast

Description and Comments   This is among Future World's most ambitious attractions. Scientists and divers conduct actual marine experiments in a 200-foot-diameter, 27-foot-deep main tank containing fish, mammals, and crustaceans in a simulation of an ocean ecosystem. Visitors view the activity through eight-inch-thick windows below the surface (including windows in Coral Reef restaurant) and aboard an adventure ride consisting of a movie dramatizing the link between the ocean and human survival, a simulated descent to the bottom of the tank, and a three-minute gondola voyage through an underwater viewing tunnel.

The underwater ride is over almost before you're settled in the gondola. No matter; the strength of this attraction lies in exhibits afterward. Visitors can view fish-breeding experiments, watch films about sea life, and more.

The Living Seas is a high-quality marine/aquarium exhibit, but it's no substitute for visiting Sea World, an outstanding marine theme park in Orlando.

Touring Tips   Exhibits at the ride's end are the best part of The Living Seas. In the morning, these are often bypassed by guests trying to stay ahead of the crowd. Linger at The Living Seas when you aren't in a hurry. Visit in late afternoon or evening, or on your second day at Epcot.

THE LAND

Description and Comments   The Land pavilion, sponsored by Nestlé, contains three attractions and several restaurants. Its original emphasis was farming, but changes in 1994 refocused it on environmental concerns.

Touring Tips   The Land is a good place for a fast-food lunch; if you want to see the attractions, don't go during mealtimes.

Living with the Land

What It Is: An indoor boat-ride adventure through the past, present, and future of U.S. farming and agriculture

Scope & Scale: Major attraction

When to Go: Before 10:30 a.m. or after 7:30 p.m.

Special Comments: Ride in early morning, but save other Land attractions for later. Located on the lower level of The Land.

Author's Rating: Interesting and fun; not to be missed; ★★★★

Appeal by Age Group:

Pre-school	Grade School	Teens	Young Adults	Over 30	Senior Citizens
★★½	★★★	★★★½	★★★★	★★★★	★★★★

Duration of Ride: About 12 minutes

Avg. Wait in Line per 100 People ahead of You: 3 minutes

Assumes: 15 boats operating

Loading Speed: Moderate

Description and Comments Boat ride takes visitors through swamps, past inhospitable environments that humankind has faced as farmers, and through a futuristic greenhouse where real crops are grown using the latest agricultural technologies. Inspiring and educational, with excellent effects and a good narrative.

Touring Tips See this attraction before the lunch crowd hits or in the evening.

If you really enjoy this ride or have a special interest in the agriculture demonstrated, take the backstage Greenhouse Tour. At $6 for adults and $4 for children ages three–nine, this one-hour guided walking tour goes behind the scenes for an in-depth examination of growing methods. Reservations are accepted, space available, at the tour waiting area (far right of restaurants on lower level).

Food Rocks

What It Is: Audio-animatronic theater show about food and nutrition

Scope & Scale: Minor attraction

When to Go: Before 11 a.m. or after 2 p.m.

Special Comments: On lower level of The Land

Author's Rating: Sugarcoated nutrition lesson; ★★½

Appeal by Age Group:

Pre-school	Grade School	Teens	Young Adults	Over 30	Senior Citizens
★★★	★★★	★★½	★★★	★★★	★★★

Duration of Presentation: About 13 minutes

Preshow Entertainment: None

Probable Waiting Time: Less than 10 minutes

Description and Comments   Audio-animatronic foods and cook-ing utensils perform in a marginally educational rock concert. Featured artists include the Peach Boys, Chubby Cheddar, Neil Moussaka, and Pita Gabriel. Little Richard is the voice of a singing pineapple. Fast-paced and imaginative, *Food Rocks* is better enter-tainment than its predecessor, *Kitchen Kabaret,* and delivers the message about as well.

Touring Tips   One of Epcot's few light entertainment offerings. Though the theater isn't large, we've never waited long, even dur-ing mealtimes.

Circle of Life Theater

What It Is: Film exploring mankind's relationship with the environment

Scope & Scale: Minor attraction

When to Go: Before 11 a.m. and after 2 p.m.

Author's Rating: Highly interesting and enlightening; ★★★½

Appeal by Age Group:

Pre-school	Grade School	Teens	Young Adults	Over 30	Senior Citizens
★★½	★★★	★★½	★★★	★★★	★★★

Duration of Presentation: About 12½ minutes

Preshow Entertainment: None

Probable Waiting Time: 10–15 minutes

Description and Comments   The featured attraction is *The Circle of Life,* starring Simba, Timon, and Pumbaa from Disney's *The Lion King.* This superb film spotlights the environmental interdependency of all creatures on Earth. It's sobering, but not too heavy-handed.

Touring Tips   Crowds are least in late afternoon. Lines are long at mealtimes.

IMAGINATION PAVILION

Description and Comments   Multiattraction pavilion on the west side of Innoventions West, down the walk from The Land. Outside is an "upside-down waterfall" and one of our favorite Future World landmarks, the "jumping water."

Touring Tips   Go in early morning or late evening.

Journey into Your Imagination

What It Is: Fantasy-adventure dark ride
Scope & Scale: Major attraction
When to Go: Before 10:30 a.m. or after 6 p.m.
Author's Rating: ★★½
Appeal by Age Group:

Pre-school	Grade School	Teens	Young Adults	Over 30	Senior Citizens
★★	★★	★★	★★★	★★★	★★★

Duration of Ride: About 6 minutes
Avg. Wait in Line per 100 People ahead of You: 2 minutes
Loading Speed: Fast

Description and Comments   Replacing its dull and vacuous predecessor, Journey into Your Imagination takes you on a tour of the zany Imagination Institute. It stimulates all of your senses with optical illusions, an experiment where noise generates colors, a room that defies gravity, and other brain teasers.

Journey into Your Imagination pales in comparison to Honey, I Shrunk the Audience, the hilarious 3-D film that occupies the other half of the Imagination Pavilion. Pleasant rather than stimulating, the ride strains to achieve mediocrity.

Touring Tips   One of the coolest interactive exhibits at Epcot is a photo-morphing computer in the interactive exhibit area. First the machine takes your picture, then you select an image from several categories into which your photo is integrated. The final result can be e-mailed on the spot to family and friends. Best of all, there's no charge. Because it's new, Journey into Your Imagination will draw large crowds. Try to ride before 10:30 a.m.

Honey, I Shrunk the Audience (FASTPASS)

What It Is: 3-D film with special effects
Scope & Scale: Headliner
When to Go: Before 10 a.m. or just before Future World closes.
Special Comments: Loud, intense show with tactile effects

frightens some young children. Adults shouldn't be put off by the sci-fi theme

Author's Rating: An absolute hoot! Not to be missed; ★★★★½

Appeal by Age Group:

Pre-school	Grade School	Teens	Young Adults	Over 30	Senior Citizens
★★★	★★★★½	★★★★½	★★★★½	★★★★½	★★★★

Duration of Presentation: About 17 minutes

Preshow Entertainment: 8 minutes

Probable Waiting Time: 12 minutes (at suggested times)

Description and Comments *Honey, I Shrunk the Audience* is a 3-D offshoot of Disney's feature film, *Honey, I Shrunk the Kids.* Rich special effects include simulated explosions, smoke, fiber optics, lights, water spray, and moving seats—all played for laughs.

Touring Tips The sound is earsplitting, frightening some children and discomforting many adults.

Though launched with little fanfare in 1994, *Honey, I Shrunk the Audience* has become one of the park's most popular attractions. It isn't necessary to ride Journey into Your Imagination to enter; the theater is to the left of the ride. Avoid seats in the first several rows. If you're too close to the screen, 3-D images don't focus properly. Be sure to use FASTPASS if the line is oppressively long.

TEST TRACK

Description and Comments Test Track, presented by General Motors, contains the Test Track ride and TransCenter, an assembly of exhibits and mini-theater productions on the transportation theme. The pavilion is to the left of Spaceship Earth, toward World Showcase from the Universe of Energy pavilion.

Many readers say Test Track is one big GM commercial. We recognize the heavy hype, but we consider Test Track one of the most creatively conceived and executed attractions in Disney World.

Test Track Ride (FASTPASS)

What It Is: Automobile test-track simulator ride

Scope & Scale: Super headliner

When to Go: Before 9:15 a.m. and just before closing

Special Comments: 40" minimum height

Author's Rating: Not to be missed; ★★★½

Pre-school	Grade School	Teens	Young Adults	Over 30	Senior Citizens
★★★★	★★★★	★★★★	★★★★	★★★★	★★★★

Duration of Ride: About 4 minutes

Avg. Wait in Line per 100 People ahead of You: 4½ minutes

Assumes: Normal operation

Loading Speed: Moderate to fast

Description and Comments Visitors test a future model car at high speeds through hairpin turns, up and down steep hills, and over rough terrain. The six-guest vehicle rocks and pitches. Unlike simulators at Star Tours, Body Wars, and Back to the Future, the Test Track model is affixed to a track and actually travels.

Touring Tips Some great technology is at work here. When it's running, it's one of the park's better attractions. Head for Test Track as soon as you're admitted to the park. If you fail to arrive early, use FASTPASS. If all the FASTPASSES are gone join the singles line, a separate line for individuals who do not object to riding alone. Because most groups are unwilling to split up, singles lines are usually shorter than the regular line and can save you a lot of time.

WONDERS OF LIFE

Description and Comments This pavilion deals with the human body, health, and medicine. Housed in a 100,000-square-foot, gold-domed structure and presented by MetLife, Wonders of Life focuses on the capabilities of the human body and the importance of keeping fit.

Body Wars

What It Is: Flight-simulator ride through the human body

Scope & Scale: Headliner

When to Go: Before 10 a.m. or after 6 p.m.

Special Comments: Not recommended for pregnant women or persons prone to motion sickness; 40" minimum height

Author's Rating: Anatomy made fun. Not to be missed; ★★★★

Appeal by Age Group:

Pre- school	Grade School	Teens	Young Adults	Over 30	Senior Citizens
★★★	★★★★	★★★★	★★★★	★★★½	★★½

Duration of Ride: 5 minutes

Avg. Wait in Line per 100 People ahead of You: 4 minutes

Assumes: All simulators operating

Loading Speed: Moderate to fast

Description and Comments   This thrill ride through the human body was developed along the lines of the Star Tours space-simulation ride. The story is that you're a passenger in a miniature capsule injected into a body to retrieve a scientist who has been inspecting a splinter in the patient's finger. The scientist, however, is sucked into the circulatory system, and you chase throughout the body to rescue her. The simulator creates a visually graphic experience as it seems to hurtle at fantastic speeds through human organs.

Touring Tips   Body Wars remains popular with all ages, but it makes a lot of riders motion sick. It isn't unusual for a simulator to be taken off-line to clean up a previous rider's mess. If you're at all susceptible to motion sickness, reconsider riding. If you're on the ride and feel nauseous, look away from the screen (at the ceiling, or side and back walls, for example). Without the visual effects, the ride isn't rough enough to disturb most guests. If you get queasy, rest rooms are nearby as you exit. (*Note:* Star Tours at Disney-MGM Studios is just as wild but makes very few people sick. Successfully riding Star Tours doesn't mean you'll tolerate Body Wars. Conversely, if Body Wars made you ill, don't assume Star Tours will, too.)

Motion sickness aside, Body Wars is too intense (even terrifying) for some, especially preschoolers and seniors.

Ride in the early morning after Test Track Ride and the attractions at the Imagination Pavilion, or the hour before closing.

Cranium Command

What It Is: Audio-animatronic theater show about the brain

Scope & Scale: Major attraction

When to Go: Before 11 a.m. or after 3 p.m.

Author's Rating: Funny, outrageous, and educational. Not to be missed; ★★★★½

Appeal by Age Group:

Pre-school	Grade School	Teens	Young Adults	Over 30	Senior Citizens
★★	★★★★	★★★★	★★★★½	★★★★½	★★★★½

Duration of Presentation: About 20 minutes

Preshow Entertainment: Explanatory lead-in to feature presentation

Probable Waiting Time: Less than 10 minutes at times suggested

Description and Comments   *Cranium Command* is Epcot's great sleeper. Stuck on the back side of Wonders of Life and far less promoted than Body Wars, this most humorous attraction is bypassed by many people. Characters called "brain pilots" are trained to operate human brains. The show consists of a day in the life of one of these Cranium Commanders as he tries to pilot the brain of an adolescent boy. Disney World could use a lot more of this type of humor.

Touring Tips   To understand the program, you need to see the preshow cartoon in the waiting area. Most preschoolers enjoy *Cranium Command,* but many don't really understand it.

The Making of Me

What It Is: Humorous movie about human conception and birth

Scope & Scale: Minor attraction

When to Go: Early in the morning or after 4:30 p.m.

Author's Rating: Sanitized sex education; ★★★

Appeal by Age Group:

Pre-school	Grade School	Teens	Young Adults	Over 30	Senior Citizens
★½	★★★½	★★½	★★★	★★★	★★★

Duration of Presentation: 14 minutes

Preshow Entertainment: None

Probable Waiting Time: About 25 minutes (or more), unless you go at recommended times

Description and Comments   This lighthearted, sensitive movie about human conception, gestation, and birth was originally considered controversial, but most viewers agree the material is tasteful and creative. The main character goes back in time to watch his parents date, fall in love, marry, and conceive and give birth to him. Look for the biological error in the film. If you spot it, write us.

Sexual material is well handled, with emphasis on loving relationships, not plumbing. Parents say the sexual information goes over the heads of children younger than age seven. In older children, however, the film precipitates questions.

Touring Tips   *The Making of Me* is excellent and should be moved from its tiny space to a larger theater. Until (and if) it is, expect long lines unless you go at recommended times.

Fitness Fairgrounds

Description and Comments   Participatory exhibits allow guests to test their senses in a funhouse, get computer-generated health analyses, work out on sophisticated equipment, and watch a video called *Goofy about Health* (starring, who else?).

Touring Tips   Save Fitness Fairgrounds for your second day or the end of your first day at Epcot.

UNIVERSE OF ENERGY: ELLEN'S ENERGY ADVENTURE

What It Is: Combination ride/theater presentation about energy

Scope & Scale: Major attraction

When to Go: Before 11:15 a.m. or after 4:30 p.m.

Special Comments: Don't be dismayed by lines; 580 people enter the pavilion each time the theater changes audiences

Author's Rating: The most improved attraction at Walt Disney World; ★★★★

Appeal by Age Group:

Pre-school	Grade School	Teens	Young Adults	Over 30	Senior Citizens
★★★	★★★★	★★★½	★★★★	★★★★	★★★★

Duration of Presentation: About 26½ minutes

Preshow Entertainment: 8 minutes

Probable Waiting Time: 20–40 minutes

Description and Comments   Audio-animatronic dinosaurs and the unique traveling theater make this Exxon pavilion one of Future World's most popular. Visitors are seated in what appears to be an ordinary theater to watch an animated film on fossil fuels. Then the theater seats divide into six 97-passenger travel-ing cars, which glide among swamps and reptiles of a prehistoric forest. Special effects include warm, moist air from the swamp, the smell of sulphur from an erupting volcano, and the sight of lava hissing and bubbling toward passengers. Nifty cinematic techniques bring you back to the leading edge of energy research and development.

The original film was scrapped in 1996 and replaced with a humorous and upbeat flick starring Ellen DeGeneres. Although the current film represents a huge improvement for adults, Uni-verse of Energy remains a toss-up for kids. The dinosaurs frighten some preschoolers, and kids of all ages lose the thread during the educational segments.

Touring Tips   Universe of Energy can operate more than one show at a time, so lines generally are tolerable. If you bypass the show, try to see the great dinosaur topiaries at the pavilion.

THE "MOM, I CAN'T BELIEVE IT'S DISNEY!" FOUNTAIN

What It Is: Combination fountain and shower
When to Go: When it's hot
Scope & Scale: Diversion
Special Comments: Secretly installed by Martians during
    IllumiNations
Author's Rating: Yes!! ★★★★
Appeal by Age Group:

Pre-school	Grade School	Teens	Young Adults	Over 30	Senior Citizens
★★★★★	★★★★★	★★★★	★★★★	★★★★	★★★★★

Duration of Experience: Indefinite
Probable Waiting Time: None

Description and Comments   This fountain on the walkway link-ing Future World and World Showcase doesn't look like much, but it offers a truly spontaneous experience, rare in Disney World.

Spouts of water erupt randomly from the sidewalk. You can swim in the water, or let it cascade down on you or blow up your britches. On a broiling Florida day, people fling themselves into the fountain, dancing, skipping, singing, and splashing. Kids throw off their clothes. It's hard to imagine so much personal freedom in carefully controlled Disney World, but here it is. Hurrah!

Touring Tips   Your kids will be in the middle of this before your brain sounds the alert. Our advice: Pack dry shorts and turn them loose.

World Showcase

World Showcase, Epcot's second theme area, is an ongoing World's Fair set on a picturesque lagoon. Architecture, culture, cuisine, and history of 11 nations are permanently displayed at pavilions replicating familiar landmarks. Representative street scenes from host countries are spaced along a 1.2-mile promenade circling the 40-acre lagoon.

Most adults enjoy World Showcase, but many children find it boring. To help this, the Camera Center in Future World sells a Passport Kit (about $9). Each contains a blank passport and stamps for each Showcase nation. As kids visit a country, they tear out the appropriate stamp and stick it in the passport. The kit also contains basic information on the countries. Parents say the kit helps children tour World Showcase with minimal impatience. Also child-friendly are Kidcot Fun Stops, tables on the sidewalk at each pavilion where kids' passports are stamped and youngsters may try simple craft projects.

Double-decker buses carry visitors around the promenade, and boats ferry guests across the lagoon. Lines at bus stops can be pushy, and it's almost always quicker to walk than to ride buses or boats. Moving clockwise around the promenade, nations represented are:

MEXICO PAVILION
Description and Comments   Pre-Columbian pyramids dominate the architecture. One forms the pavilion's facade; the other overlooks the restaurant and plaza beside the boat ride, El Río del Tiempo.

Touring Tips   Romantic and exciting testimony to Mexico's charms, this pavilion also contains authentic and valuable artifacts. The village scene is beautiful and exquisitely detailed. See this pavilion before 11 a.m. or after 6 p.m.

El Río del Tiempo

What It Is: Indoor scenic boat ride

Scope & Scale: Minor attraction

When to Go: Before 11 a.m. or after 3 p.m.

Author's Rating: Light and relaxing; ★★

Appeal by Age Group:

Pre-school	Grade School	Teens	Young Adults	Over 30	Senior Citizens
★★	★★	★½	★★	★★	★★½

Duration of Ride: About 7 minutes (plus 1½-minute wait to disembark)

Avg. Wait in Line per 100 People ahead of You: 4½ minutes

Assumes: 16 boats in operation

Loading Speed: Moderate

Description and Comments El Río del Tiempo (River of Time) winds among audio-animatronic and cinematic scenes depicting Mexico's history. Special effects include simulated fireworks.

Pleasant and relaxing, but not particularly interesting, El Río del Tiempo isn't worth a long wait.

Touring Tips The ride is crowded in early afternoon.

NORWAY PAVILION

Description and Comments The Norway pavilion is complex, beautiful, and architecturally diverse. Surrounding a courtyard are traditional Scandinavian buildings, including a replica of the 14th-century Akershus Castle, a wooden stave church, red-tiled cottages, and replicas of historic buildings. The pavilion also offers an adventure boat ride, a movie, and, in the stave church, an art gallery. A Viking ship play area was added in 1999. Located between China and Mexico, Norway houses the sit-down Restaurant Akershus (priority seating required) serving *koldtbord* (cold buffet) and hot Norwegian fare. An outdoor cafe and a bakery cater to the hurried. Shoppers can browse native handicrafts.

Maelstrom

What It Is: Indoor adventure boat ride

Scope & Scale: Major attraction

When to Go: Before noon or after 4:30 p.m.

Author's Rating: Too short, but has its moments; ★★★

Appeal by Age Group:

Pre-school	Grade School	Teens	Young Adults	Over 30	Senior Citizens
★★★½	★★★½	★★★	★★★	★★★	★★★

Duration of Ride: 4½ minutes, followed by a 5-minute film
  with a short wait in between; about 14 minutes total

Avg. Wait in Line per 100 People ahead of You: 4 minutes

Assumes: 12–13 boats operating

Loading Speed: Fast

Description and Comments   In one of Disney's shorter boat rides, guests board dragon-headed ships for an adventure voyage through waters of Viking history and legend. They encounter trolls, gorges, waterfalls, and a storm at sea. Impressive special effects combine visual, tactile, and auditory stimuli. After this fast-paced and often humorous odyssey, guests see a five-minute film on Norway. A vocal minority of readers considers the ride too brief and resents the "travelogue." If you don't want to see the film, be one of the first to enter the theater, and follow the exiting audience out.

Touring Tips   Return later if several hundred guests from a recently concluded performance of *Wonders of China* have arrived en masse.

CHINA PAVILION

Description and Comments   A half-sized replica of the Temple of Heaven in Beijing identifies this pavilion. Gardens and reflecting ponds simulate those in Suzhou, and an art gallery features a "Lotus Blossom" gate and saddle roofline.

Pass through the Hall of Prayer for Good Harvest to see the Circle-Vision 360° movie, *Wonders of China*. Warm and appealing, the film is a brilliant introduction to the nation. A fast-food eatery and a lovely full-service establishment are available.

Touring Tips   A beautiful, serene pavilion, yet exciting. The audience stands for the movie, but lines are usually short. If you're touring World Showcase counterclockwise and plan to go next to Norway and ride Maelstrom, stand on the far left of the theater (as you face the podium). After the show, be one of the first to exit, and beat the horde.

Wonders of China

What It Is: Film about Chinese people and country
Scope & Scale: Major attraction
When to Go: Anytime
Special Comments: Audience stands
Author's Rating: Well produced, though film glosses over political unrest; ★★★
Appeal by Age Group:

Pre-school	Grade School	Teens	Young Adults	Over 30	Senior Citizens
★★	★★½	★★★	★★★½	★★★★	★★★★

Duration of Presentation: Approximately 19 minutes
Preshow Entertainment: None
Probable Waiting Time: 10 minutes

GERMANY PAVILION

Description and Comments   A clock tower rises above the Platz (plaza) marking the Germany pavilion. Dominated by a fountain depicting St. George and the dragon, the Platz is encircled by buildings in traditional architecture. The Biergarten, a buffet (priority seating) restaurant, features German food and beer, yodeling, folk dancing, and oompah music.

Also, be sure to check out the elaborate model railroad situated just beyond the rest rooms as you walk from Germany toward Italy.

Touring Tips   Pleasant and festive; visit Germany anytime.

ITALY PAVILION

Description and Comments   The entrance to Italy is marked by a 105-foot bell tower mirroring that of Venice's St. Mark's Square. To the left is a replica of the 14th-century Doge's Palace. Other buildings are composites of Italian architecture. The pavilion has a waterfront on the lagoon with gondolas tied to striped moorings.

Touring Tips   Streets and courtyards in the pavilion are among the most realistic in World Showcase. Since there is no film or ride at Italy, touring is recommended anytime.

THE AMERICAN ADVENTURE

What It Is: Patriotic mixed-media and audio-animatronic
   theater presentation on U.S. history

Scope & Scale: Headliner

When to Go: Anytime

Author's Rating: Disney's best historic/patriotic attraction. Not
   to be missed; ★★★★

Appeal by Age Group:

Pre-school	Grade School	Teens	Young Adults	Over 30	Senior Citizens
★★	★★★	★★★	★★★★	★★★★½	★★★★★

Duration of Presentation: About 29 minutes

Preshow Entertainment: Voices of Liberty choral singing

Probable Waiting Time: 16 minutes

Description and Comments   The United States pavilion, generally referred to as The American Adventure, encompasses a fast-
food restaurant and a patriotic audio-animatronic show. A new,
upscale, full-service American restaurant is in the works—stay
tuned. *The American Adventure* is a composite of everything Disney does best. Presented in an imposing brick structure reminiscent of colonial Philadelphia, the production is a stirring rendi-
tion of American history narrated by Mark Twain and Ben
Franklin. Behind a stage almost half the size of a football field is
a 28-by-155-foot rear-projection screen (the largest ever used) on
which images are interwoven with the action onstage.

Touring Tips   The American Adventure isn't as interesting   architecturally as most other pavilions, but the show is the best patriotic attraction in the Disney repertoire. It usually plays to capacity audiences from noon to 3:30 p.m., but it isn't hard to get into
because the theater is large. Even during busy times, the wait averages 25–40 minutes. *The American Adventure* is decidedly less
compelling to non-Americans.

   The adjacent Liberty Inn restaurant serves a quick, nonethnic
meal.

JAPAN PAVILION

Description and Comments   A five-story, blue-roofed pagoda
inspired by a seventh-century shrine in Nara sets this pavilion

apart. A hill garden behind blends waterfalls, rocks, flowers, lanterns, paths, and bridges. The building on the right of the entrance echoes the coronation hall of the Imperial Palace at Kyoto. This one, however, contains restaurants and a retail store.

Through the center entrance and to the left is the Bijutsu-kan Gallery, exhibiting some exquisite Japanese artifacts. A second gallery, Karakuri, showcases an unusual collection of mechanical dolls.

Touring Tips   Tasteful and elaborate, Japan can be toured anytime.

MOROCCO PAVILION

Description and Comments   The bustling market, winding streets, lofty minarets, and stuccoed archways re-create the intrigue of Marrakesh and Casablanca. Attention to detail makes Morocco one of the most exciting World Showcase pavilions. It also has a museum of Moorish art and Restaurant Marrakesh, which serves North African specialties.

Touring Tips   Morocco has neither ride nor theater; tour anytime.

FRANCE PAVILION

Description and Comments   Predictably, a replica of the Eiffel Tower is this pavilion's centerpiece. In the foreground, streets recall La Belle Epoque, the "beautiful time" between 1870 and 1910. The sidewalk cafe and the restaurant are very popular, as is the pastry shop (for its croissants).

Impressions de France is an 18-minute movie projected over 200° onto five screens. The audience sits to view this well-made introduction to the people, cities, and natural wonders of France.

Touring Tips   Detail enriches the atmosphere of this pavilion, but the small streets become congested when lines form for the film. Waits can be long.

Impressions de France

What It Is: Film essay on the French people and country

Scope & Scale: Major attraction

When to Go: Before noon and after 4 p.m.

Author's Rating: Exceedingly beautiful film; ★★★½

Appeal by Age Group:

Pre-school	Grade School	Teens	Young Adults	Over 30	Senior Citizens
★½	★★½	★★★	★★★★	★★★★	★★★★

Duration of Presentation: About 18 minutes

Preshow Entertainment: None

Probable Waiting Time: 12 minutes (at suggested times)

UNITED KINGDOM PAVILION

Description and Comments   A variety of architectural styles are used to capture Britain's city, town, and rural atmospheres. The pavilion is mostly shops. The Rose & Crown Pub and Dining Room is World Showcase's only full-service restaurant with dining on the promenade's water side.

Touring Tips   There are no attractions to create congestion; tour anytime. Priority seating isn't required for the Rose & Crown Pub; stop for a beer in midafternoon. Smoking indoors is allowed.

MILLENNIUM VILLAGE

What It Is: World's Fair–type exhibit hall

Scope & Scale: Major diversion

When to Go: On your second day at Epcot or after you've seen all the major attractions

Special Comments: Scheduled to close after January 1, 2001

Author's Rating: Not much depth here; ★★½

Appeal by Age Group:

Pre-school	Grade School	Teens	Young Adults	Over 30	Senior Citizens
★	★½	★½	★★	★★½	★★½

Description and Comments   Located between and behind the United Kingdom and Canadian pavilions, Millennium Village is an eclectic mix of entertainment, shopping, snacking opportunities, and exhibits. Countries represented include Brazil, Ethiopia, Indonesia, Israel, Kenya, Namibia, New Zealand, Saudi Arabia, South Africa, and the United States among others. The theme is world brotherhood and "a globe without boundaries." Some of the exhibits are truly dumbfounding.

Touring Tips There's a lot of stuff jammed into Millennium Village, but most of it will not demand the level of cerebral energy required by Innoventions.

CANADA PAVILION

Description and Comments Thirty-foot totem poles embellish an Indian village at the foot of a château-style hotel in this large pavilion. Near the hotel is a rugged stone building modeled after a landmark near Niagara Falls. A fine film, *O Canada!,* demonstrates the immense pride Canadians have in their beautiful country. Visitors leave the theater through Victoria Gardens, inspired by British Columbia's famed Butchart Gardens.

Touring Tips Because Canada is the first pavilion as one travels counterclockwise around the lagoon, *O Canada!* is crowded in late morning. View the stand-up movie in late afternoon or early evening. Le Cellier, a steak house on the pavilion's lower level, accepts priority seating but also welcomes walk-ins.

O Canada!

What It Is: Film essay on the Canadian people and country
Scope & Scale: Major attraction
When to Go: Late afternoon or early evening
Special Comments: Audience stands
Author's Rating: Makes you want to catch the first plane to
  Canada!; ★★★½
Appeal by Age Group:

Pre-school	Grade School	Teens	Young Adults	Over 30	Senior Citizens
★★	★★½	★★★	★★★½	★★★★	★★★★

Duration of Presentation: About 18 minutes
Preshow Entertainment: None
Probable Waiting Time: 10 minutes

Live Entertainment in Epcot

Live entertainment in World Showcase reflects the nations represented. Future World spotlights new and experimental performances. Obtain specifics on either at Guest Relations.

Here are performers you're apt to encounter:

In Future World   A roving brass band, a musical crew of drumming janitors, socializing robots (EpBOTS), and gymnasts in *Alien* attire striking statuesque poses work near the front entrance and at Innoventions Plaza (between the two Innoventions buildings and by the fountain) according to the daily entertainment schedule.

Innoventions Fountain Show   Numerous times each day, the fountain between the two Innoventions buildings comes alive with pulsating, arching plumes of water synchronized to a musical score. There is no posted schedule of performances, so the fountain show surprises many guests.

Disney Characters   Disney characters once were considered inconsistent with the image of Epcot. That's changed. They now appear for meals at the Garden Grill Restaurant at The Land pavilion and in shows at the American Gardens Theatre and Showcase Plaza between Mexico and Canada. Times are listed in the free guide map from Guest Relations. And characters now appear throughout the park.

American Gardens Theatre   International talent plays the American Gardens Theatre near The American Adventure, facing World Showcase Lagoon. Many shows highlight the performer's home country.

Tapestry of Nations Parade   This parade features 120 giant "puppets" and 32 drummers accompanied by a recorded musical score. The puppets evoke culture and costume around the world. Performed twice nightly according to the daily entertainment schedule, the parade route winds around World Showcase Lagoon. If you watch the second parade, you won't have much time after the parade to find a viewing spot for *IllumiNations*.

IllumiNations   A not-to-be-missed multimedia program performed after dark on World Showcase Lagoon when the park is open late.

Around World Showcase   Impromptu performances occur in and near World Showcase pavilions. They include strolling mariachis in Mexico, street actors in Italy, and a fife-and-drum corps or singing group (The Voices of Liberty) at The American Adventure. Street entertainment occurs at pavilions about every half hour (though not necessarily on the hour or half hour).

Dinner & Lunch Shows   World Showcase restaurants offer floor shows during mealtimes. Find singing waiters in Italy and belly dancers in Morocco, for example. Entertainment is at dinner only in Italy, but at both lunch and dinner in Germany and Morocco.

IllumiNations

IllumiNations integrates fireworks, laser lights, neon, and music in a stirring nightly tribute to nations of the world. Presented on the lagoon, it's Epcot's great outdoor spectacle.

IllumiNations 2000 preempts the regular show during the 15-month Millennium Celebration and owing to its popularity will probably be retained after January 1, 2001. Unlike earlier *IllumiNations* renditions, this one has a plot as well as a theme and is loaded with symbolism. This modest little number traces the history of the universe from the Big Bang and winds up with a fireworks and laser crescendo heralding the dawn of a new age. One practical change affecting *IllumiNations* is that the Tapestry of Nations Parade directly precedes it. Prior to *IllumiNations* you are facing away from the lagoon to watch the parade, then after the parade you must turn around to view *IllumiNations*. It's almost impossible to have an ideal viewing spot for both. We recommend placing your priority on scoring a good *IllumiNations* viewing spot. The puppets in the parade are 20 feet tall, so you'll be able to see fairly well even if you're not in the front row.

Getting out of Epcot after *IllumiNations*

Pick your viewing spot after you decide how quickly you want to leave the park after the show. *IllumiNations* ends the day at Epcot. Afterward, only a few shops remain open. With nothing to do, the crowd exits en masse, jamming Package Pick-up, the monorail station, and the Disney bus stop. Parking-lot trams are at capacity.

If you're staying at an Epcot resort (Swan and Dolphin Hotels, Yacht and Beach Club Resorts, and BoardWalk Inn and Villas), watch *IllumiNations* from the southern (American Adventure) half of the lagoon, then exit through International Gateway and walk or take a boat back to your hotel. If you have a car and are visiting Epcot for dinner and *IllumiNations,* park at the Yacht or Beach Club. After the show, duck through International Gateway and be on the road in 15 minutes. If you're staying at any other Disney World hotel and don't have a car, join the exodus through the main gate and catch a bus or monorail.

More groups get separated, and more children lost, after *IllumiNations* than at any other time. In summer, the audience numbers up to 30,000 people. Anticipate this congestion and designate a spot in the Epcot entrance area where you'll reassemble if you're separated. We recommend the fountain just inside the main entrance. No one in your party should exit the turnstiles until the whole group is together.

The main problem with having a car is getting to it. If you know where it is, skip the tram and walk. But hang on tightly to your children; the parking lot is extremely busy at this time.

Good Locations for Viewing *IllumiNations* and Other World Showcase Lagoon Performances

A seat on the lakeside veranda of Cantina de San Angel in Mexico is the best place to watch any show on World Showcase Lagoon. Come early (at least 90 minutes for *IllumiNations*) and relax with a cold drink while waiting for the show. The Rose & Crown Pub in the United Kingdom also has lagoonside seating, but a small wall downgrades the view.

If you want to combine dinner on the Rose & Crown's veranda with *IllumiNations,* make a priority seating for about an hour and 15 minutes before show time. Report a few minutes early for your seating and ask the host for a table outside where you can view *IllumiNations.* Our experience is that the Rose & Crown folks will bend over backward to accommodate you. If you can't get a table outside, eat inside and linger until show time. When lights dim for *IllumiNations,* you'll be allowed onto the terrace.

Because most guests run for the exits after a presentation, and because islands in the southern half of the lagoon block the view from some places, the most popular spectator positions are along the northern waterfront from Norway and Mexico to Canada and the United Kingdom. The view is excellent; the trade-off is that you have to claim a spot 35–60 minutes before *IllumiNations.* For anyone who doesn't want to stand by a rail for 45 minutes, there

are some good viewing spots along the southern perimeter (counterclockwise from United Kingdom to Germany) that often go
unnoticed until 10–20 minutes before show time:

1. International Gateway Island The pedestrian bridge across
the canal near International Gateway spans an island that offers
great viewing spots. It normally fills 30 minutes or more before
show time.

*2. Second-Floor (Restaurant-Level) Deck of the Mitsukoshi
Building in Japan* An oriental arch slightly blocks your sightline,
but this covered deck offers shelter if it rains. Only Cantina de
San Angel is more protected. Finally, the deck is the only vantage
point that works equally well for *IllumiNations* and the Tapestry
of Nations Parade.

3. Gondola Landing at Italy The elaborate waterfront promenade is excellent, but you must claim a spot at least 30 minutes
before show time.

4. The Boat Dock Opposite Germany The dock generally fills
30 minutes before show time.

5. Waterfront Promenade by Germany Views are good from the
90-foot lagoonside walkway between Germany and China.

None of these viewpoints are reserved for *Unofficial Guide* readers, and on busier nights many are claimed early. But we still won't
hold down a slab of concrete for two hours before *IllumiNations,*
as some people do. Most nights, you can find an acceptable spot
15–30 minutes before show time. And you needn't be right on the
rail or have an unobstructed view of the water. Most of the action
is significantly above ground. It's important, however, not to
stand under a tree, awning, or anything that would block your
overhead perspective.

Other Things to Know about Epcot

SHOPPING IN EPCOT

Merchandise available in Future World generally is also sold elsewhere, except for Epcot and Disney trademark souvenirs.

World Showcase shops add realism and atmosphere to the settings. Much of the merchandise, however, is overpriced. But some shops really are special. In China, visit Yong Feng Shangdian (crafts, rugs, carvings, furniture); and Japan, Mitsukoshi Department Store (porcelain, bonsai trees, pearls from a live oyster). Village Traders, a new shop between China and Germany, sells Kenyan African woodcarvings for about the same price you'd pay at the carving center in Mombasa where they're made.

Clerks will forward purchases to Package Pick-up. Allow three hours, and retrieve them when you leave the park. Specify whether you'll depart through the main entrance or International Gateway. Disney resort guests can have packages sent to their rooms.

BEHIND-THE-SCENES TOURS IN EPCOT

Readers rave about guided walking tours that explore the architecture of the international pavilions. The three-and-a-half-hour Hidden Treasures East and West costs $49 plus Epcot admission, which includes lunch and park admission. Two-hour tours halve World Showcase into East and West, and cost $35 each plus park admission. For $85, you can take the Hidden Treasures Plus Tour, which includes everything in Hidden Treasures East and West, plus lunch and a backstage tour of Epcot.

The three-hour Gardens of the World explores Disney landscaping. The cost is $49 plus park admission.

All tours are open to persons age 16 and older. For a discount, charge the tour on an American Express card. For reservations, call (407) 939-8687.

A shorter option is the Behind the Seeds Tour, which goes behind the scenes at vegetable gardens in The Land. Make sameday reservations on the lower level of The Land (to the far right of the fast-food windows). The cost of the hour-long tour is $6 for adults and $4 for children ages three–nine.

TRAFFIC PATTERNS IN EPCOT

After admiring the traffic flow at the Magic Kingdom, we were amazed by Epcot, which has no feature such as the Magic Kingdom's Main Street, which funnels visitors to a central hub that distributes them almost equally to the lands.

Spaceship Earth, Epcot's premier landmark and a headliner attraction, is just inside the main entrance. Arriving visitors head straight for it, and crowds form as soon as the park opens. The congestion, however, provides opportunities for avoiding lines at other Future World attractions.

Epcot's top draw is Test Track, and everybody in the know makes a fast break for this attraction as soon as they clear the park's entrance turnstiles. Unless you ride Test Track within the first 20 minutes Epcot is open (or use FASTPASS), you're in for a 60–90 minute wait.

Crowds in Future World build from 9 to 11 a.m. Even after World Showcase opens (usually 11 a.m.), more people enter Future World than leave it for World Showcase. Throngs continue to grow between noon and 2 p.m., when guests head for lunch in World Showcase. Exhibits at the far end of World Showcase play to capacity audiences from about noon through 7:30 p.m. Not until evening do crowds equalize in Future World and World Showcase. Attendance throughout Epcot is lighter then.

Some guests leave Epcot after dinner, but most stay for *Illumi-Nations* and exit en masse. Even so, the crush isn't as intense as it is when the Magic Kingdom closes, primarily because the parking lot is next to the park and guests don't have to use a monorail or boat to reach their cars.

Epcot Touring Plans

The Epcot touring plans are field-tested, step-by-step itineraries for seeing all major attractions with minimal waiting. They keep you ahead of the crowds in the morning and place you at less-crowded attractions during busier times of day. They assume you'd prefer a *little* extra walking to a lot of standing in line.

Touring Epcot is much more strenuous than touring the other theme parks. Epcot requires twice as much walking, and it has no effective transportation system; wherever you want to go, it's always quicker to walk. Touring plans help you avoid bottlenecks on days of moderate to heavy attendance, and organize your visit on days of lighter attendance. In either case, they can't shorten the walk.

There are four Epcot touring Plans:

- Epcot One-Day Touring Plan
- Author's Selective Epcot One-Day Touring Plan
- Epcot Two-Day Sunrise/Starlight Touring Plan
- Epcot Two-Day Early Riser Touring Plan

The One-Day Touring Plan packs as much as possible in one long day and requires a lot of stamina. It can be used on early-entry and non-early-entry days.

The Author's Selective One-Day Touring Plan eliminates some lesser attractions and is more relaxing if you have only one day. Use it with or without early entry.

The Sunrise/Starlight Touring Plan combines the easy touring of early morning on one day with the live pageantry of evening on the second day. The first day requires some backtracking and hustle but is more laid-back than either one-day plan. Use it with or without early entry.

The Early Riser Touring Plan is the most efficient itinerary, eliminating 90% of backtracking while still providing a comprehensive tour. Use it only on mornings when early entry isn't in effect.

ABOUT THE INTERNATIONAL GATEWAY

The International Gateway is a secondary entrance to Epcot between the United Kingdom and France in World Showcase. It provides easy access by boat or foot to lodgers at Disney's Swan and Dolphin Hotels, the BoardWalk Inn and Villas, and Disney's Yacht and Beach Club Resorts. Stroller and wheelchair rentals are available. If you enter here in the morning before World Showcase opens (around 11 a.m.), you'll be taken to Future World on double-decker buses.

Epcot One-Day Touring Plan

For: Adults and children age 8 and older
Assumes: Willingness to experience all major
rides and shows.

The plan isn't recommended for families with young children, who are advised instead to use the Author's Selective Epcot One-Day Touring Plan.

Break after lunch and return to your hotel to rest. Return to the park in late afternoon. Also, if you allocate two days at Epcot, use a two-day touring plan.

This plan requires a lot of walking and some backtracking in order to avoid long lines. You may not be able to complete the tour. How far you get depends on how quickly you move among attractions, how often you rest or eat, how quickly the park fills, and the park's closing time.

1. If you're a Disney resort guest, arrive 100 minutes before official opening on *early-entry days* and 40 minutes before on *non-early-entry days*. If you're a day-guest, arrive at the parking lot 45 minutes before official opening on a *non-early-entry day.*

   If you're taking advantage of early entry, expect Spaceship Earth, Test Track, and Wonders of Life to be open. Hit Test Track first, followed by Body Wars in the Wonders of Life pavilion. Also at Wonders of Life, see *Cranium Command*. Save Spaceship Earth for last. Pick up the touring plan, skipping steps directing you to attractions you already experienced.

2. When admitted, move quickly around the left of Spaceship Earth. If inclined, make priority seatings at Guest Relations. Continue through the plaza with Innoventions East on your left until you see a passage through the building. Turn left through this passage. Emerge on the far side of Innoventions East, turn right, and head to Test Track. If you do not want to experience Test Track, skip to Step 3.

3. After Test Track bear right and head for the Wonders of Life pavilion. Ride Body Wars. Be sure to read our motion sickness warning. If you don't want to ride, skip to Step 4.

4. After Body Wars, skip the other attractions in the Wonders of Life pavilion for now. Head back to the central plaza. Cross the plaza and pass through Innoventions West. On the far side of Innoventions West bear left to Imagination Pavilion. Enjoy the ride here first, then see *Honey, I Shrunk the Audience*.

5. Exit Imagination Pavilion, stay left, and head to The Land pavilion next door. Ride Living with the Land. If *Food Rocks* and *The Circle of Life* interest you, see them now.

Note: If you're hungry, feel free to stop for lunch or a snack any time after this.

6. Exit The Land and turn left into The Living Seas. Experience The Living Seas.

7. After The Living Seas, bear left and pass back through

Innoventions West. Ride Spaceship Earth. Bypass the communications electronics exhibit at the exit.

8. Return to the Test Track side of Future World. Bear left to the Universe of Energy and see the show. The line might appear daunting, but your wait should be tolerable.

9. Exit the Universe of Energy, turn left, and return to the Wonders of Life pavilion. See *Cranium Command*.

10. Depart Wonders of Life and turn left. Depart Future World and go to the World Showcase, initiating a counterclockwise circuit. If you are primarily interested in the attractions, try to limit your shopping.

11. At Canada, see the movie.

12. Skip Millennium Village for now, unless you're a World Showcase veteran and have previously experienced all the permanent attractions. Note that Millennium Village is scheduled to close permanently after January 1, 2001.

13. Next, tour United Kingdom.

14. Proceed across the bridge to France. See the movie.

15. After France, visit Morocco next door.

Note: Check your watch. If it's time for your dinner priority seating, suspend touring and eat. Check the daily entertainment schedule for the times of Tapestry of Nations and *IllumiNations*. Give yourself at least 30 minutes after dinner to locate a good viewing spot.

16. Continue counterclockwise to Japan.

17. After Japan, see *The American Experience.*

18. Continue counterclockwise to Italy.

19. Next go to Germany.

20. Proceed to China. See the movie.

21. After China, continue to Norway. Ride Maelstrom if the wait is not prohibitive.

22. Next tour Mexico and ride El Río del Tiempo.

23. This concludes the touring plan. Unless a holiday schedule is in effect, everything at Epcot closes after *IllumiNations* except a few shops. Thirty or forty thousand people bolt for the exits at once. See pages 171–172 for tips on coping with the exodus.

Author's Selective Epcot
One-Day Touring Plan

For: All parties
Assumes: Willingness to experience all major
rides and shows.

This touring plan includes only what the author believes is the best Epcot has to offer. The exclusion of an attraction doesn't mean it isn't worthwhile.

1. If you're a Disney resort guest, arrive 100 minutes before official opening on *early-entry days* and 40 minutes before official opening on *non-early-entry days*. If you're a day-guest, arrive at the parking lot 45 minutes before Epcot's stated opening time on a *non-early-entry day*.

   If you're taking advantage of early entry, expect Spaceship Earth, Test Track, and Wonders of Life to be open. Hit Test Track first, followed by Body Wars in the Wonders of Life pavilion. Also at Wonders of Life, see *Cranium Command*. Save Spaceship Earth for last. After Spaceship Earth, pick up the touring plan, skipping steps directing you to attractions you already experienced.

2. When admitted, move quickly around the left of Spaceship Earth. If inclined, make priority seatings at Guest Relations. Continue through the plaza with Innoventions East on your left until you see a passage through the building. Turn left through this passage. Emerge on the far side of Innoventions East, turn right, and head to Test Track. If you do not want to experience Test Track, skip to Step 3.

3. After Test Track bear right and head for the Wonders of Life pavilion. Ride Body Wars. Be sure to read our motion sickness warning (page 158). If you don't want to ride, skip to Step 4.

4. After Body Wars, skip the other attractions in the Wonders of Life pavilion for now. Head back to the central plaza. Cross the plaza and pass through Innoventions West. On the far side of Innoventions West bear left to Imagination Pavilion. Enjoy the ride here first, then see *Honey, I Shrunk the Audience.*

5. Exit Imagination Pavilion, stay left, and head to The Land pavilion next door. Ride Living with the Land. Skip the other two attractions in this pavilion.

Note: If you're hungry, feel free to stop for lunch or a snack any time after this.

6. Exit The Land and turn left into The Living Seas. Experience The Living Seas.

7   After The Living Seas, bear left and pass back through Innoventions West. Ride Spaceship Earth. Bypass the communications electronics exhibit at the exit.

8. Return to the Test Track side of Future World. Bear left to the Universe of Energy and see the show. The line might appear daunting, but your wait should be tolerable.

9. Exit the Universe of Energy, turn left, and return to the Wonders of Life pavilion. See *Cranium Command.*

10. Depart Wonders of Life and turn left. Depart Future World and go to the World Showcase, initiating a counterclockwise circuit. If you are primarily interested in the attractions, try to limit your shopping. We recommend you spend time enjoying the architecture, gardens, and street entertainment of the different countries. Try to relax and not hurry.

11. There are three movies, two boat rides, and an audioanimatronic attraction (*The American Adventure*) in the World Showcase. We recommend you experience *The American Adventure,* see the films at France and China, and take the boat ride at Norway (if the wait is manageble).

12. To the left of Canada is Millennium Village. Skip it for now, unless you're a World Showcase veteran and have previously experienced all the permanent attractions. Note that Millennium Village is scheduled to close permanently after January 1, 2001.

Note: Check your watch. If it's time for your dinner priority seating, suspend touring and eat. Check the daily entertainment schedule for the times of Tapestry of Nations and *IllumiNations.* Give yourself at least 30 minutes after dinner to locate a good viewing spot.

13. This concludes the touring plan. Unless a holiday sched-

ule is in effect, everything at Epcot closes after *IllumiNations* except a few shops. Thirty or forty thousand people bolt for the exits at once. See pages 171–172 for tips on coping with the exodus.

Epcot Two-Day Sunrise/Starlight Touring Plan

For: All visitors who want to tour Epcot comprehensively over two days. Day One takes advantage of early-morning touring opportunities. Day Two begins in late afternoon and continues until the park closes.

Many guests spend part of their Disney World arrival day traveling and settling into their hotel. They go to the theme parks in the afternoon. The second day of this plan is ideal for these visitors.

Families with children younger than age eight using this touring plan should review Epcot attractions in the Small Child Fright-Potential Chart (page 296). Rent a stroller for any child small enough to fit into one. Break off Day One no later than 2:30 p.m. and return to your hotel for rest. If you missed attractions called for in Day One, add them to your itinerary on Day Two.

Day One

1. If you're a Disney hotel guest, arrive at Epcot 100 minutes before official opening on *early-entry days* and 40 minutes before on *non-early-entry days*. If you're a day-guest, arrive at the parking lot 45 minutes before official opening on a *non-early-entry day.*

   If you're taking advantage of early entry, expect Spaceship Earth, Test Track and the Wonders of Life to be open. Hit Test Track first, followed by Body Wars in the Wonders of Life pavillion. Also at the Wonders of Life see *Cranium Command.* Save Spaceship Earth for last. After Spaceship Earth, pick up the Touring Plan, skipping steps directing you to attraction that you already experienced.

2. When admitted, move quickly around the left of Spaceship Earth. If inclined, make priority seatings at Guest Relations. Continue through the plaza with Innoventions East on your left until you see a passage through the building.

Turn left through this passage. Emerge on the far side of Innoventions East, turn right, and head to Test Track. If you do not want to experience Test Track, skip to Step 4.

3. Ride Test Track.

4. Exit Test Track. Cross Future World to the Imagination Pavilion. Experience the ride and then see *Honey, I Shrunk the Audience.*

5. Skip other attractions at the Imagination Pavilion. Exit left to The Land pavilion. Ride Living with the Land.

6. Postpone other Land attractions. Backtrack to the Wonders of Life pavilion. Ride Body Wars. *Warning:* This ride gives many people motion sickness (page 158).

7. See *Cranium Command* at Wonders of Life. Don't miss the cartoon preshow or you may not understand the main presentation.

8. Exit Wonders of Life. Turn right into Universe of Energy and see the show.

9. Turn left out of Universe of Energy. Head back, passing Test Track. Go left on the path leading to Odyssey Center. Cut through Odyssey Center to World Showcase.

10. Turn left and proceed clockwise around World Showcase Lagoon. Experience El Río del Tiempo boat ride in Mexico. The ride is in the far left corner of the courtyard, not well marked. Consign any purchases to Package Pick-up for collection when you leave the park.

11. Continue left to Norway. Ride Maelstrom.

Note: If your lunch priority seating is soon, eat. Afterward, resume the plan.

12. Continue left to China. See *Wonders of China.*

13. Visit Germany and Italy. Enjoy the settings; there are no rides or films. If you don't have a restaurant priority seating, consider Sommerfest (fast food) at Germany.

14. Continue clockwise to The American Adventure. See the show. If you don't have restaurant priority seatings, consider the Liberty Inn (fast food; left side of The American Adventure).

15. Visit Japan and Morocco. Consign any purchases to Package Pick-up for collection when you leave the park.

16. This concludes the touring plan for Day One. Attractions and pavilions not included today will be experienced

tomorrow. If you wish to continue touring, follow the Epcot One-Day Touring Plan, starting at Step 17. If you've had enough, exit through International Gateway or leave through the main entrance. To reach the main entrance without walking around the lagoon, catch a boat at the dock near Morocco.

Day Two

1. Enter Epcot about 2 p.m. Go to Guest Relations for a guidemap containing the daily entertainment schedule.

2. While at Guest Relations, make dinner priority seatings, if you haven't done so already.

    You can eat your evening meal in any Epcot restaurant without interrupting the efficiency of the touring plan. We recommend a 7 p.m. priority seating. This timing is important if you want to see *IllumiNations* on the lagoon at 9 p.m.

    If your preferred restaurants are filled, try for a priority seating at Morocco or Norway. These nations' ethnic dishes are little known to Americans, and seatings may be available.

3. Ride Spaceship Earth.

4. Pass through Innoventions West and proceed to The Living Seas. For efficiency, be one of the last to enter the theater from the preshow area. Sit as close to the end of a middle row as possible. This will position you to be first on the ride that follows. Afterward, enjoy exhibits in Sea Base Alpha.

5. Exit right from The Living Seas to The Land. See *Food Rocks* and the film at the Circle of Life Theater.

Note: If your dinner priority seating is soon, eat. Afterward, check the entertainment schedule for the time of *IllumiNations*. Allow 30 minutes to find a good viewing spot (pages 172–173).

6. Leave Future World. Walk counterclockwise around World Showcase Lagoon to Canada. See *O Canada!*

7. Turn right and tour Millennium Village.

8. Exit right and visit the United Kingdom.

9. Exit right to France. See *Impressions de France.*

10. This concludes the touring plan. Enjoy dinner and *IllumiNations*. If you have time, shop or revisit your favorite attractions.

11. Unless a holiday schedule is in effect, all but a few shops close at Epcot after *IllumiNations*. Thirty thousand or more people bolt for the exits. See pages 171–172 for tips on coping with the exodus.

Epcot Two-Day Early Riser Touring Plan

For: All parties

This efficient plan eliminates backtracking and takes advantage of easy touring in morning's light crowds. Most folks will complete each day of the plan by midafternoon.

The plan doesn't include *IllumiNations,* other evening festivities, or dinner, but they can be added. It's designed to be used on *non-early-entry days.*

Families with children younger than eight using this plan should review Epcot attractions in the Small Child Fright-Potential Chart (page 296). Rent a stroller for any child small enough to fit it.

Day One

1. Arrive 45 minutes before official opening.
2. When admitted, move quickly around the left of Spaceship Earth to Guest Relations and make lunch and dinner priority seatings, if needed. If not, skip to Step 3.
3. Ride Spaceship Earth.
4. Cross Future World Plaza, pass through Innoventions West, and bear left to Imagination Pavilion. Enjoy the ride here first, then see *Honey, I Shrunk the Audience.*
5. Exit left and proceed to The Land. Ride Living with the Land.
6. In the same pavilion, see *Food Rocks* and *The Circle of Life.* Start with the first scheduled.
7. Exit The Land and bear left to The Living Seas. Ride, then see the exhibits at Sea Base Alpha at your leisure.

Note: If your priority seating is soon, eat. Afterward, resume the plan.

8. Bear left from The Living Seas and transit Innoventions West. Cross the plaza behind Spaceship Earth and go

through Innoventions East to Universe of Energy. Enjoy the show.

9. From Universe of Energy, return to Innoventions. Explore Innoventions East and West.

10. This concludes Day One of the plan. If you linger over exhibits at The Living Seas and Innoventions East and West, it may be late in the day. Consider staying for dinner and *IllumiNations.* If you toured faster, you'll probably complete the plan by about 2:30 p.m., even with a full-service lunch.

Day Two

1. Arrive 45 minutes before official opening.

2. When admitted, move quickly around the left of Spaceship Earth to Guest Relations and make lunch and dinner priority seatings, if needed. If not, skip to Step 3.

3. After making priority seatings, continue through the plaza keeping Innoventions East on your left until you see a passage through the building. Turn left through this passage. Emerge on the far side of Innoventions East, turn right, and head to Test Track. If you do not want to experience Test Track, skip to Step 5.

4. Ride Test Track.

5. Exit Test Track to the right and proceed to the Wonders of Life pavilion. Ride Body Wars. *Warning:* This ride gives many people motion sickness (page 158)

6. In the same pavilion, see *The Making of Me.*

7. Also in the same pavilion, see *Cranium Command.* Afterward, enjoy the exhibits and interactive displays.

8. Exit left from the pavilion and return to Test Track. To the left of Test Track, bear left on the path to Odyssey Center. Cut through Odyssey Center to World Showcase.

9. Turn left and proceed clockwise around World Showcase Lagoon. Ride El Río del Tiempo at Mexico. It's in the far left corner of the courtyard, not well marked. Consign any purchases to Package Pick-up for retrieval when you leave the park.

10. Go left to Norway. Ride Maelstrom.

11. Go left to China. See *Wonders of China.*

12. Visit Germany and Italy. Enjoy the settings; there are no

rides or films. If you don't have a restaurant priority seating, consider Sommerfest (fast food) at Germany.

13. Continue clockwise to The American Adventure. See the show. If you don't have restaurant priority seatings, consider the Liberty Inn (fast food; left side of The American Adventure).

14. Visit Japan and Morocco. Consign any purchases to Package Pick-up for collection when you leave the park.

15. Continue left to France. See *Impressions de France.*

16. Continue left and visit the United Kingdom.

17. Check out Millennium Village (closed permanently after January 1, 2001) between the United Kingdom and Canada.

18. Go left to Canada. See *O Canada!*

19. This concludes Day Two of the touring plan. If you lingered in World Showcase shops and it's late, consider staying for dinner and *IllumiNations.* If you caught *IllumiNations* after Day One, consider leaving Epcot through International Gateway (between the United Kingdom and France) and exploring Disney's BoardWalk. It's a five-minute walk from International Gateway.

Part Eleven

Disney's Animal Kingdom

Not to Be Missed at the Animal Kingdom	
Safari Village	*It's Tough to Be a Bug!*
Camp Minnie-Mickey	*Festival of the Lion King*
Africa	Kilimanjaro Safaris
DinoLand U.S.A.	Dinosaur

With its lush flora, winding streams, meandering paths, and exotic setting, the Animal Kingdom is a stunningly beautiful theme park. The landscaping alone conjures images of rain forest, veldt, and even formal garden. Soothing, mysterious, and exciting all at once, every vista is a feast for the eye. Add to this loveliness a population of more than 1,000 animals, replicas of Africa's and Asia's most intriguing architecture, and a diverse array of singularly original attractions, and you have the most unique of all Disney theme parks. In the Animal Kingdom, Disney has created an environment to savor. And though you will encounter the typical long lines, pricey food, and shops full of Disney merchandise, you will also (with a little effort) experience a day of stimulating private discoveries.

At 500 acres, Disney's Animal Kingdom is five times the size of the Magic Kingdom and more than twice the size of Epcot. But like Disney-MGM Studios, most of the Animal Kingdom's vast geography is only accessible on guided tours or as part of attractions. When complete, the Animal Kingdom will feature seven sections or "lands": The Oasis, Safari Village, DinoLand

U.S.A., Camp Minnie-Mickey, Africa, Asia, and an as-yet unnamed land inspired by mythical beasts. Built in phases, The Oasis, Safari Village, Camp Minnie-Mickey, Africa, and DinoLand U.S.A. were all operational for the park's opening in 1998, and Asia opened in early 1999. "Beastie Land" (our suggestion) may or may not be developed. In any event it's certainly not on the front burner..

Its size notwithstanding, the Animal Kingdom features a limited number of attractions. To be exact, there are four rides, several walk-through exhibits, an indoor theater, four amphitheaters, a conservation exhibit, and a children's playground. Two of the attractions, however, Dinosaur and Kilimanjaro Safaris, are among the best in the Disney repertoire.

The Animal Kingdom has received mixed reviews. Guests complain about the park layout, congested walkways, lack of shade, poor signage, and insufficient air conditioning. Most attractions, however, have been well received. Also lauded are the natural habitats for animal exhibits and park architecture and landscaping.

ARRIVING

The Animal Kingdom is situated off Osceola Parkway in the southwest corner of Walt Disney World and is not too far from Blizzard Beach, the Coronado Springs Resort, and the All-Star Resorts. The Animal Kingdom Lodge adjoins the park on its northwest side. From I-4, take Exit 25B, US 192, to the so-called Walt Disney World main entrance (World Drive) and follow the signs to the Animal Kingdom. The Animal Kingdom has its own 6,000-car pay parking lot with close parking for the disabled. Once parked, you can walk to the entrance or catch a ride on one of Disney's trademark trams. The new park is connected to other Walt Disney World destinations by the Disney bus system.

A Word about Admission

Be forewarned that unused days on multiday "hopper" passports issued prior to the opening of the Animal Kingdom are good only for admission to the Magic Kingdom, Epcot, and Disney-MGM Studios. Thus holders of these older passes must purchase a separate admission for the Animal Kingdom.

Operating Hours and Early Entry

The Animal Kingdom, not unexpectedly, hosted tremendous crowds during its first three years. Consequently, Disney management has done a fair amount of fiddling and experimenting with operating hours and opening procedures. Generally, the Animal Kingdom opens earlier than the other three parks. In the summer of 2000 it was common practice to advertise 7 or 8 a.m. as the official opening time, but to open certain sections of the park as early as 6 or 7 a.m. Opening early allows the Animal Kingdom to also close early (usually 8 p.m. or so) and still provide guests with approximately 12–13 hours of touring time. Because the Animal Kingdom opens so early anyway, there are no designated early-entry days as at the other three parks. This means that everyone has the same opportunity to be among the first to enter the park.

On holidays and other days of projected heavy attendance, Disney will open the entire park 30 or 60 minutes early. Our advice is to arrive, admission in hand, an hour before official opening during the summer and holiday periods, and 40 minutes before official opening the rest of the year.

When to Go

For the time being, expect to encounter large crowds at the Animal Kingdom. The best days of the week to go are Saturday and Sunday in the summer, and Wednesday and Thursday, year-round. Next best is Friday. Avoid Saturday and Sunday during the school year, and Monday regardless of season.

Because the park opens so early, many guests wrap up their tour and leave by 3:30 or 4 p.m. Lines for the major rides and the 3-D movie in the Tree of Life will usually thin appreciably between 4:30 p.m. and closing time. If you arrive at 3 p.m. and take in a couple of stage shows (described later), waits should be tolerable by the time you hit the Tree of Life and the rides.

GETTING ORIENTED

At the entrance plaza are ticket kiosks fronting the main entrance. To your right before the turnstiles are the kennel and an ATM. Passing through the turnstiles, wheelchair and stroller rentals are

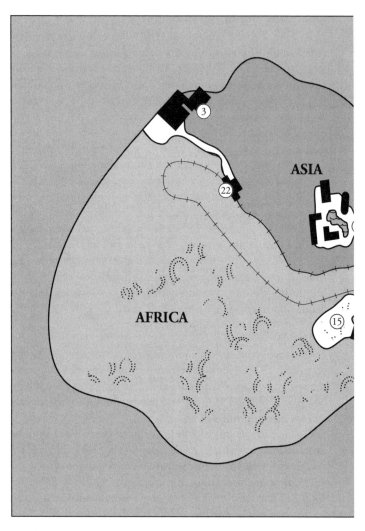

1. The Boneyard
2. Character Greeting Area
3. Conservation Station
4. Cretaceous Trail
5. Dinosaur
6. *Festival of the Lion King*

7. *Flights of Wonder*
8. Gibbon Pool
9. Guest Relations
10. Harambe Village
11. Kali River Rapids
12. Kilimanjaro Safaris

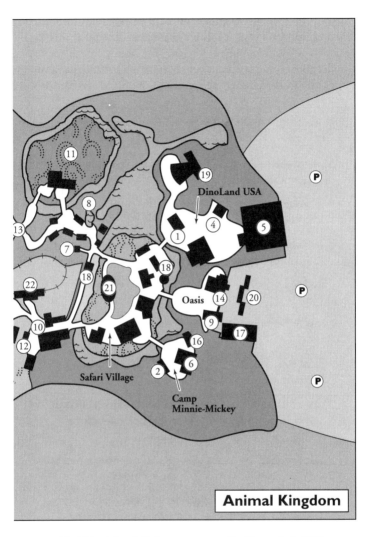

Animal Kingdom

13. Maharaja Jungle Trek
14. Main Entrance
15. Pangani Forest Exploration Trail
16. Pocahontas
17. Rainforest Cafe
18. River Cruise
19. Theater in the Wild
20. Ticket Booths
21. Tree of Life/
    It's Tough to Be Bug!
22. Wildlife Express (Train)

191

to your right. Guest Relations, the park headquarters for information, handout park maps, entertainment schedules, missing persons, and lost and found, is to the left. Nearby are rest rooms, public phones, and rental lockers. Beyond the entrance plaza you enter The Oasis, a lushly vegetated network of converging path-

---

Animal Kingdom Services

Most of the park's service facilities are located inside the main entrance and in Safari Village as follows:

Wheelchair & Stroller Rentals	Inside the main entrance to the right
Banking Services	ATMs are located at the main entrance and at Safari Village.
Storage Lockers	Inside the main entrance to the left
Lost & Found	Inside the main entrance to the left
Guest Relations/ Information	Inside the main entrance to the left
Live Entertainment/ Parade Information	Included in the park guidemap, available free at Guest Relations
Lost Persons	Lost persons can be reported at Guest Relations.
First Aid	In Safari Village, next to the Creature Comforts Shop
Baby Center/ Baby-Care Needs	In Safari Village, next to the Creature Comforts Shop
Film & Cameras	Just inside the main entrance at Garden Gate Gifts, in Safari Village at Disney Outfitters, and in Africa at Duka La Filimu

ways winding through a landscape punctuated with streams, waterfalls, and misty glades, and inhabited by what Disney calls "colorful and unusual animals."

The park is arranged somewhat like the Magic Kingdom, in a hub-and-spoke configuration. The lush, tropical Oasis serves as Main Street, funneling visitors to Safari Village on an island at the center of the park. Dominated by the park's central icon, the 14-story-tall, handcarved Tree of Life, Safari Village is the park's retail and dining center. From Safari Village, guests can access the respective theme areas: Africa, Camp Minnie-Mickey, Asia, and DinoLand U.S.A. Safari Village additionally hosts two attractions: a boat ride and a theater in the Tree of Life.

To help you plan your day, we have profiled all of the Animal Kingdom's major attractions. We suggest, however, that you be open-minded and try everything. For the time being you should easily be able to take in the Animal Kingdom in one day.

The Oasis

Though the functional purpose of The Oasis is the same as that of Main Street in the Magic Kingdom (i.e., to funnel guests to the center of the park), it also serves as what Disney calls a "transitional experience." In plain English, this means that it sets the stage and gets you into the right mood to enjoy the Animal Kingdom. The Oasis immediately envelops you in an environment that is replete with choices. There is not one broad thoroughfare, but rather multiple paths. Each will deliver you to Safari Village at the center of the park.

The natural-habitat zoological exhibits in The Oasis are representative of those throughout the park. Although extraordinarily lush and beautiful, the exhibits are primarily designed for the comfort and well-being of the animals. This means in essence that you must be patient and look closely if you want to see the animals. A sign will identify the animal(s) in each exhibit, but there's no guarantee the animals will be immediately visible. Animal-watching Disney-style requires a sharp eye and a bit of effort.

Touring Tips The Oasis is a place to linger and appreciate, and although this is exactly what the designers intended, it will be largely lost on Disney-conditioned guests who blitz through at warp speed to queue up for the big attractions. If you are a blitzer in the morning, plan to spend some time in The Oasis on your way out of the park. The Oasis usually opens 30 minutes before and closes 30–60 minutes after the rest of the park.

Safari Village

Safari Village is an island of tropical greenery and whimsical equatorial African architecture, executed in vibrant hues of teal, yellow, red, and blue. Connected to the other lands by bridges, the island is the hub from which guests can access the park's various theme areas. The village is arrayed in a crescent around the base of the Animal Kingdom's signature landmark, the Tree of Life. Towering 14 stories above the village, the Tree of Life is this park's version of Cinderella Castle or Spaceship Earth. Flanked by pools, meadows, and exotic gardens, the Tree of Life houses a theater attraction inspired by the Disney/Pixar film, *A Bug's Life*.

Safari Village is the park's central shopping, dining, and services headquarters. It is here that you will find the First Aid and Baby-Care Centers. For the best selection of Disney trademark merchandise, try the Island Mercantile or Disney Outfitters shops. Counter-service food and snacks are available, but there are no full-service restaurants at Safari Village (the only full-service restaurant in the park is the Rainforest Cafe, located to the left of the main entrance).

The Tree of Life/It's Tough to Be a Bug!

What It Is: 3-D theater show

Scope & Scale: Major attraction

When to Go: Before 10 a.m. and after 4 p.m.

Special Comments: The theater is inside the tree

Author's Rating: Zany and frenetic; ★★★★

Appeal by Age Group:

Pre-school	Grade School	Teens	Young Adults	Over 30	Senior Citizens
★★½	★★★★★	★★★★★	★★★★	★★★★	★★★★

Duration of Presentation: Approximately 7½ minutes

Probable Waiting Time: 12–30 minutes

Description and Comments The Tree of Life, apart from its size, is quite a work of art. Although from afar it is certainly magnificent and imposing, it is not until you examine the tree at close range that you truly appreciate its rich detail. What appears to be ancient gnarled bark is in fact hundreds of carvings depicting all manner of wildlife, each integrated seamlessly into the trunk, roots, and limbs of the tree. A stunning symbol of the interdependence of all living things, the Tree of Life is the most visually compelling structure to be found in any Disney park.

In sharp contrast to the grandeur of the tree is the subject of the attraction housed within its trunk. Called *It's Tough to Be a Bug!*, this humorous 3-D film is about the difficulties of being a very small creature. *It's Tough to Be a Bug!* also contrasts with the relatively serious tone of the Animal Kingdom in general, standing virtually alone in providing some much needed levity and whimsy. *It's Tough To Be A Bug!* is similar to *Honey, I Shrunk the Audience* at Epcot in that it combines a 3-D film with an arsenal of tactile and visual special effects. In our view, the special effects are a bit overdone and the film somewhat anemic. Even so, we rate the bugs as not to be missed.

Touring Tips   Because it's situated in the most eye-popping structure in the park, and also because there aren't that many attractions anyway, you can expect *It's Tough to Be a Bug!* to be mobbed most of the day. We recommend going in the morning after Kilimanjaro Safaris, Kali River Rapids, and Dinosaur. If you miss the bugs in the morning, try again in the late afternoon.

Be advised that *It's Tough to Be a Bug!* is very intense and the special effects will do a number on young children as well as anyone who is squeamish about insects.

River Cruise

What It Is: Boat ride around Safari Village
Scope & Scale: Minor attraction
When to Go: Before 10 a.m. or one hour before closing
Author's Rating: Not worth the wait; ★
Appeal by Age Group:

Pre-school	Grade School	Teens	Young Adults	Over 30	Senior Citizens
★★	★	½	½	★	★

Duration of Ride: 8–9 minutes
Avg. Wait in Line per 100 People ahead of You: 14 minutes

Assumes: All boats operating

Loading Speed: Slow

Description and Comments   Every theme park has at least one dumb and totally vacuous attraction. At the Animal Kingdom it's River Cruise. For an average wait of 45 minutes, the cruise treats you to the same sights you can see from Safari Village bridges— wow! In 2000, the River Cruise, originally called Discovery River Boats, was closed for much of the year and even removed from the park map. The new attraction is essentially the same: boats make the same trip around Safari Village Island and see the same sights.

Touring Tips   Skip it. If you go anyway, try to get on before 10 a.m. or after 6 p.m. Boats load from two docks (near Asia Bridge and Oasis Bridge). You make the same circuit and see the same sights regardless of where you board.

Camp Minnie-Mickey

This land is designed to be the Disney characters' Animal King-dom headquarters. A small land, Camp Minnie-Mickey is about the size of Mickey's Toontown Fair but has a rustic and woodsy theme like a summer camp. In addition to a character meeting and greeting area, Camp Minnie-Mickey is home to two live stage productions featuring Disney characters.

Situated in a cul-de-sac, Camp Minnie-Mickey is a pedestrian nightmare. Lines for the two stage shows and from the character greeting areas spill out into the congested walkways, making move-ment almost impossible. To compound the problem, hundreds of parked strollers clog the paths, squeezing the flow of traffic to a trickle. Meanwhile, hordes of guests trying to enter Camp Minnie-Mickey collide with guests trying to exit on the bridge connecting the camp to Safari Village. To make matters worse, Disney positions vendor carts on the approaches to the bridge. It's a planning error of the first order.

Character Trails

Description and Comments   Characters can be found at the end of each of several "character trails" named Jungle, Forest, or some such, and Mickey and Minnie.

Touring Tips   Waiting in line to see the characters can be very time-consuming. We recommend visiting early in the morning or late in the afternoon.

Festival of the Lion King

What It Is: Theater-in-the-round stage show
Scope & Scale: Major attraction
When to Go: Before 11 a.m. or after 4 p.m.
Special Comments: Performance times are listed in the handout park map
Author's Rating: Upbeat and spectacular; ★★★★
Appeal by Age Group:

Pre-school	Grade School	Teens	Young Adults	Over 30	Senior Citizens
★★★★	★★★★½	★★★★	★★★★	★★★★	★★★★

Duration of Presentation: 25 minutes
Preshow Entertainment: None
Probable Waiting Time: 20–35 minutes

Description and Comments   This energetic production, inspired by Disney's *Lion King* feature film, is part stage show, part parade, and part circus. There is a great deal of parading around, some acrobatics, and a lot of singing and dancing.

Touring Tips   This show is both popular and difficult to see. Your best bet is to go to the first show in the morning or to one of the last two performances in the evening. To see the show during the more crowded middle of the day, you'll need to get in line at least 35 minutes before show time. Though the theater is covered and air is circulated by fans, there is no air conditioning.

Pocahontas and Her Forest Friends at Grandmother Willow's Grove

What It Is: Conservation-themed stage show
Scope & Scale: Major attraction
When to Go: Before 11 a.m. or after 4 p.m.
Special Comments: Performance times are listed in the park map
Author's Rating: A little sappy; ★★½

Appeal by Age Group:

Pre-school	Grade School	Teens	Young Adults	Over 30	Senior Citizens
★★★½	★★★½	★★★	★★★½	★★★	★★★

Duration of Presentation: 15 minutes

Preshow Entertainment: None

Probable Waiting Time: 20–30 minutes

Description and Comments   This show, featuring Pocahontas, addresses the role of humans in protecting the natural world. Various live creatures of the forest, including a raccoon, a snake, and a turkey, as well as a couple of animatronic trees (Grandmother Willow and Twig), assist Pocahontas in making the point. The presentation is gushy and overacted but has its moments, nonetheless.

Touring Tips   Because the theater is relatively small, and because Camp Minnie-Mickey stays so mobbed, the Pocahontas show is hard to get into. To avoid the hassle, try to catch the show before 11 a.m. or after 4 p.m. Regardless of the time of day, arrive at least 20 minutes before show time.

Africa

The largest of the Animal Kingdom's lands, guests enter through Harambe, Disney's idealized and immensely sanitized version of a modern, rural African town. There is a market (with modern cash registers), and counter-service food is available. What distinguishes Harambe is its understatement. Far from the stereotypical great-white-hunter image of an African town, Harambe is definitely (and realistically) not exotic. The buildings, while interesting, are quite plain and architecturally simple.

Kilimanjaro Safaris (FASTPASS)

What It Is: Truck ride through an African wildlife reservation

Scope & Scale: Super headliner

When to Go: As soon as the park opens or in the two hours before closing

Author's Rating: Truly exceptional; ★★★★★

Appeal by Age Group:

Pre-school	Grade School	Teens	Young Adults	Over 30	Senior Citizens
★★★★	★★★★★	★★★★½	★★★★½	★★★★½	★★★★★

Duration of Ride: About 20 minutes

Avg. Wait in Line per 100 People ahead of You: 4 minutes

Assumes: Full-capacity operation with 18-second dispatch interval

Loading Speed: Fast

Description and Comments   The park's premier zoological attraction, Kilimanjaro Safaris offers an exceptionally realistic, albeit brief, imitation of an actual African photo safari. Thirty-two guests at a time board tall, open safari vehicles and are dispatched into a simulated African veldt habitat. Animals such as zebra, wildebeest, impala, Thomson's gazelle, giraffe, and even rhinos roam apparently free, while predators such as lions, as well as potentially dangerous large animals like hippos, are separated from both prey and guests by all-but-invisible, natural-appearing barriers.

Having traveled in Kenya and Tanzania, we can tell you that Disney has done an amazing job of replicating the sub-Saharan/east African landscape. The main difference that an east African would notice is that Disney's version is greener and, generally speaking, less barren. And, like on a real African safari, what animals you see (and how many) is pretty much a matter of luck. We tried Disney's safari upwards of a dozen times and had a different experience on each trip.

Touring Tips   Kilimanjaro Safaris is the Animal Kingdom's top draw. When the park opens, as many as 90% of guests head for the safari—and later-arriving guests do the same thing. If you want to see Kilimanjaro Safaris without a long wait, be among the first guests through the turnstiles and make a beeline for Africa. *Hint:* A less-crowded park entrance turnstile can be accessed by passing through the retail area of Rainforest Cafe. The Rainforest Cafe retail shop usually opens about ten minutes before guests are admitted to the park. Waits for Kilimanjaro Safaris diminish in late afternoon, usually between 3:30 and 5:30 p.m. If the wait exceeds 30 minutes when you arrive, use FASTPASS. The downside to FASTPASS with this attraction is that there aren't many other attractions in Africa to occupy attention while you wait for your FASTPASS return time. Your best bet is to see the attraction first thing in the morning.

If you want to take photos on your safari, be advised that the vehicle doesn't stop very often, so be prepared to snap while under way. Also, don't worry about the ride itself: it really isn't very rough. Finally, the only thing that a young child might find intimidating is crossing an "old bridge" that pretends to collapse under your truck.

Pangani Forest Exploration Trail

What It Is: Walk-through zoological exhibit
Scope & Scale: Major attraction
When to Go: Before 10 a.m. or after 3:30 p.m.
Author's Rating: ★★★
Appeal by Age Group:

Pre-school	Grade School	Teens	Young Adults	Over 30	Senior Citizens
★★★½	★★★	★★½	★★★	★★★	★★★

Duration of Tour: About 20–25 minutes

Description and Comments   Because guests disembark from the safari at the entrance to the Pangani Forest Exploration Trail, most guests try the trail immediately after the safari. Winding between the domain of two troops of lowland gorillas, it's hard to see what, if anything, separates you from the primates. Also on the trail are a hippo pool with an underwater viewing area, a naked mole rat exhibit (I promise I'm not making this up), and some hyenas. A highlight of the trail is an exotic bird aviary so craftily designed that you can barely tell you're in an enclosure.

Touring Tips   The Gorilla Falls Exploration Trail is lush, beautiful, and jammed with people most of the time. When the safari is operating at full tilt, it spews hundreds of guests every couple of minutes onto the Exploration Trail. The one-way trail in turn becomes so clogged that nobody can move or see much of anything.

Clearly this attraction is either badly designed, misplaced, or both. Your only real chance for enjoying it is to walk through before 10 a.m. (i.e., before the safari hits full stride) or after 3:30 p.m.

Wildlife Express

What It Is: Scenic railroad ride to Conservation Station
Scope & Scale: Major attraction
When to Go: Before 11 a.m. or after 3 p.m.
Special Comments: Most guests will take the train after returning to Harambe from the Kilimanjaro Safari
Author's Rating: Ho hum; ★★
Appeal by Age Group:

Pre-school	Grade School	Teens	Young Adults	Over 30	Senior Citizens
★★★	★★★	★½	★★½	★★½	★★½

Duration of Ride: About 5–7 minutes one way
Avg. Wait in Line per 100 People ahead of You: 9 minutes
Loading Speed: Moderate

Description and Comments A transportation ride that snakes behind the African wildlife reserve as it makes its loop connecting Harambe to Conservation Station. En route to Conservation Station, you see the nighttime enclosures for the animals that populate the Kilimanjaro Safaris. Similarly, returning from Conservation Station to Harambe, you see the backstage areas of Asia. Regardless which direction you're heading, the sights are not especially interesting.

Touring Tips Most guests will embark for Conservation Station after experiencing Kilimanjaro Safaris and Gorilla Falls Exploration Trail. Thus, the train begins to get crowded between 10 and 11 a.m. Though you may catch a glimpse of several species from the train, it can't compare to Kilimanjaro Safaris for seeing the animals.

Conservation Station

What It Is: Behind-the-scenes walk-through educational exhibit
Scope & Scale: Minor attraction
When to Go: Before 11 a.m. or after 3 p.m.
Author's Rating: Evolving; ★★★
Appeal by Age Group:

Pre-school	Grade School	Teens	Young Adults	Over 30	Senior Citizens
★★½	★★	★½	★★½	★★½	★★½

Probable Waiting Time: None

Description and Comments   Conservation Station is the Animal Kingdom's veterinary and conservation headquarters. Located on the perimeter of the African section of the park, Conservation Station is, strictly speaking, a backstage, working facility. Here guests can meet wildlife experts, observe some of the Station's ongoing projects, and learn about the behind-the-scenes operations of the park. The Station includes, among other things, a rehabilitation area for injured animals and a nursery for recently born (or hatched) critters. Vets and other experts are on hand to answer questions.

You can access Conservation Station by taking the Wildlife Express train directly from Harambe. To return to the center of the park, continue the loop from Conservation Station back to Harambe.

Touring Tips   Conservation Station is interesting, but you have to invest a little effort and it helps to be inquisitive. Because it's on the far-flung border of the park, you'll never bump into Conservation Station unless you take the train.

Asia

Crossing the Asia Bridge from Safari Village, you enter Asia through the village of Anandapur, a veritable collage of Asian themes inspired by the architecture and ruins of India, Thailand, Indonesia, and Nepal. Situated near the bank of the Chakranadi River (translation: the river that runs in circles) and surrounded by lush vegetation, Anandapur provides access to a gibbon exhibit and to Asia's two feature attractions, the Kali River Rapids whitewater raft ride and the Maharaja Jungle Trek. Also in Asia is *Flights of Wonder,* an educational production about birds.

Kali River Rapids (FASTPASS)

What It Is: Whitewater raft ride

Scope & Scale: Headliner

When to Go: Before 10 a.m. or after 4:30 p.m.

Special Comments: You are guaranteed to get wet; 42" height minimum

Author's Rating: Short but scenic ★★★½

Appeal by Age Group:

Pre-school	Grade School	Teens	Young Adults	Over 30	Senior Citizens
★★★★	★★★★	★★★★	★★★½	★★★½	★★★

Duration of Ride: About 5 minutes

Avg. Wait in Line per 100 People ahead of You: 5 minutes

Loading Speed: Moderate

Description and Comments   The ride consists of an unguided trip down a man-made river in a circular rubber raft with a platform seating 12 persons mounted on top. The raft essentially floats free in the current and is washed downstream through rapids and waves. Because the river is fairly wide with numerous currents, eddies, and obstacles, there is no telling exactly where the raft will go. Thus, each trip is different and exciting. At the end of the ride a conveyor belt hauls the raft up to be unloaded and prepared for the next group of guests.

What distinguishes Kali River Rapids from other theme park raft rides is Disney's trademark attention to visual detail. Kali River Rapids flows through a dense rain forest, past waterfalls, temple ruins, and bamboo thickets, emerging into a cleared area where loggers have ravaged the forest, and finally drifting back under the tropical canopy as the river cycles back to Anandapur. Though the visuals here are first-class (the queuing area is one of the most striking and interesting of any Disney attraction), Kali River Rapids is marginal in two important respects: You're on the water only about three and a half minutes, and it's a weenie ride. Sure you get wet, but otherwise the drops and rapids are not all that exciting.

Touring Tips   This attraction is hugely popular, especially on hot summer days. Ride Kali River Rapids before 10 a.m., after 4:30 p.m., or use FASTPASS. You can expect to get wet and possibly drenched on this ride. Our recommendation is to wear shorts to the park and bring along a jumbo trash bag as well as a smaller plastic bag. Before boarding the raft, take off your socks and punch holes in your jumbo bag for your head. Though you can also cut holes for your arms, you will probably stay dryer with your arms inside the bag. Use the smaller plastic bag to wrap around your shoes. There's also a water-resistant compartment in the middle of the raft for any small items you want to stow.

Maharaja Jungle Trek

What It Is: Walk-through zoological exhibit

Scope & Scale: Headliner

When to Go: Anytime

Author's Rating: A standard setter for natural habitat design;
    ★★★★

Appeal by Age Group:

Pre-school	Grade School	Teens	Young Adults	Over 30	Senior Citizens
★★★	★★★½	★★★	★★★½	★★★★	★★★★

Duration of Tour: About 20–30 minutes

Description and Comments   The Maharaja Jungle Trek is a zoo-logical nature walk similar to the Pangani Forest Exploration Trail, but with an Asian setting and Asian animals. You start with Komodo dragons and then work up to Malayan tapirs. Next is a cave with fruit bats. Ruins of the maharaja's palace provide the setting for Bengal tigers. From the top of a parapet in the palace you can view a herd of blackbuck antelope and Asian deer. The trek concludes with an aviary.

Touring Tips   The Jungle Trek does not get as jammed as Pangani Forest Exploration Trail and is a good choice for midday touring when most other attractions are crowded. The downside is the exhibit showcases tigers, tapirs, and other creatures that might not be as active in the heat of the day as the proverbial mad dogs and Englishmen.

Flights of Wonder at the Caravan Stage

What It Is: Stadium show about birds

Scope & Scale: Major attraction

When to Go: Anytime

Special Comments: Performance times are listed in the handout park map

Author's Rating: Unique; ★★★★

Appeal by Age Group:

Pre-school	Grade School	Teens	Young Adults	Over 30	Senior Citizens
★★★★	★★★★	★★★½	★★★★	★★★★	★★★★

Duration of Presentation: 30 minutes

Preshow Entertainment: None

Probable Waiting Time: 20 minutes

Description and Comments Both interesting and fun, *Flights of Wonder* is well paced and showcases a surprising number of bird species. The focus of *Flights of Wonder* is on the natural talents and characteristics of the various species, so don't expect to see any parrots riding bicycles. The natural behaviors, however, far surpass any tricks learned from humans. Overall, the presentation is fascinating and exceeds most guests' expectations.

Touring Tips *Flights of Wonder* plays at the stadium, located near the Asia Bridge on the walkway into Asia. The stadium is covered but not air-conditioned, thus early-morning and late-afternoon performances are more comfortable. Though we did not have any problem getting a seat for *Flights of Wonder,* the show's attendance has picked up since the rest of Asia opened. To play it safe, arrive about 10–15 minutes before show time.

DinoLand U.S.A.

This most typically Disney of the Animal Kingdom's lands is a cross between an anthropological dig and a quirky roadside attraction. Accessible via the bridge from Safari Village, DinoLand U.S.A. is home to a children's play area, a nature trail, a 1,500-seat amphitheater, a couple of natural history exhibits, and Dinosaur, one of the Animal Kingdom's two thrill rides.

Dinosaur (FASTPASS)

What It Is: Motion-simulator dark ride

Scope & Scale: Super headliner

When to Go: Before 10 a.m. or in the hour before closing

Special Comments: Must be 40'' tall to ride (see "Switching off" on page 54)

Author's Rating: Really improved; ★★★★½

Appeal by Age Group:

Pre-school	Grade School	Teens	Young Adults	Over 30	Senior Citizens
†	★★★★★	★★★★½	★★★★½	★★★★½	★★★★

† Sample size too small for an accurate rating.

Duration of Ride: $3^1/3$ minutes

Average Wait in Line per 100 People ahead of You: 3 minutes
Assumes: Full-capacity operation with 18-second dispatch interval
Loading Speed: Fast

Description and Comments   Dinosaur, formerly known as Count-down to Extinction, is a combination track ride and motion simulator. In addition to moving along a cleverly hidden track, the ride vehicle also bucks and pitches (the simulator part) in sync with the visuals and special effects encountered. The plot has you traveling back in time on a mission of rescue and conservation. Your objective, believe it or not, is to haul back a living dinosaur before the species becomes extinct. Whoever is operating the clock, however, cuts it a little close, and you arrive on the prehistoric scene just as a giant asteroid is hurling toward Earth. General mayhem ensues as you evade carnivorous predators, catch Barney, and make your escape before the asteroid hits. Although the ride is jerky, it's not too rough for seniors. The menacing dinosaurs, however, along with the intensity of the experience, make Dinosaur a no-go for younger children. To our surprise and joy, Dinosaur has been refined and cranked up a couple of notches on the intensity scale after its first year of operation. The latest version is darker, more interesting, and much zippier.

Touring Tips   We recommend that you ride early after experiencing Kilimanjaro Safaris and the Kali River Rapids. If you bump into a long line, use FASTPASS.

Theater in the Wild

What It Is: Open-air venue for live stage shows
Scope & Scale: Major attraction
When to Go: Anytime
Special Comments: Performance times are listed in the handout park map
Author's Rating: Tarzan lays an egg; ★★½
Appeal by Age Group:

Pre-school	Grade School	Teens	Young Adults	Over 30	Senior Citizens
★★★	★★★★	★★★	★★★	★★★	★★★

Duration of Presentation: 25–35 minutes

Preshow Entertainment: None

Probable Waiting Time: 20–30 minutes

Description and Comments   The Theater in the Wild is a 1,500-seat covered amphitheater. The largest stage production facility in the Animal Kingdom, the theater can host just about any type of stage show. In summer 1999, Theater in the Wild unveiled a rock musical production based on Disney's animated movie *Tarzan*. Called *Tarzan Rocks!,* the show features aerial acts and acrobatic stunts including extreme skating. If this sounds like a hodgepodge, you're right. Although the performers are both talented and enthusiastic, attempting to attach such disparate elements to the Tarzan plot (in a musical context yet!) produces a lumbering, uneven, and hugely redundant affair. We like parts of the presentation taken individually, but every time the show comes close to taking off, it fumbles into an awkward transition and loses its momentum.

Touring Tips   To get a seat, show up 20–25 minutes in advance for morning and late-afternoon shows, and 30–35 minutes in advance for shows scheduled between noon and 4:30 p.m.

The Boneyard

What It Is: Elaborate playground

Scope & Scale: Diversion

When to Go: Anytime

Author's Rating: Stimulating fun for children; ★★★½

Appeal by Age Group:

Pre-school	Grade School	Teens	Young Adults	Over 30	Senior Citizens
★★★★½	★★★★½	—	—	—	—

Duration of Visit: Varies

Waiting Time: None

Description and Comments   This attraction is an elaborate playground, particularly appealing to kids ages ten and younger, but visually appealing to all ages. Arranged in the form of a rambling open-air dig site, The Boneyard offers plenty of opportunity for exploration and letting off steam. Playground equipment consists of the skeletons of Triceratops, *Tyrannosaurus rex,* Brachiosaurus, and the like, on which children can swing, slide, and climb. In addition, there are sand pits where little ones can scrounge around for bones and fossils.

Touring Tips   Not the cleanest Disney attraction, but certainly one where younger children will want to spend some time. Aside from getting dirty, or at least sandy, be aware that The Boneyard gets mighty hot in the Florida sun. Also, be aware that The Boneyard rambles over about a half-acre and is multistoried. It's pretty easy to lose sight of a small child in the playground. Fortunately, there's only one entrance and exit.

Live Entertainment in the Animal Kingdom

Stage Shows   Stage shows are performed daily at the Theater in the Wild in DinoLand U.S.A., at Grandmother Willow's Grove, at the Lion King Theater in Camp Minnie-Mickey, and at the stadium in Asia. Presentations at Camp Minnie-Mickey and DinoLand U.S.A. feature Disney characters.

Street Performers   Street performers can be found most of the time at Safari Village, at Harambe in Africa, at Anandopur in Asia, and in DinoLand U.S.A.

Afternoon Parade   The Animal Kingdom sometimes offers a modest parade. Though not as elaborate as parades at the Magic Kingdom or Disney-MGM Studios, the parade is pleasant enough. Parades in the Animal Kingdom start next to the Creature Comforts shop in Safari Village and cross the Africa Bridge. Turning right, the parade proceeds along the path connecting Africa and Asia before making a right turn over the Asia Bridge back into Safari Village. From here the parade completes the circuit through Safari Village back to the starting point.

If a parade is offered, and if you are a big fan of Disney parades, check it out. Otherwise, for the moment, we don't think that the parade is worth a special effort.

Animal Encounters   Throughout the day, knowledgeable Disney staff conduct impromptu short lectures on specific animals at the park. Look for a cast member in safari garb holding a bird, reptile, or small mammal.

Goodwill Ambassadors A number of Asian and African natives are on hand throughout the park. Both gracious and knowledgeable, they are delighted to discuss their county and its wildlife.

Shopping in the Animal Kingdom

While most of the shopping at the Animal Kingdom is concentrated in Safari Village, Harambe in Africa, Anandapur in Asia, and DinoLand U.S.A., any nook or hut large enough to house a cash register is likely to sell something. Typical items for sale include wildlife- and conservation-inspired merchandise à la The Nature Company, along with African woodcarvings, crafts, and garb, as well as safari attire, dinosaur specialty items, and the inevitable assortment of Disney character goods. The two largest shops, both located in Safari Village, are Island Mercantile and Disney Outfitters.

Traffic Patterns in the Animal Kingdom

For starters, because the Animal Kingdom is new, expect huge crowds for the foreseeable future, even during the off-season. The four crowd magnets are *It's Tough to Be a Bug!* in the Tree of Life, Kilimanjaro Safaris in Africa, Dinosaur in Dino-Land U.S.A., and Kali River Rapids in Asia.

Most guests arrive in the morning, with a sizable number on-hand prior to opening and a larger wave arriving between 8 and 9:30 a.m. Guests continue to stream in through the late morning and into the early afternoon, with the crowds peaking at around 2 p.m. From about 2:30 p.m. on, departing guests outnumber arriving guests by a wide margin, as guests who arrived early complete their tour and leave. Crowds thin appreciably by late afternoon and continue to decline into the early evening.

Because the number of attractions, including theater presentations, are limited, most guests complete a fairly comprehensive tour in two-thirds of a day if they arrive early. Thus, generally speaking, your best bet for easy touring is either to be on hand when the park opens or to arrive at about 3 p.m., when the early birds are heading for the exits. If you decide to visit during the late afternoon, you might have to return on another afternoon to see everything.

Guests who have boned up on the Animal Kingdom make straight for Kilimanjaro Safaris in Africa and Dinosaur in Dino-Land U.S.A. Kali River Rapids in Asia and *It's Tough to Be a Bug!* in the Tree of Life are also early-morning favorites.

Animal Kingdom
One-Day Touring Plan

For: Visitors of All Ages

Touring the Animal Kingdom is not as complicated as touring the other parks because it offers a smaller number of attractions. Also, most Animal Kingdom rides, shows, and zoological exhibits are oriented to the entire family, thus eliminating differences of opinion regarding how to spend the day. At the Animal Kingdom the whole family can pretty much see and enjoy everything together.

Since there are fewer attractions than at the other parks, expect the crowds at the Animal Kingdom to be more concentrated. If a line seems unusually long, ask an Animal Kingdom cast member what the estimated wait is. If the wait exceeds your tolerance, try the same attraction again after 3 p.m.

The Animal Kingdom One-Day Touring Plan assumes a willingness to experience all major rides and shows. Be forewarned that Dinosaur and Kali River Rapids are sometimes frightening to children under age eight. Similarly, the theater attraction at the Tree of Life might be too intense for some preschoolers. When following the touring plan, simply skip any attraction you do not wish to experience.

Before You Go

1. Call (407) 824-4321 before you go to learn the park's hours of operation.
2. Purchase your admission prior to arrival.

At the Animal Kingdom

1. Arrive at the park one hour before the official opening time during the summer and holiday periods, and 40 minutes

before the official opening time the rest of the year. At the entrance plaza, pick up a park map. Wait at the entrance turnstiles or at the Rainforest Cafe turnstile to be admitted.

2. When admitted through the tunstiles, move quickly through The Oasis and cross the bridge into Safari Village. Turn left after the bridge and walk clockwise around the Tree of Life until you reach the bridge to Africa. Cross the bridge and continue straight ahead to Kilimanjaro Safaris. Experience Kilimanjaro Safaris.

3. After the safari, head back toward the Africa bridge to Safari Village, but turn left before crossing. Follow the walkway to Asia. In Asia, ride Kali River Rapids. If the weather is cool or it's just too early to get wet, use FAST-PASS and ride later. Also, be sure to check our suggestions for staying dry on page 203.

4. After the raft trip, return to the entrance of Asia and turn left over the Asia bridge into Safari Village. Pass Beastly Bazaar and Flame Tree Barbeque and turn left and cross the bridge into DinoLand U.S.A. After passing beneath the brontosaurus skeleton, angle right and follow the signs to Dinosaur. Ride.

5. Next, retrace your steps to Safari Village and bear left after you cross the DinoLand bridge. See *It's Tough to Be a Bug!* in the Tree of Life.

6. By now you will have most of the Animal Kingdom's potential bottlenecks behind you. Check your daily entertainment schedule for shows at the Theater in the Wild in DinoLand U.S.A., for Flights of Wonder in Asia, and for *Festival of the Lion King* and Pocahontas in Camp Minnie-Mickey. Plan the next part of your day around eating lunch and seeing these four shows. Before 11 a.m., arrive about 15–20 minutes prior to show time. During the middle of the day (11 a.m.–4 p.m.), you should queue up as follows:

For Theater in the Wild:	30 minutes before show time
For the Caravan Stage:	15 minutes before show time
For Pocahontas:	25–30 minutes before show time
For the Lion King Theater:	25–35 minutes before show time

7. Between shows, check out The Boneyard in DinoLand U.S.A. and the zoological exhibits around the Tree of Life and in The Oasis. This is also a good time to meet the characters at Camp Minnie-Mickey.

8. Return to Asia and take the Maharajah Jungle Trek.

9. Return to Africa and take Wildlife Express to Conservation Station. Tour the exhibits. If you want to experience the safari again, obtain a FASTPASS before boarding the train.

10. Depart Conservation Station and catch the train back to Harambe.

11. In Harambe, walk the Pangani Forest Exploration Trail.

Part Twelve

Disney-MGM Studios and Universal Florida

Disney-MGM Studios vs. Universal Studios Florida

The Disney-MGM Studios and Universal Studios Florida are direct competitors. Because both are large, expensive, and require at least one day to see, some guests must choose one park over the other. To help you decide, we present head-to-head comparisons of the parks, followed by a detailed description of each. In the summer of 1999, Universal launched its second major theme park, Universal's Islands of Adventure, which competes with the Magic Kingdom.

Both Disney-MGM and Universal Studios draw their inspiration from film and television. Both offer movie- and TV-themed rides and shows. Some are just for fun; others teach about the cinematic arts. Both include working film and television studios.

Nearly half of Disney-MGM is off-limits except by guided tour. Virtually all of Universal Studios is accessible. Universal emphasizes that it's first a working motion-picture and television studio, then a tourist attraction. Guests are more likely to see movie or television production in progress at Universal.

Universal is about twice as large as Disney-MGM, eliminating most of the congestion familiar at Disney-MGM. Attractions at both parks are excellent, though Disney-MGM attractions move people more efficiently. This disadvantage to Universal is somewhat offset by its having more major rides and shows.

Each park has a stellar, groundbreaking attraction. Universal offers *Terminator 2: 3-D,* which we consider the most extraordinary theater attraction in any American theme park, and Men in Black

Alien Attack, an interactive high-tech ride where the actions of guests determine the ending of the story. Disney-MGM features *The Twilight Zone* Tower of Terror, our pick as Disney's best attraction.

Although Universal has pioneered innovative rides, its attractions break down more often than Disney-MGM's. Jaws and Kongfrontation, in particular, are notorious for breakdowns.

Each offers a distinct product mix, so a person can visit both parks with little redundancy. Both offer good exposure to the cinematic arts, though Universal's presentations are more informative.

Try one park. If you enjoy it, you'll probably enjoy the other. If you have to choose between them, consider:

Touring Time   It takes 7–8 hours to see Disney-MGM (including one meal). Because Universal Studios Florida is larger and has more attractions, touring requires 9–11 hours (including one meal). Readers complain that much of that time is spent in lines.

Convenience   If you're lodging on International Drive, I-4's northeast corridor, the Orange Blossom Trail (US 441), or in Orlando, Universal Studios is closer. If you're on US 27, on FL 192, or in Disney World or Kissimmee, Disney-MGM is more convenient.

Endurance   Universal is larger and requires more walking, but it's less congested. Wheelchairs and disabled access are available at both parks.

Cost   Both cost about the same for one-day admission, food, and incidentals.

Best Days to Go   Tuesdays, Mondays, Thursdays, and Wednesdays are best, in that order, for Universal Studios. At Disney-MGM Studios, go when early entry isn't in effect.

Young Children   Both parks offer relatively adult entertainment. By our reckoning, half the rides and shows at Disney-MGM and about two-thirds at Universal Studios have significant potential for frightening young children.

Food   Food is generally much better at Universal Studios.

Disney-MGM Studios

Disney-MGM Studios was hatched from a corporate rivalry and a wild, twisted plot. At a time when the Disney Company was weak and fighting off greenmail—hostile takeover bids—Universal's parent company, MCA, announced plans to build an Orlando clone of their successful Universal Studios Hollywood theme park. MCA was courting the real estate–rich Bass brothers of Texas, hoping to secure the brothers' investment in the project, but the Bass brothers defected to the Disney camp and helped Disney squelch the hostile takeovers. The Bass brothers were front and center when Michael Eisner suddenly announced Disney would also build a movie theme park in Florida. A construction race ensued, but Universal was midprocess in the development of new attraction technologies and was no match for Disney, who could import proven concepts and attractions from their other parks. In the end, Disney-MGM Studios opened almost two years before Universal Studios Florida.

THE MGM CONNECTION

To broaden appeal and lend additional historical impact, Disney obtained rights to the MGM (Metro-Goldwyn-Mayer) name, film library, motion-picture and television titles, excerpts, costumes, music, sets, and even Leo, the MGM lion. Probably the two most recognized names in motion pictures, Disney and MGM account for almost a century of movie history.

COMPARING DISNEY-MGM STUDIOS TO THE MAGIC KINGDOM AND EPCOT

The Magic Kingdom entertains. Epcot educates. Disney-MGM Studios does both. All rely heavily on special effects and Audio-Animatronics (robotics).

The Studios and Magic Kingdom are about the same size, each half as big as Epcot. Unlike the others, Disney-MGM Studios is a working motion-picture and television production facility, meaning that about half is open only to guests on guided tours or observation walkways.

If you're interested in the history and technology of film and TV, Disney-MGM Studios offers plenty. If you just want to be entertained, the Studios provide megadoses of action, suspense,

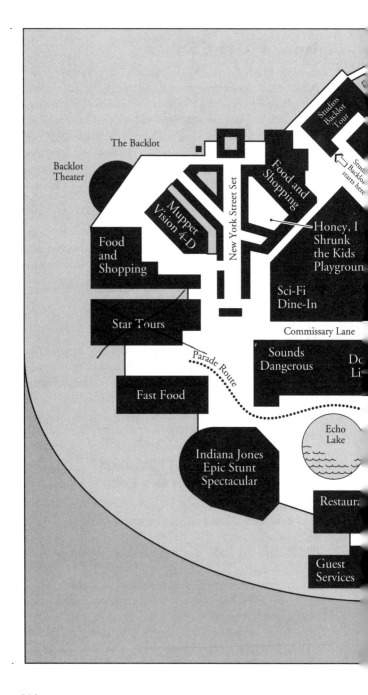

The Backlot

Backlot
Theater

Studios
Backlot
Tour

Studios
Backlot
starts here

Food and
Shopping

Honey, I
Shrunk
the Kids
Playgroun

Muppet
Vision 4-D

New York Street Set

Food
and
Shopping

Sci-Fi
Dine-In

Star Tours

Commissary Lane

Sounds
Dangerous

Do
Li

Parade Route

Fast Food

Echo
Lake

Indiana Jones
Epic Stunt
Spectacular

Restaur

Guest
Services

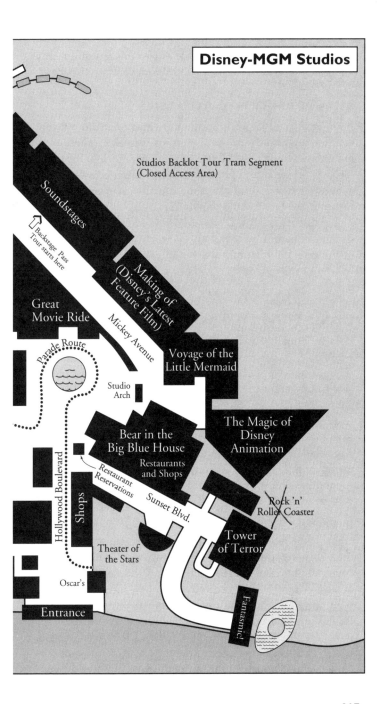

Disney-MGM Studios

Studios Backlot Tour Tram Segment
(Closed Access Area)

Soundstages

Backstage Pass
Tour starts here

Great
Movie Ride

Making of
(Disney's Latest
Feature Film)

Mickey Avenue

Voyage of the
Little Mermaid

Parade Route

Studio
Arch

Bear in the
Big Blue House

The Magic of
Disney
Animation

Restaurants
and Shops

Hollywood Boulevard

Restaurant
Reservations

Sunset Blvd.

Rock 'n'
Roller Coaster

Shops

Theater of
the Stars

Tower
of
Terror

Oscar's

Fantasmic!

Entrance

surprise, and fun. This formula has proven so successful that it has been used again at the new Animal Kingdom theme park.

HOW MUCH TIME TO ALLOCATE

It's impossible to see all of Epcot or the Magic Kingdom in one day. Disney-MGM Studios is more manageable. There's less ground to cover by foot. Trams run through much of the backlot and working areas, and attractions in the open-access parts are concentrated in an area about the size of Main Street, Tomorrowland, and Frontierland combined.

Because it's smaller, Disney-MGM Studios is more affected by large crowds. Our touring plans will keep you a step ahead of the mob and minimize waits in line. Even when the park is heavily attended, however, you can see almost everything in a day.

DISNEY-MGM STUDIOS IN THE EVENING

Because Disney-MGM Studios can be seen in a day, many guests who arrive in early morning run out of things to do by 3:30 or 4 p.m. and leave. Their departure thins the crowds and makes the park ideal for evening touring. Lines for most attractions are manageable, and the park is cooler. Outdoor theater productions are infinitely more enjoyable after midday's heat. A drawback to evening touring is that activity wanes on soundstages and in the Animation Building. Also, you might get stuck eating dinner here. If you eat, try Mama Melrose's or the Hollywood Brown Derby for full-service dining, or the Hollywood & Vine cafeteria.

In 1998, the Studios launched *Fantasmic!* (see pages 229–230), arguably the most spectacular nighttime entertainment event in the Disney repertoire. Staged nightly (weather permitting) in its own theater behind the Tower of Terror, *Fantasmic!* is "not to be missed." Unfortunately, evening crowds have increased substantially at the studios because of *Fantasmic!* Crowds build as performance time approaches, making *Fantasmic!* a challenge to get into. Also adversely affected are the Tower of Terror and Rock 'n' Roller Coaster, both situated near the entrance to *Fantasmic!* Crowd levels throughout the rest of the park, however, are generally light.

Not to Be Missed at Disney-MGM Studios

~~Star Tours~~ m 5
Disney-MGM Studios Backlot Tour
Indiana Jones Epic Stunt Spectacular
The Great Movie Ride
MuppetVision 4D
Fantasmic!
Voyage of the Little Mermaid
The Twilight Zone Tower of Terror
The Magic of Disney Animation
~~Rock 'n' Roller Coaster~~ m 5

ARRIVING

Disney-MGM Studios has its own pay parking lot and is served by the Disney transportation system. Many larger hotels out of the World offer shuttles to the Studios. If you drive, Disney World's ubiquitous trams will transport you to the ticketing area and entrance gate.

GETTING ORIENTED

Guest Relations, to the left of the entrance, is the park headquarters and information center. Check here for a map with a schedule of live performances, lost persons, Package Pick-up, lost and found, emergencies, and general information. To the right of the entrance are lockers and stroller and wheelchair rentals.

About half of the Studios is a theme park. The main street is Hollywood Boulevard of the 1920s and '30s. At the boulevard's end is a replica of Hollywood's famous Chinese Theater. While not as imposing as the Magic Kingdom's Cinderella Castle or Epcot's Spaceship Earth, the theater is Disney-MGM Studios' central landmark and is a good meeting place if your group becomes separated.

The Studios' theme park areas are at the theater end of Hollywood Boulevard, off Sunset Boulevard (branching right from Hollywood Boulevard), and around Echo Lake (to the left of Hollywood Boulevard as you face the theater). Attractions include rides and shows. The remainder of the complex has working soundstages, technical facilities, wardrobe shops, administrative offices, animation studios, and backlot sets with restricted access.

WHAT TO SEE

Try everything. Disney rides and shows are always surprising. (In the following descriptions of attractions, we give ratings based on a scale of zero to five stars; five stars is the best rating.)

FASTPASS AT DISNEY-MGM

Disney-MGM offers four FASTPASS attractions. Strategies for using FASTPASS are explained in detail on page 20. Disney-MGM FASTPASS attractions include

The Twilight Zone Tower of Terror   ~~Star Tours~~
Voyage of the Little Mermaid   ~~Rock 'n' Roller Coaster~~

Hollywood Boulevard Services	
Most park services are centered on Hollywood Boulevard, including:	
Baby Center/ Baby-Care Needs	Guest Relations; Oscar's sells baby food and other necessities
Banking Services	An automated bank teller is right of the entrance turnstiles (outside the park)
Film	The Darkroom, right side of Hollywood Boulevard, just beyond Oscar's
First Aid	Guest Relations
Live Entertainment/ Parade Information/ Character Information	Listed in the free park guidemap available at Guest Relations and other locations in the park
Lost & Found	Package Pick-up, right of the entrance
Lost Persons	Guest Relations
Storage Lockers	Right of the entrance on Hollywood Boulevard, left side of Oscar's

Hollywood Boulevard Services (continued)	
Walt Disney World & Local Attraction Information	Guest Relations
Wheelchair & Stroller Rental Service	Right of the entrance at Oscar's

DISNEY-MGM STUDIOS IN DETAIL

Hollywood Boulevard

Hollywood Boulevard is a palm-lined re-creation of Hollywood's main drag during the city's golden age. The architecture is streamlined *moderne* with Art Deco embellishments. Most service facilities are here, interspersed with eateries and shops. Merchandise includes Disney trademark items, Hollywood and movie-related souvenirs, and one-of-a-kind collectibles obtained from studio auctions and estate sales.

Hollywood characters and roving performers entertain on the boulevard, and daily parades pass this way.

Sunset Boulevard

Sunset Boulevard, evoking the 1940s, is a major recent addition to Disney-MGM Studios. The first right off Hollywood Boulevard, it provides another venue for dining, shopping, and street entertainment.

The Twilight Zone Tower of Terror (FASTPASS)

What It Is: Sci-fi-theme indoor thrill ride
Scope & Scale: Super headliner
When to Go: Before 9:30 a.m. and after 6 p.m.
Special Comments: 40" minimum height
Author's Rating: Walt Disney World's best attraction; ★★★★★
Appeal by Age Group:

Pre-school	Grade School	Teens	Young Adults	Over 30	Senior Citizens
★★★	★★★★★	★★★★★	★★★★★	★★★★★	★★★★½

Duration of Ride: About 4 minutes plus preshow

Avg. Wait in Line per 100 People ahead of You: 4 minutes
Assumes: All elevators operating
Loading Speed: Moderate

Description and Comments   Tower of Terror is a new species of
thrill ride, though it borrows elements of the Magic Kingdom's
Haunted Mansion. The idea is that you're touring the ruins of a
once-famous Hollywood hotel. The queuing area draws guests
into the adventure, taking them through the hotel's once-opulent
public rooms. From the lobby, they enter the hotel's library, where
Rod Serling (the host of the *Twilight Zone* series), speaking on a
black-and-white television, greets them and introduces the plot.

About the Tower of Terror is a whopper, 13-plus-stories tall. You can see
the entire park from the top, but you have to look quickly.

The ride vehicle, one of the hotel's elevators, takes guests on a
tour of the haunted hostelry. It begins innocuously, but by the fifth
floor things get weird. You have just entered the Twilight Zone.
Guests are subjected to special effects as they encounter unexpected
horrors and illusions. The climax occurs when the elevator reaches
the top floor (13th, of course) and the cable snaps.

Though the final plunges are calculated to thrill, the soul of
the attraction is its extraordinary visual and audio effects. There's
enough richness and subtlety to keep the ride stimulating through
many repetitions.

The Tower has great potential for terrifying children and rat-
tling adults.

Touring Tips   This ride is worth your admission to Disney-
MGM Studios. Due to its height, it's a beacon luring the curious. Due to its popularity with teens and young adults, count on
a footrace to this attraction, as well as Rock 'n' Roller Coaster,
when the park opens. It's mobbed most of the day. Experience it
first thing in the morning, in the evening before the park closes,
or use FASTPASS.

If you're on hand when the park opens and want to ride Tower
of Terror first, position yourself on the far right side of Sunset
Boulevard, as close to the rope barrier as possible. When the park
opens, cast members will walk the rope up the street toward Rock
'n' Roller Coaster and Tower of Terror. Stay on the far right sidewalk and you'll be among the first to make the right turn to the
entrance of the Tower.

When you enter the library waiting area, stand in the far back corner across from the door where you entered and at the opposite end of the room from the TV set. When the loading doors open, you'll be among the first admitted. If you have children or anyone else apprehensive about this attraction, ask the attendant about switching off (page 54).

Rock 'n' Roller Coaster (FASTPASS)

What It Is: Rock music–themed roller coaster

Scope & Scale: Headliner

When to Go: Before 10 a.m. or in the hour before closing

Special Comments: Children must be 48" tall to ride. Those younger than age 7 must ride with an adult. Switching off option provided (page 54).

Author's Rating: Disney's wildest American coaster; not to be missed; ★★★★

Appeal by Age Group:

Pre-school	Grade School	Teens	Young Adults	Over 30	Senior Citizens
★★★	★★★★	★★★★	★★★★	★★★★	★★★

Duration of Ride: Almost 1¼ minutes

Average Wait in Line per 100 People ahead of You: 2½ minutes

Assumes: All trains operating

Loading Speed: Moderate to fast

Description and Comments Exponentially wilder than Space Mountain or Big Thunder Mountain, Rock 'n' Roller Coaster is an attraction for fans of cutting-edge thrill rides. Although the rock icons and synchronized music add measurably to the experience, the ride itself is the focus here. Rock 'n' Roller Coaster offers loops, corkscrews, and drops that make Space Mountain seem like the Jungle Cruise. What really makes this metal coaster unusual, however, is that it's in the dark (like Space Mountain only with Southern California nighttime scenes instead of space) and you're launched up the first hill like a jet off a carrier deck. By the time you crest the hill you'll have gone from 0 to 57 mph in less than 3 seconds. When you enter the first loop you'll be pulling 5 gs—that's two more gs than astronauts experience at liftoff on the space shuttle! Is Rock 'n' Roller the baddest coaster in Florida? Hard to say, but it definitely ranks along with the Incredible Hulk Coaster at Universal's Islands of Adventure and Montu at Busch Gardens.

Touring Tips   This ride is not for everyone. If Space Mountain or Big Thunder push your limits, stay away from Rock 'n' Roller Coaster. Expect long lines except in the first hour after opening and during the late-evening performance of *Fantasmic!* Ride first thing in the morning or use FASTPASS.

If you're on hand when the park opens, position yourself on the far left side of Sunset Boulevard, as close to the rope barrier as possible. When the park opens, cast members will walk the rope toward Rock 'n' Roller Coaster and Tower of Terror. Stay on the far left sidewalk and you'll be among the first to make the left turn to the entrance of the coaster.

The Great Movie Ride

What It Is: Movie history indoor adventure ride
Scope & Scale: Headliner
When to Go: Before 10 a.m. and after 5 p.m.
Special Comments: Elaborate, with several surprises
Author's Rating: Unique; ★★★½
Appeal by Age Group:

Pre-school	Grade School	Teens	Young Adults	Over 30	Senior Citizens
★★½	★★★½	★★★½	★★★★	★★★★	★★★★

Duration of Ride: About 19 minutes
Avg. Wait in Line per 100 People ahead of You: 2 minutes
Assumes: All trains operating
Loading Speed: Fast

Description and Comments   Entering through a re-creation of Hollywood's Chinese Theater, guests board vehicles for a fast-paced tour through famous scenes from classic films, including *Casablanca, The Wizard of Oz, Alien,* and *Raiders of the Lost Ark.* Each is populated with new-generation audio-animatronic robots and an occasional human, all augmented by dazzling special effects. One of Disney's larger and more ambitious dark rides, The Great Movie Ride encompasses 95,000 square feet. Plans are afoot to either modernize The Great Movie Ride or replace it altogether with a new attraction.

Touring Tips   The ride draws large crowds from the moment the park opens. Its high capacity keeps lines moving, but even so, waits can exceed an hour after midmorning.

Doug Live!

What It Is: Audience participation television production based on Disney's *Doug* cartoon

Scope & Scale: Major attraction

When to Go: After 10 a.m.

Author's Rating: Pure schmaltz; ★★★

Appeal by Age Group:

Pre-school	Grade School	Teens	Young Adults	Over 30	Senior Citizens
★★★½	★★★½	★★	★★★	★★½	★★½

Duration of Presentation: 30 minutes

Preshow Entertainment: Participants are selected from guests in the preshow area

Probable Waiting Time: 10–20 minutes

Description and Comments   This stage show is a live musical adaptation of the *Doug* cartoon show. The plot revolves around shy Doug as he tries to muster the courage to ask Patti, his would-be girlfriend, to go to a rock concert. If Disney has ever come up with anything sappier, we must have missed it. However, the characters and storyline are true to the television show, so if you like the cartoon you'll probably enjoy the stage show. Guests are chosen (sometimes conscripted) prior to the show to play minor roles in the production.

Touring Tips   The theater seats 1,000, so it's usually easy to get in. If you want to be in the production, however, it's essential that you enter the preshow holding area at least 30 minutes before the next performance. Participants for the show are drafted from both genders and all age groups. Those who stand near the casting director and those who are outlandishly attired seem to be selected most often. One visitor who screamed, "Honeymooners!" was picked.

Star Tours (FASTPASS)

What It Is: Space-flight simulation indoor ride

Scope & Scale: Headliner

When to Go: First hour and a half the park is open

Special Comments: Pregnant women or anyone prone to motion sickness are advised against riding. The ride is too intense for many children younger than age 8. 40" height minimum

Author's Rating: Not to be missed; ★★★★

Appeal by Age Group:

Pre-school	Grade School	Teens	Young Adults	Over 30	Senior Citizens
★★★★	★★★★	★★★★	★★★★	★★★★	★★★★

Duration of Ride: About 7 minutes

Avg. Wait in Line per 100 People ahead of You: 5 minutes

Assumes: All simulators operating

Loading Speed: Moderate to fast

Description and Comments   Based on the continuing Star Wars movie series, guests ride in a flight simulator modeled after those used to train pilots and astronauts. The pilot is a droid on his first flight with real passengers. Mayhem ensues, scenery flashes by, and the simulator bucks and pitches. After several minutes, the droid manages to land the spacecraft.

Touring Tips   Star Tours hasn't been as popular at Disney-MGM Studios as at Disneyland in California. Except on unusually busy days, waits rarely exceed 30–40 minutes. Even so, see Star Tours before 11 a.m. or use FASTPASS. If you have children who are apprehensive about this attraction, ask the attendant about switching off (page 54).

Star Tours is near the exit of the 2,000-seat stadium that houses the *Indiana Jones Epic Stunt Spectacular.* When *Indiana Jones* lets out, Star Tours is temporarily inundated. The same goes for *MuppetVision 4D* and the *ABC Sound Studio* nearby. If you arrive amid this mayhem, return later.

Sounds Dangerous

What It Is: Show demonstrating sound effects

Scope & Scale: Minor attraction

When to Go: Before 11 a.m. or after 5 p.m.

Author's Rating: Funny and informative; ★★★

Appeal by Age Group:

Pre-school	Grade School	Teens	Young Adults	Over 30	Senior Citizens
★★½	★★★½	★★★	★★★	★★★	★★★★

Duration of Presentation: 12 minutes

Preshow Entertainment: David Letterman and Jimmy McDonald video

Probable Waiting Time: 15–30 minutes

Description and Comments   *Sounds Dangerous*, a film presentation starring Drew Carey as a blundering detective, is the vehicle for a crash course on movie and TV sound effects. Funny, educational, and well paced, *Sounds Dangerous* is entertaining and worthwhile. Earphones make the sounds seem very real—perhaps too real for some younger children during a part when the theater is plunged into darkness.

Touring Tips   Because the theater is small, long waits (partly in the sun) are common. *Sounds Dangerous* is inundated periodically by throngs from just-concluded performances of *Doug Live!* or *Indiana Jones.* Don't line up with them; come back in 20 minutes.

One reader took in *Sounds Dangerous* just before the afternoon parade, exiting just in time to see the marchers. If the parade starts on Hollywood Boulevard, it takes about 15–18 minutes to reach the theater.

Indiana Jones Epic Stunt Spectacular

What It Is: Movie stunt demonstration and action show

Scope & Scale: Headliner

When to Go: First 3 morning shows or last evening show

Special Comments: Performance times are posted at the theater entrance

Author's Rating: Done on a grand scale; ★★★★

Appeal by Age Group:

Pre-school	Grade School	Teens	Young Adults	Over 30	Senior Citizens
★★★	★★★★	★★★★	★★★★	★★★★	★★★★

Duration of Presentation: 30 minutes

Preshow Entertainment: Selection of "extras" from audience

Probable Waiting Time: None to approximately 30 minutes

Description and Comments   Coherent and educational, though somewhat unevenly paced, this popular production showcases professionals who demonstrate dangerous stunts. Sets, props, and special effects are elaborate. *Indiana Jones* was closed for renovation for several months in 2000. Though the sets and props have been refurbished and the special effects modernized, the content of the show remains essentially the same.

Touring Tips   Stunt Theater holds 2,000; capacity audiences are common. The first performance is easiest to get into. If it's at 9:30 a.m. or earlier, you can usually walk in. If it's at 9:45 or later, arrive 20 minutes early. For the second performance, go 20–35 minutes early. For subsequent shows, arrive 30–45 minutes early. If you tour in late afternoon and evening, attend the last performance. If you want to beat the crowd out of the stadium, sit near the top on the far right (as you face the stage).

To be chosen as an "extra" in the stunt show, arrive early, sit in front, and display boundless enthusiasm.

Theater of the Stars

What It Is: Live Hollywood-style musical, usually featuring Disney characters; performed in open-air theater

Scope & Scale: Major attraction

When to Go: In the evening

Special Comments: Performance times are listed in the daily entertainment schedule

Author's Rating: Excellent; ★★★★

Appeal by Age Group:

Pre-school	Grade School	Teens	Young Adults	Over 30	Senior Citizens
★★★★	★★★★	★★★	★★★★	★★★★	★★★★

Duration of Presentation: 25 minutes

Preshow Entertainment: None

Probable Waiting Time: 20–30 minutes

Description and Comments   *Theater of the Stars* combines Disney characters with singers and dancers in upbeat and humorous Hollywood musical productions. *Beauty and the Beast,* in particular, is outstanding. The theater, on Sunset Boulevard, offers a clear view from almost every seat. Best of all, a canopy protects the audience.

Touring Tips Unless you visit during cooler months, see this show in the late afternoon or the evening. Show up 20–50 minutes before any show.

Fantasmic!

What It Is: Mixed-media nighttime spectacular

Scope & Scale: Super headliner

When to Go: Only staged in the evening

Special Comments: Disney's best nighttime event

Author's Rating: Not to be missed; ★★★★★

Appeal by Age Group:

Pre-school	Grade School	Teens	Young Adults	Over 30	Senior Citizens
★★★★	★★★★★	★★★★½	★★★★½	★★★★½	★★★★½

Duration of Presentation: 25 minutes

Probable Waiting Time: 50–60 minutes if you want a seat; 30 minutes for standing room

Description and Comments *Fantasmic!* is a mixed-media show presented one or more times each evening when the park is open late. Located off Sunset Boulevard behind the Tower of Terror, *Fantasmic!* is staged on a newly created lagoon and island opposite a 6,900-seat amphitheater. By far the largest theater facility ever created by Disney, the amphitheater can accommodate an additional 3,000 standing guests for a total audience of nearly 10,000.

Fantasmic! is far and away the most extraordinary and ambitious outdoor spectacle ever attempted in any theme park. Starring Mickey Mouse in his role as the Sorcerer's Apprentice from *Fantasia,* the production uses lasers, images projected on a shroud of mist, fireworks, lighting effects, and music in combinations so stunning you can scarcely believe what you have seen. The plot is simple: good versus evil. The story gets lost in all the special effects at times, but no matter, it is the spectacle, not the story line, that is so overpowering. While beautiful, stunning, and powerful are words that immediately come to mind, they fail to convey the uniqueness of this presentation. It could be argued, with some validity, that *Fantasmic!* alone is worth the price of the Disney-MGM Studios admission.

Touring Tips   Fantasmic! provides a whole new dimension to nighttime at Disney-MGM Studios. As a day-capping event, it is to the Studios what *IllumiNations* is to Epcot. While it's hard to imagine running out of space in a 10,000-person stadium, it happens almost every day. On evenings when there are two performances, the second show will always be less crowded. If you attend the first (or only) scheduled performance, line up at least an hour in advance. If you opt for the second show, arrive 50 minutes early. Also, hang on to your children after *Fantasmic!* and give them explicit instructions for regrouping in the event you are separated.

Voyage of the Little Mermaid (FASTPASS)

What It Is: Musical stage show featuring characters from the
  Disney movie *The Little Mermaid*
Scope & Scale: Major attraction
When to Go: Before 9:30 a.m. or just before closing
Author's Rating: Romantic, lovable, and humorous in the best
  Disney tradition. Not to be missed; ★★★★
Appeal by Age Group:

Pre-school	Grade School	Teens	Young Adults	Over 30	Senior Citizens
★★★★	★★★★	★★★½	★★★★	★★★★	★★★★

Duration of Presentation: 15 minutes
Preshow Entertainment: Taped ramblings about the holding
  area's decor
Probable Waiting Time: Before 9:45 a.m., 10–30 minutes; after
  9:30 a.m., 35–70 minutes

Description and Comments   Voyage of the Little Mermaid is a winner, appealing to every age. Cute without being saccharine, and infinitely lovable, *Little Mermaid* is the most tender and romantic entertainment in Disney World. The story is simple and engaging; the special effects are impressive; and the characters are memorable.

*Touring Tips   Because it's excellent and located at a busy pedestrian intersection, the show plays to capacity crowds all day. Unless you make the first or second show or use FASTPASS, you'll probably have to wait an hour or more.

When you enter the preshow lobby, stand near the theater doors. When you enter, pick a row and let about six to ten people enter ahead of you. The strategy is to get a good seat and be near the exit doors.

The Making of (Disney's Lastest Feature Film)

What It Is: Documentary about the making of Disney's latest animated feature

Scope & Scale: Minor attraction

When to Go: Anytime

Author's Rating: Disney infomercial; ★★

Appeal by Age Group:

Pre-school	Grade School	Teens	Young Adults	Over 30	Senior Citizens
★★	★★★	★★★½	★★★½	★★★½	★★★½

Duration of Presentation: 17 minutes

Preshow Entertainment: Tour of post-production facilities

Probable Waiting Time: 20 minutes

Description and Comments   Short documentary about latest Disney film follows a tour of post-production studios, where sound and film animation is explained.

Touring Tips   Although this attraction offers perspective on how movies are made, its primary purpose is to lure you to the box office. Transparent self-promotion aside, presentations at least marginally teach about filmmaking. Presentation is usually uncrowded.

Jim Henson's MuppetVision 4D

What It Is: 4-D movie starring the Muppets

Scope & Scale: Major attraction

When to Go: Before 11 a.m. and after 4 p.m.

Author's Rating: Uproarious. Not to be missed; ★★★★½

Appeal by Age Group:

Pre-school	Grade School	Teens	Young Adults	Over 30	Senior Citizens
★★★★½	★★★★★	★★★★½	★★★★½	★★★★½	★★★★½

Duration of Presentation: 17 minutes

Preshow Entertainment: Muppets on television
Probable Waiting Time: 12 minutes

Description and Comments   *MuppetVision 4D* provides a total
sensory experience, with wild 3-D action augmented by auditory,
visual, and tactile special effects. If you're tired and hot, this zany
presentation will make you feel brand-new.

Touring Tips   Before noon, waits are about 20 minutes. From
noon until about 4 p.m., expect long lines. Also, watch out for
crowds arriving from just-concluded performances of the *Indiana
Jones Epic Stunt Spectacular.* Don't line up with them; return later.

Honey, I Shrunk the Kids Movie Set Adventure

What It Is: Small but elaborate playground
Scope & Scale: Diversion
When to Go: Before 10 a.m. or after dark
Author's Rating: Great for young children, expendable for
    adults; ★★½
Appeal by Age Group:

Pre-school	Grade School	Teens	Young Adults	Over 30	Senior Citizens
★★★★½	★★★½	★★	★★½	★★★	★★½

Duration of Presentation: Varies
Avg. Wait in Line per 100 People ahead of You: 20 minutes

Description and Comments   This elaborate playground especially
appeals to kids ages 11 and younger. The idea is that you've been
"miniaturized" and have to make your way through a yard full of
20-foot-tall grass blades, giant ants, lawn sprinklers, and other
oversized features.

Touring Tips   This imaginative playground has tunnels, slides,
rope ladders, and oversized props. All surfaces are padded, and
Disney personnel help control children. Only 240 people are
allowed "on the set" at once—not nearly the number who'd like
to play. By 10:30 or 11 a.m., the area is usually full, with dozens
waiting (some impatiently).

There's no provision for getting people to leave. Kids play as
long as parents allow. This creates uneven traffic flow and unpre-
dictable waits. If this attraction weren't poorly ventilated and hot
as a swamp, there's no telling when anyone would leave.

One reader accessed the playground through the Backstage Plaza fast-food and retail area and bought snacks and beverages while the kids were playing. When the youngsters emerged, refreshments were waiting.

New York Street Backlot

What It Is: Walk-through backlot movie set

Scope & Scale: Diversion

When to Go: Anytime

Author's Rating: Interesting, with great detail; ★★★

Appeal by Age Group:

Pre-school	Grade School	Teens	Young Adults	Over 30	Senior Citizens
★½	★★★	★★★	★★★	★★★	★★★

Duration of Presentation: Varies

Avg. Wait in Line per 100 People ahead of You: No waiting

Description and Comments   This part of the Studios' backlot was previously accessible only on the tram segment of the Backstage Tour. Now guests can stroll the elaborate New York Street set. Opening this area also relieves congestion in the Hollywood Boulevard and Echo Lake areas.

Touring Tips   There's never a wait; save it until you've seen attractions that develop long lines. Mickey Mouse signs autographs on the steps of the hotel in the middle of the block. It has no visible name but has flags above the entrance. Consult the daily entertainment schedule for autograph sessions.

Backlot Theater

What It Is: Hollywood-style musical, usually based on a Disney film; performed in open-air theater

Scope & Scale: Major attraction

When to Go: First show in the morning or in the evening

Special Comments: Consult the daily entertainment schedule for performances

Author's Rating: Excellent; ★★★★

Appeal by Age Group:

Pre-school	Grade School	Teens	Young Adults	Over 30	Senior Citizens
★★★	★★★½	★★★	★★★★	★★★★	★★★★

Duration of Presentation: 25–35 minutes
Preshow Entertainment: None
Probable Waiting Time: 20–30 minutes

Description and Comments   The Backlot Theater, like *Theater of the Stars,* is an open-air venue for musicals and concerts. Most productions spring from Disney films or animated features. The theater is well designed but has several obtrusive support columns. The audience is out of the elements, but the theater can get terribly hot.

Touring Tips   Unless you visit during cooler times, see the first morning show or the last evening show. To reach the obscurely located Backlot Theater, walk down New York Street toward Washington Square. At the square, turn left for a short block.

Arrive 25 minutes before any show to avoid sitting behind the columns.

Bear in the Big Blue House

What It Is: Live show for children
Scope & Scale: Minor attraction
When to Go: Per the daily entertainment schedule
Author's Rating: A must for families with preschoolers; ★★★
Appeal by Age Group:

Pre-school	Grade School	Teens	Young Adults	Over 30	Senior Citizens
★★★★	★★★½	★★	★★½	★★½	★★½

Duration of Presentation: 20 minutes
Special Comments: Audience sits on the floor
Probable Waiting Time: 10 minutes

Description and Comments   The *Bear in the Big Blue House* is based on and features characters from the Disney Channel television show of the same name. The show includes singing, dancing, and puppetry as well as a good deal of audience participation. The bear (who oozes love and goodness) rallies throngs of tots and preschoolers to sing and dance along with him. Even for adults without children of their own it's a treat to watch the tikes rev up. If you have a younger child in your party, all the better.

Touring Tips   The Bear is located to the immediate right of the Animation Tour. Show up about 15 minutes or so in advance.

The Magic of Disney Animation

What It Is: Walking tour of the Disney Animation Studio

Scope & Scale: Major attraction

When to Go: Before 11 a.m. and after 5 p.m.

Author's Rating: A masterpiece; not to be missed; ★★★★

Appeal by Age Group:

Pre-school	Grade School	Teens	Young Adults	Over 30	Senior Citizens
★★★	★★★	★★★	★★★★	★★★★	★★★★

Duration of Presentation: 36 minutes

Preshow Entertainment: Gallery of animation art in waiting area

Avg. Wait in Line per 100 People ahead of You: 7 minutes

Description and Comments   The public, for the first time, sees Disney artists at work.

The animation tour exceeds expectations. It's dynamic, fast paced, educational, and fun. After entering the Animation Building, you enter a theater for an eight-minute film about animation narrated by Walter Cronkite and Robin Williams.

After the film, you enter the studio and watch artists and technicians through large windows. Each workstation and task is explained by Cronkite and Williams via video monitors. Next, guests gather to see a multimonitor video where a Disney animator shares his perspective on the creative process. It entertains but is warm, endearing, and worthwhile in its own right. Finally, the group enters a theater for a film that melds all elements of animation production. Clips from Disney animation classics are featured.

The tour depends on live, video, and film narration and only secondarily on animators in the studio. Though animation is well explained, you may be disappointed if you thought you'd see lots of animators working.

Touring Tips   Some days, the animation tour doesn't open until 11 a.m.; check the daily entertainment schedule and try to go before noon. Lines begin to build on busy days by mid- to late morning.

After the introductory film, stay as long as you like in the studio. The narrative repeats at each workstation every two to three minutes. Let most of your 160-person tour group pass you at the first station. Then take your time watching artists. You'll likely catch up with your group. If not, move with the next group.

Disney-MGM Studios Backlot Tour

What It Is: Tram tour of modern film and video production

Scope & Scale: Headliner

When to Go: Anytime

Special Comments: Can be combined with soundstage tour described below

Author's Rating: Educational and fun; not to be missed; ★★★★

Appeal by Age Group:

Pre-school	Grade School	Teens	Young Adults	Over 30	Senior Citizens
★★★	★★★★	★★★★	★★★★	★★★★	★★★★

Duration of Presentation: About 25 minutes

Preshow Entertainment: Video before special effects segment and another in tram boarding area

Avg. Wait in Line per 100 People ahead of You: 2 minutes

Assumes: 16 tour departures per hour

Loading Speed: Fast

Description and Comments   A working film and television facility occupies about two-thirds of Disney-MGM Studios. Actors, artists, and technicians work there year-round. This tour takes visitors behind the scenes to learn about methods and technologies of motion-picture and TV production.

The tour begins on the edge of the backlot with the special effects segment. The tram segment follows. After that, guests can leave or continue on to the sound stage segment.

To reach the tour's start, take Hollywood Boulevard and turn right through the Studio Arch into the Animation Courtyard. Bear left at the corner where *Little Mermaid* is and go down the street to a red brick warehouse facade on the right. Go inside and up the ramp.

Guests then continue to the tram tour. The highlight is Catastrophe Canyon, an elaborate special effects set where a storm, earthquake, fire, and flood are simulated.

The tram tour ends at Backstage Plaza, where guests can use rest rooms, eat, or shop before taking the soundstage tour. To access the soundstage tour, go back past the entrance of the special effects/tram tour toward *Little Mermaid.* The soundstage tour begins on the far left end of the building next to the special effects/tram tour.

Touring Tips Because the Backlot Tour is one of Disney's most efficient attractions, you will rarely wait more than 15–20 minutes. Take the tour at your convenience, but preferably before 5 p.m., when the workday ends for the workshops.

Backstage Pass

What It Is: Walking tour of modern film and video production soundstages

Scope & Scale: Minor attraction

When to Go: Anytime

Special Comments: Can be combined with Disney-MGM Studios Backlot Tour described above

Author's Rating: Latest version not the best, but improved; ★★★

Appeal by Age Group:

Pre-school	Grade School	Teens	Young Adults	Over 30	Senior Citizens
★½	★★	★★	★★★	★★★	★★★

Duration of Presentation: About 25 minutes

Special Comments: The preshow video starring Bette Midler is the best part of the tour.

Probable Waiting Time: 10 minutes

Description and Comments The soundstage tour is a thinly disguised promo for a Disney film, so the name changes and is usually derived from the movie. Recently, for example, it was called Backstage Pass to "101 Dalmatians." Check your guidemap for the name in use when you visit.

You can take the soundstage tour before the Backlot Tour. In the Disney guidemap, the Backlot Tour and soundstage tours are listed separately. For continuity, start with the Backlot Tour, then tour the soundstages.

On the soundstage tour, soundproofed observation platforms allow unobtrusive viewing of ongoing productions. At the next stop, you inspect sets and props used in a Disney film and watch a video explaining how the film was produced.

Touring Tips While the Backlot Tour is worthwhile, the educational value of the soundstage tour is marginal. Though revised in 2000, what was once a compelling educational experience is now little more than a promo for Disney flicks. Waiting time for the tour is usually less than 20 minutes. The soundstage tour is roughly next door and to the right of the Backlot Tour on Mickey Avenue.

LIVE ENTERTAINMENT
AT DISNEY-MGM STUDIOS

Live entertainment, parades, and special events at the Studios are as fully developed or elaborate as those at the Magic Kingdom or Epcot. In the fall of 1998, Disney-MGM launched a new edition of *Fantasmic!,* a water, fireworks, and laser show that draws rave reviews. *Fantasmic!,* staged in its own specially designed 10,000-person amphitheater, makes the Studios the park of choice for spectacular nighttime entertainment. *Fantasmic!* is profiled in detail on pages 229–230.

Afternoon Parade   Staged one or more times a day, the parade features floats and characters from Disney animated features. One route begins near the park's entrance, continues down Hollywood Boulevard, circles in front of The Great Movie Ride, passes *Doug Live!* and *Sounds Dangerous,* and ends at Star Tours. The alternate route begins at the far end of Sunset Boulevard and turns right onto Hollywood Boulevard.

The parade is colorful, creative, and upbeat, but it brings pedestrian traffic to a standstill along its route and complicates movement within the park. If you're on the route when the parade begins, stay put and enjoy. Our favorite vantage point is the steps of *Doug Live!*

Theater of the Stars   This covered amphitheater on Sunset Boulevard showcases a variety of revues, usually featuring music from Disney movies and starring Disney characters. Performance times are posted at the theater and listed in the entertainment schedule in the park's guidemap.

Backlot Theater   This stage offers musical productions featuring Disney characters and/or films. To find it, follow New York Street toward the back of the park and turn left at the end of the street.

Disney Characters   See them at *Theater of the Stars,* Backlot Theater, parades, Studio Courtyard on New York Street (usually in front of the Animation Building), in Backstage Plaza, or along Mickey Avenue (next to the soundstages). Mickey appears regularly on Sunset Boulevard at times listed in the daily entertainment schedule. A character breakfast or lunch is offered most days at the Hollywood and Vine Cafeteria.

Sorcery in the Sky   An excellent fireworks show based on Mickey Mouse's exploits as the sorcerer's apprentice in *Fantasia* is held daily at closing when the park stays open after dark. In the off-season, it's held only on weekends, if at all. Watch anywhere along Hollywood Boulevard. It is conceivable that in the near future Sorcery in the Sky will be discontinued, revised, or incorporated into the finale of *Fantasmic!*

Shopping at Disney-MGM Studios

Movie-oriented merchandise and Disney trademark souvenirs star in shops throughout the park. Most are on Sunset and Hollywood Boulevards.

Animation Gallery, in the Animation Building, sells reproductions of cels from animated features and other animation art. Sid Cahuenga's near the park entrance sells vintage movie posters and celebrity autographs. Find Disney collectibles at Celebrity 5 & 10 on Sunset Boulevard. Planet Hollywood Super Store on Hollywood Boulevard is the place for celebrity memorabilia and Planet Hollywood trademark apparel. Sunset Boulevard Shop offers custom watches.

Disney-MGM Studios
One-Day Touring Plan

For: Adults and children of any age
Assumes: Willingness to experience all major rides
and shows

Because it offers fewer attractions, Disney-MGM Studios isn't as complicated to tour as the Magic Kingdom or Epcot.

Since there are fewer attractions here, expect crowds to be more concentrated. If a line seems unusually long, ask an attendant what the wait is. If it exceeds your tolerance, try again while *Indiana Jones,* a parade, or a special event is in progress.

The Rock 'n' Roller Coaster, Star Tours, The Great Movie Ride, the Tower of Terror, and the Catastrophe Canyon segment of the

Backstage Studio Tour may frighten young children. Star Tours and Rock 'n' Roller Coaster may cause motion sickness.

When following the touring plan, skip any attraction you don't wish to experience.

Early Entry at Disney-MGM Studios

Two days each week (usually Wednesday and Sunday), Disney resort guests are invited to enter Disney-MGM Studios 90 minutes before official opening. During the early-entry period, guests usually can enjoy Rock 'n' Roller Coaster, *MuppetVision 4D,* Star Tours, and *The Twilight Zone* Tower of Terror.

Early entry at Disney-MGM Studios offers some real advantages. Attractions that open early are those that are not to be missed and draw huge crowds. If you experience these first, the remainder of your touring will be a cinch. If you participate in early entry, be at the turnstiles 90 minutes before official opening. Once in the park, hurry to to the Rock 'n' Roller Coaster, then to the Tower of Terror, then to Star Tours and *MuppetVision 4D*. If you use our touring plan, skip steps that call for seeing these attractions.

If you aren't eligible for early entry, arrive 40 minutes before official opening on a day when early entry isn't in effect.

Before You Go

1. Call (407) 824-4321 to learn park hours and which days early entry is in effect.
2. Buy your admission.
3. Make advance dining priority seatings at (407) 939-3463. Disney resort guests can dial 55 or 56 from their rooms.

At Disney-MGM Studios

1. Arrive at the park 100 minutes before official opening if you're a Disney resort guest taking advantage of early entry. *On non-early-entry days,* arrive 40 minutes before official opening. Persons ineligible for early entry should avoid the park on those days.
2. When you're admitted, go to Guest Services and get a free guidemap with the daily entertainment schedule. Proceed down Hollywood Boulevard, turn right at Sunset Boule-

vard, and go to the Rock 'n' Roller Coaster. If you are held up at a rope barrier en route, position yourself on the far left sidewalk and stay put until you're allowed to proceed. Ride the Rock 'n' Roller Coaster. If you have children or adults who don't wish to ride, switch off (page 54).

3. After the coaster, return to Sunset Boulevard and bear left to Tower of Terror. Ride. Once again, take advantage of switching off if you have young children or adults who are still woozy from the coaster. FASTPASS is available for the Tower of Terror, but you shouldn't need it this early in the day.

4. After Tower of Terror, cross the park to Star Tours as follows: Return via Sunset Boulevard to Hollywood Boulevard. Go right on Hollywood Boulevard until you see a lake to your left. Bear left around the top of the lake and then right to Star Tours. Experience Star Tours.

5. Exit Star Tours to the right and return to Hollywood Boulevard. At the opposite end of Hollywood Boulevard from the park entrance is The Great Movie Ride. Ride.

6. After The Great Movie Ride, exit left and pass through the Studios Arch. To your immediate left through the arch is *Voyage of the Little Mermaid*. See the show if the wait is 25 minutes or less; otherwise, use FASTPASS.

7. Exit *Little Mermaid*, cross the Animation Courtyard, and go to the Animation building (on your left). Take the Magic of Disney Animation tour.

8. Head back through the Studios Arch, return to the Star Tours area, and pass Star Tours on your left. Proceed straight and slightly left to *MuppetVision 4D*. Enjoy the show.

Note: Stops for meals, refreshments, or rest room breaks will not adversely affect the touring plan after this step. If you have small children, now is a good time to visit the *Honey, I Shrunk the Kids* playground.

9. You have now experienced all the rides and most of the attractions that cause major bottlenecks. There are four live shows that are worthwhile. Plan the next part of your day to work them in, checking respective show times in the daily entertainment schedule in your park map.

Show	When to Line Up
*Indiana Jones Stunt Spectacular**	30 minutes before show time
The stage show at Theater of the Stars	30 minutes before show time
The stage show at Backlot Theater	30 minutes before show time
Doug Live!	20 minutes before show time
The Bear in the Big Blue House	15 minutes before show time

10. Between or after the shows see *Sounds Dangerous.* If the line is long, it's probably because the audience from a recently concluded performance of *Indiana Jones* or *Doug Live!* descended en masse. Come back in 30 minutes and the line will have disappeared.
11. Take the Backlot Tour.
12. Take the Backstage Pass tour.
13. See The Making of Disney's latest film, next door to *Little Mermaid.*
14. At your leisure, check out the New York Street set.

Universal Florida

Universal Florida is close to completion in the expansion project that has transformed it into a destination resort with two theme parks; a shopping, dining, and entertainment complex; and two hotels. The second theme park, Islands of Adventure (described later in this section), opened in 1999 with five theme areas.

A new system of roads and two multistory parking facilities are connected by moving sidewalks to CityWalk, a shopping, dining, and nighttime entertainment complex that also serves as a gateway to both the Universal Studios Florida and the Islands of Adventure theme parks. CityWalk includes the world's largest Hard Rock Cafe, complete with its own concert facility; an Emeril's restaurant; a NASCAR Cafe, with an auto-racing theme; a Pat O'Brien's New Orleans nightclub, with dueling pianos; a Motown Cafe; a Bob Marley restaurant and museum; a multi-faceted Jazz Center; an E! Entertainment production studio; Jimmy Buffett's Margaritaville; and a 16-screen cinema complex.

The Portofino Bay Resort opened in 1999 with 750 rooms, followed by a Hard Rock Hotel in late 2000.

---

* There's a possibility that *Indiana Jones* will become a FASTPASS attraction. If this occurs by all means take advantage of it.

ARRIVING

The Universal Florida complex can be accessed directly from I-4. Once on-site, you will park in one of two multitiered parking garages. Parking runs $6 for cars and $8 for RVs. Be sure to write down the location of your car before heading for the parks. From the garages, moving sidewalks deliver you to Universal CityWalk (described above). From CityWalk you can access the main entrances of both Universal Studios Florida and Universal's Islands of Adventure theme parks.

Universal offers 1-Day, 2-Day, 3-Day, and Annual Passes. Multi-day passes allow you to visit both Universal theme parks on the same day, and unused days are good forever. Multiday passes also allow for early entry on select days. Passes can be obtained in advance with your credit card at (800) 711-0080. All prices are the same regardless whether you buy your admission at the gate or in advance. Prices below include tax.

	Adults	Children (3–9)
1-Day, One Park Pass	$49	$40
2-Day Escape Pass	$90	$74
3-Day Escape Pass (sold at gate)	$106	$85
Two-Park Annual Pass	$201	$175

The main Universal Florida information number is (407) 363-8000. Reach Guest Services at (407) 224-6035, schedule a character lunch at (407) 224-6339, and order tickets by mail at (800) 224-3838.

UNIVERSAL, KIDS, AND SCARY STUFF

Although there's plenty for younger children to enjoy at the Universal parks, the majority of major attractions have the potential to frighten kids under age eight. At Universal Studios Florida, forget Alfred Hitchcock, *Twister*, Kongfrontation, Earthquake, Jaws, Men in Black, Back to the Future, and *Terminator 2: 3-D*. Most young children take The Funtastic World of Hanna-Barbera in stride. Ditto for the stunt show, though gunfire and explosions are involved. E.T. is a toss-up. Interestingly, very few families report problems with *Beetlejuice's Rock 'n' Roll Graveyard Revue* or *The Gory, Gruesome, & Grotesque Horror Make-Up Show*. Anything not listed here is pretty benign.

At Islands of Adventure watch out for the Incredible Hulk Coaster, Dr. Doom's Fearfall, The Adventures of Spider-Man,

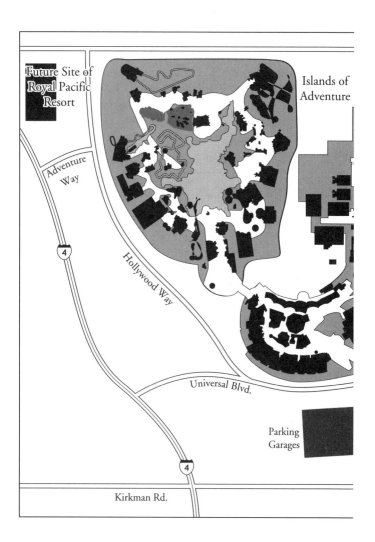

Future Site of
Royal Pacific
Resort

Islands of
Adventure

Adventure Way

Hollywood Way

Universal Blvd.

Parking
Garages

Kirkman Rd.

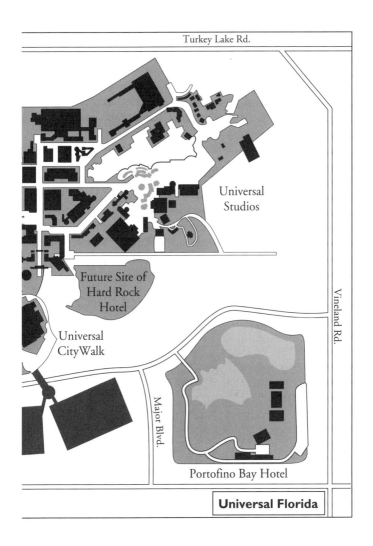

Turkey Lake Rd.

Universal
Studios

Future Site of
Hard Rock
Hotel

Universal
CityWalk

Vineland Rd.

Major Blvd.

Portofino Bay Hotel

Universal Florida

Jurassic Park River Adventure, Dueling Dragons, and *Poseidon's Fury*. Popeye & Bluto's Bilge-Rat Barges is wet and wild, but most younger children handle it well. Dudley Do-Right's Ripsaw Falls should be considered only if your kids liked Splash Mountain. The *Sinbad* stunt show includes some explosions and startling special effects, but children tolerate it well. Nothing else should pose a problem.

Universal Studios Florida

Universal Studios Florida opened in June 1990. At that time, it was almost four times the size of Disney-MGM Studios (Disney-MGM has since expanded), with much more of the facility accessible to visitors. Like its sister facility in Hollywood, Universal Studios Florida is spacious, beautifully landscaped, meticulously clean, and delightfully varied in its entertainment. Rides are exciting and innovative. However, many lack the capacity to handle the number of guests who frequent major Florida tourist destinations. Happily, most shows and theater performances at Universal Studios Florida are in theaters that accommodate large crowds. Since many shows run continuously, waits usually don't exceed twice the show's performance time (40–50 minutes).

Universal Studios Florida is laid out in an upside-down **L**. Beyond the entrance, a wide boulevard stretches past shows and rides to a New York City backlot set. Branching right from this pedestrian thoroughfare are five streets that access other areas of the studios and intersect a promenade circling a large lake.

The park is divided into five sections: the Front Lot/Produc-

---

Not to Be Missed at Universal Studios Florida

Back to the Future
Earthquake—The Big One
Jaws
Men in Black Alien Attack
Terminator 2: 3-D
The Wild, Wild, Wild West Stunt Show

tion Central, New York, Hollywood, San Francisco/Amity, and Expo Center. The area open to visitors is about the size of Epcot.

Almost all guest services, including stroller rental and lockers, are in the Front Lot, just inside the main entrance. Most of the park is accessible to disabled guests, and TDDs are available for the hearing impaired.

UNIVERSAL STUDIOS FLORIDA ATTRACTIONS

Terminator 2: 3-D

What It Is: 3-D thriller mixed-media presentation

Scope & Scale: Super headliner

When to Go: After 3:30 p.m.

Special Comments: Very intense for some preschoolers and grade-schoolers

Author's Rating: Furiously paced high-tech; the best theater attraction in any U.S. theme park; not to be missed; ★★★★★

Appeal by Age Group:

Pre-school	Grade School	Teens	Young Adults	Over 30	Senior Citizens
★★★	★★★★★	★★★★★	★★★★★	★★★★★	★★★★

Duration of Presentation: 20 minutes, plus 8-minute preshow

Probable Waiting Time: 20–40 minutes

Description and Comments   The Terminator cop from the *Terminator 2* movie "morphs" to life and battles Arnold Schwarzenegger's T-100 cyborg character. If you missed the Terminator flicks, don't worry. The attraction is all action; you don't need to understand much. What's interesting in this version is that it uses 3-D film and sophisticated technology to integrate the real with the imaginary. Remove your 3-D glasses momentarily to see that the motorcycle is actually onstage.

Touring Tips   The theater holds 700 and changes audiences about every 19 minutes. Even so, expect to wait 30–45 minutes. *Note to families:* The violence characteristic of the Terminator movies is largely absent here. There's suspense and action, but not much blood.

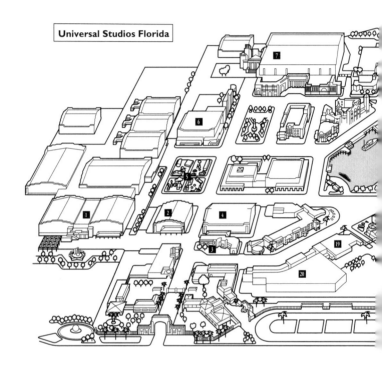

Universal Studios Florida

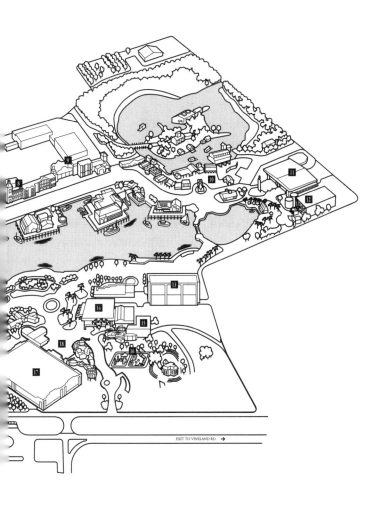

EXIT TO VINELAND RD. →

The Funtastic World of Hanna-Barbera

What It Is: Flight-simulation ride

Scope & Scale: Major attraction

When to Go: Before 11 a.m.

Special Comments: Very intense for some preschoolers; 40" height minimum

Author's Rating: A delight for all ages; ★★★½

Appeal by Age Group:

Pre-school	Grade School	Teens	Young Adults	Over 30	Senior Citizens
★★★★	★★★★	★★★½	★★★½	★★★½	★★★½

Duration of Ride: 4½ minutes, with a 3½-minute preshow

Loading Speed: Moderate to slow

Description and Comments   Flight-simulation ride in the same family as Disney's Body Wars, but all visuals are cartoons. Guests accompany Yogi Bear in a chase to rescue a kidnapped child.

Touring Tips   Large lines build early at this slow-loading ride and move glacially. Ride during the first two hours the park is open.

"Alfred Hitchcock: The Art of Making Movies"

What It Is: Mini-course on filming action sequences and a testimonial to Alfred Hitchcock

Scope & Scale: Major attraction

When to Go: After 3:30 p.m.

Special Comments: May frighten young children

Author's Rating: A little slow-moving, but well done; ★★★½

Appeal by Age Group:

Pre-school	Grade School	Teens	Young Adults	Over 30	Senior Citizens
★★½	★★★	★★★½	★★★½	★★★½	★★★½

Duration of Presentation: 40 minutes

Probable Waiting Time: 22 minutes

Description and Comments   Guests view a variety of clips of famous scenes from Hitchcock films (including some unreleased 3-D footage) and then exit to a soundstage where the stabbing scene from *Psycho* is re-created with audience volunteers. In a third area, the technology of filming action scenes is explained.

The Hitchcock "greatest hits" film is disjointed and confusing unless you recall the movies. The stabbing reenactment is informative and entertaining, as are sets and techniques shown in the third area.

Touring Tips   Lines are long but usually disappear quickly. Nevertheless, see this attraction just before you leave in the evening.

Nickelodeon Studios Walking Tour

What It Is: Behind-the-scenes guided tour
Scope & Scale: Minor attraction
When to Go: When Nickelodeon shows are in production (usually weekdays)
Author's Rating: ★★★
Appeal by Age Group:

Pre-school	Grade School	Teens	Young Adults	Over 30	Senior Citizens
★★½	★★★★	★★★	★★★	★★★	★★★

Duration of Tour: 36 minutes
Probable Waiting Time: 30–45 minutes

Description and Comments   Walking tour of the Nickelodeon studio examines set construction, soundstages, wardrobe, props, lighting, video production, and special effects. While much of the same information is presented more creatively in "Alfred Hitchcock" and the *Horror Make-Up Show,* the Nickelodeon Tour is specifically geared toward kids.

Touring Tips   While grade-schoolers, in particular, enjoy this tour, it's expendable for everyone else. Go on a second day at Universal. If Nickelodeon isn't in production, forget it.

Twister

What It Is: Theater presentation featuring characters and special effects from the movie *Twister*
Scope & Scale: Major attraction
When to Go: Immediately after experiencing all rides
Special Comments: High potential for frightening young children
Author's Rating: Gutsy; ★★★½

Appeal by Age Group:

Pre-school	Grade School	Teens	Young Adults	Over 30	Senior Citizens
★★	★★★★	★★★★	★★★★	★★★★	★★★★

Duration of Presentation: 15 minutes

Probable Waiting Time: 26 minutes

Description and Comments   Replacing the *Ghostbusters* attraction, *Twister* combines an elaborate set and special effects, climaxing with a five-story-tall simulated tornado created by circulating more than two million cubic feet of air per minute.

Touring Tips   The wind, pounding rain, and freight-train sound of the tornado are deafening, and the entire presentation is exceptionally intense. School-age children are mightily impressed, while younger children are terrified and overwhelmed. Unless you want the kids hopping in your bed whenever they hear thunder, try this attraction yourself before taking your kids.

Kongfrontation

What It Is: Indoor adventure ride featuring King Kong

Scope & Scale: Major attraction

When to Go: Before 11 a.m.

Special Comments: May frighten young children

Author's Rating: ★★★★

Appeal by Age Group:

Pre-school	Grade School	Teens	Young Adults	Over 30	Senior Citizens
★★★½	★★★★	★★★½	★★★½	★★★	★★★

Duration of Ride: 4½ minutes

Loading Speed: Moderate

Description and Comments   Guests board an aerial tram to ride from Manhattan to Roosevelt Island. En route, they hear that the giant ape has escaped. The tram passes evidence of Kong's rampage and encounters the monster, who hurls their tram to the ground.

Touring Tips   Ride in the morning after Men in Black, Back to the Future, E.T. Adventure, and Jaws.

The Gory Gruesome & Grotesque Horror Make-Up Show

What It Is: Theater presentation on the art of makeup

Scope & Scale: Major attraction

When to Go: After you've experienced all rides

Special Comments: May frighten young children

Author's Rating: A gory knee-slapper; ★★★½

Appeal by Age Group:

Pre-school	Grade School	Teens	Young Adults	Over 30	Senior Citizens
★★★	★★★½	★★★½	★★★½	★★★½	★★★½

Duration of Presentation: 25 minutes

Probable Waiting Time: 20 minutes

Description and Comments   A lively, well-paced look at how makeup artists create film monsters, realistic wounds, severed limbs, and other unmentionables. Excellent and enlightening, if somewhat gory, introduction to cinema monster-making.

Touring Tips   *The Horror Make-Up Show* exceeds most guests' expectations and is Universal's sleeper attraction. The humor transcends gruesome effects, and even preschoolers take the blood and guts in stride. It usually isn't hard to get into.

Earthquake—The Big One

What It Is: Combination theater presentation and adventure ride

Scope & Scale: Major attraction

When to Go: Before 11 a.m.

Special Comments: May frighten young children

Author's Rating: Not to be missed; ★★★★

Appeal by Age Group:

Pre-school	Grade School	Teens	Young Adults	Over 30	Senior Citizens
★★★	★★★★	★★★★	★★★★	★★★★	★★★★

Duration of Presentation: 20 minutes

Loading Speed: Moderate

Description and Comments   Guests view a film on how miniatures are used to create special effects in earthquake movies, followed by a demonstration starring audience volunteers. They then board a subway and experience an earthquake. Special effects range from fires and runaway trains to exploding tanker trucks and tidal waves. One of Universal's more compelling rides.

Touring Tips   Experience Earthquake in the morning after Men in Black, Back to the Future, E.T., Jaws, and Kongfrontation.

Jaws

What It Is: Adventure boat ride

Scope & Scale: Headliner

When to Go: Before 11 a.m.

Special Comments: Will frighten young children

Author's Rating: Not to be missed; ★★★★

Appeal by Age Group:

Pre-school	Grade School	Teens	Young Adults	Over 30	Senior Citizens
★★½	★★★★	★★★★	★★★★	★★★★	★★★★

Duration of Ride: 5 minutes

Loading Speed: Fast

Description and Comments   Unlike its predecessor, this version of the ride is mechanically reliable (usually). It delivers five minutes of nonstop action, with the huge shark attacking repeatedly. The story line is predictable, but the shark is quite realistic. Jaws builds an amazing degree of suspense and anticipation using inventive sets and powerful special effects. It's first-rate.

A variable is the enthusiasm and acting ability of your boat guide. The guide sets the tone, reveals the plot, pilots the boat, and fights the shark—every eight minutes. Most guides are quite good.

Touring Tips   Jaws handles crowds well; waits aren't long if all boats are operating. People on the boat's left side get splashed more. Skip Jaws if your children frighten easily, or you can switch off (page 54).

Men in Black Alien Attack

What It Is: Interactive dark thrill ride

Scope & Scale: Super headliner

When to Go: First thing in the morning

Special Comments: May induce motion sickness. 42" height minimum. Switching off available (page 54).

Author's Rating: Buzz Lightyear on steroids; not to be missed; ★★★★½

Appeal by Age Group:

Pre-school	Grade School	Teens	Young Adults	Over 30	Senior Citizens
†	★★★★½	★★★★★	★★★★★	★★★★★	★★★★

† Sample size too small for an accurate rating.

Duration of Ride: 4 minutes

Loading Speed: Moderate to Fast

Description and Comments   Based on the movie of the same name, Men in Black has you volunteering as a Men in Black (MIB) trainee. After the introductory warning that aliens "live among us," you are familiarized with your training vehicle and your alien "zapper." Then you are dispatched on an innocuous training mission in which only you are in a position to prevent aliens from taking over the universe. It's both a wild ride and one where movies, sets, Audio-Animatronics, and your vehicle are all integrated into a fairly seamless package. Your marksmanship and ability to blast yourself out of some tricky situations will determine how the story ends.

Touring Tips   Each of the 120 or so alien audio-animatronic figures has sensors that activate audio-animatronic effects and respond to your zapper—many of the aliens shoot back, causing your vehicle to veer or spin. Notice that there is a vehicle of guests next to you on a dual track traveling simultaneously in order to instill a spirit of competition. Although there are many possible endings, long lines at this headliner attraction will probably dissuade you from experiencing all but one or two. Hotfoot it to MIB as soon as the park opens.

Back to the Future—The Ride

What It Is: Flight-simulator thrill ride

Scope & Scale: Super headliner

When to Go: First thing in the morning after Men in Black

Special Comments: Very rough ride; may induce motion sickness. Must be 40" tall to ride; switching off available (page 54)

Author's Rating: Not to be missed, if you have a strong stomach; ★★★★★

Appeal by Age Group:

Pre-school	Grade School	Teens	Young Adults	Over 30	Senior Citizens
†	★★★★★	★★★★★	★★★★★	★★★★	★★½

† Sample size too small for accurate rating

Duration of Ride: 4½ minutes

Loading Speed: Moderate

Description and Comments   This is Universal's most popular thrill ride. Guests in Doc Brown's lab join a high-speed chase spanning a million years. Extremely intense, Back to the Future is similar to Star Tours and Body Wars at Disney World, but much rougher. The story line makes little sense, but the visual effects are wild and powerful. Vehicles (DeLorean time machines) are much smaller than those of Star Tours and Body Wars, so the ride feels more personal.

Because the height requirement has been lowered from 46 inches to 40 inches, younger children are riding. One reader suggests preparing them by reassuring them that (1) it's only a movie and (2) the car doesn't go anywhere, it just shakes.

Touring Tips   When the park opens, there's a stampede to Men in Black and Back to the Future. Be in it. If you don't ride before 10 a.m., you'll encounter long lines. Sitting in the car's rear seat makes the ride more realistic.

E.T. Adventure

What It Is: Indoor adventure ride based on the movie *E.T.*

Scope & Scale: Major attraction

When to Go: Before 10 a.m.

Author's Rating: ★★★★
Appeal by Age Group:

Pre-school	Grade School	Teens	Young Adults	Over 30	Senior Citizens
★★★★	★★★★	★★★½	★★★½	★★★½	★★★½

Duration of Ride: 4½ minutes
Loading Speed: Moderate

Description and Comments Guests board a bicycle-like conveyance to escape with E.T. from earthly law-enforcement officers and then journey to E.T.'s planet. Wilder and more elaborate than Disney's Peter Pan's Flight. Guests who balk at sitting on the bicycle can ride in a gondola.

Touring Tips Most preschoolers and grade-school children love E.T. We thought it worth a 20- to 30-minute wait, but nothing longer. Lines build quickly, and waits on busy days can be two hours. The wait to enter the building may be short, but the wait inside is much longer. Ride in the morning, right after Men in Black and Back to the Future.

Woody Woodpecker's KidZone

What It Is: Interactive playground and kid's roller coaster
Scope & Scale: Minor attraction
When to Go: Anytime
Author's Rating: Good place to let off steam; ★★★

Appeal by Age Group:

Pre-school	Grade School	Teens	Young Adults	Over 30	Senior Citizens
★★★★	★★★	—	—	—	—

Description and Comments KidZone consists of Woody Woodpecker's Nuthouse Coaster and an interactive playground called Curious George Goes to Town. The child-sized roller coaster is small enough for kids to enjoy but sturdy enough for adults; its moderate speed might unnerve some smaller children. The Curious George playground exemplifies Universal's obsession with wet stuff. Kids who want to stay dry can mess around in the foam-ball playground, also equipped with chutes, tubes, and ball-blasters.

Touring Tips   Universal employees have already dubbed this new children's area "Peckerland." Visit the playground after you've experienced all the major attractions.

Animal Actors Stage

What It Is: Trained-animals stadium performance
Scope & Scale: Major attraction
When to Go: After you've experienced all rides
Author's Rating: Warm and delightful; ★★★½
Appeal by Age Group:

Pre-school	Grade School	Teens	Young Adults	Over 30	Senior Citizens
★★★★½	★★★★	★★★½	★★★½	★★★½	★★★½

Duration of Presentation: 20 minutes
Probable Waiting Time: 25 minutes

Description and Comments   Humorous demonstration of how animals are trained for film work. Well-paced and informative, the show stars cats, dogs, monkeys, birds, and others. Animals sometimes don't behave as expected, but that's half the fun.

Touring Tips   We wish guests were allowed to enter the theater at their leisure. Instead, they must wait in line to be admitted. The show is presented six to ten times daily; check the daily entertainment guide for times. Go at your convenience; line up about 15 minutes before show time.

The Wild, Wild, Wild West Stunt Show

What It Is: Stunt show with western theme
Scope & Scale: Major attraction
When to Go: After you've experienced all rides, go at your convenience
Author's Rating: Solid and exciting; ★★★★
Appeal by Age Group:

Pre-school	Grade School	Teens	Young Adults	Over 30	Senior Citizens
★★★★½	★★★★	★★★★	★★★★	★★★★	★★★★

Duration of Presentation: 16 minutes

Probable Waiting Time: None

Description and Comments A Wild West stunt show with shoot-outs, fistfights, horse tricks, and high falls. Staged about ten times daily in a 2,000-seat covered stadium. Quick-paced, exciting, and well-executed. Unlike the stunt show on the lagoon, the action is easy to follow.

Touring Tips The daily entertainment guide lists show times. In summer, the stadium is more comfortable after dusk.

Fievel's Playland

What It Is: Children's play area with water slide

Scope & Scale: Minor attraction

When to Go: Anytime

Author's Rating: A much-needed attraction for preschoolers; ★★★★

Appeal by Age Group:

Pre-school	Grade School	Teens	Young Adults	Over 30	Senior Citizens
★★★★	★★★★	★★★	★★★	★★★	★★★

Probable Waiting Time: 20–30 minutes for the water slide; otherwise, no waiting

Description and Comments Imaginative playground where ordinary household items are reproduced on a giant scale, as a mouse would experience them. Kids climb nets and a cow skull, walk through a big boot, splash in a sardine-can fountain, and seesaw on huge spoons. Though most of Fievel's Playland is reserved for preschoolers, a water slide/raft ride is open to everyone.

Touring Tips Younger children love the oversized items, and there's enough to keep teens and adults busy while little ones frolic. Stay as long as you want.

Beetlejuice's Rock 'N Roll Graveyard Revue

What It Is: Rock-and-roll stage show

Scope & Scale: Minor attraction

When to Go: At your convenience

Author's Rating: Outrageous; ★★★½

Appeal by Age Group:

Pre-school	Grade School	Teens	Young Adults	Over 30	Senior Citizens
★★★★	★★★★	★★★★	★★★½	★★★½	★★★½

Duration of Presentation: 18 minutes
Probable Waiting Time: None

Description and Comments The *Graveyard Revue* is a high-powered rock-and-roll stage show starring Beetlejuice, Frankenstein, the Bride of Frankenstein, Wolfman, Dracula, and the Phantom of the Opera. In addition to fine vintage rock, the show features exuberant choreography. Sets and special effects are impressive.

Touring Tips Mercifully, this attraction has been moved under cover.

A Day in the Park with Barney

What It Is: Live character stage show
Scope & Scale: Major children's attraction
When to Go: Anytime
Author's Rating: A hit with preschoolers; ★★★★
Appeal by Age Group:

Pre-school	Grade School	Teens	Young Adults	Over 30	Senior Citizens
★★★★½	★★★	★★	★★½	★★★	★★★

Duration of Presentation: 12 minutes plus character greeting
Probable Waiting Time: 15 minutes

Description and Comments Barney, the purple dinosaur of public-television fame, and his sidekicks Baby Bop and BJ lead a sing-along augmented by effects that include wind, falling leaves, snow, and clouds and stars in a simulated sky. Afterward, Barney greets children, hugging each and posing for photos.

Touring Tips If your kids like Barney, this show is a must. It's happy and upbeat, and the character greeting afterward is the best-organized we've seen: no lines and no fighting for attention. Relax by the rail and await your hug.

Lucy, a Tribute

What It Is: Walk-through tribute to Lucille Ball
Scope & Scale: Diversion

When to Go: Anytime
Author's Rating: A touching remembrance; ★★★
Appeal by Age Group:

Pre-school	Grade School	Teens	Young Adults	Over 30	Senior Citizens
★	★	★★	★★★	★★★	★★★

Probable Waiting Time: None

Description and Comments   Exhibit traces the life and career of comedienne Lucille Ball of TV's *I Love Lucy*. Well-designed and informative, the attraction succeeds admirably in honoring the beloved redhead.

Touring Tips   Go during midafternoon heat or on your way out of the park. Adults could spend 15–30 minutes here; children get restless sooner.

Universal Studios Florida One-Day Touring Plan

This plan is for all visitors. Skip rides or shows that don't interest you and go to the plan's next step. Move briskly among attractions and stop for lunch after Step 10.

Buying Admission to Universal Studios Florida

Universal Studios never opens enough ticket windows in the morning to accommodate the crowd. Buy your admission before you arrive. Passes are sold by mail directly through Universal (phone (800) 224-3838) and at hotels' concierge desk or box office. Guest Services at the Radisson Twin Towers (phone (407) 351-1000), at the intersection of Major Boulevard and Kirkman Avenue, also sells them.

Many hotels sell admission vouchers that are redeemed at the park. Fortunately, the voucher window is separate from ticket sales and redemption is quick.

Touring Plan

1. Call (407) 363-8000 the day before your visit for the official opening time.

2. Eat breakfast before you go. Arrive 50 minutes before opening with your admission pass or voucher in hand. Redeem your voucher.

3. Obtain a map and daily entertainment schedule at the front gate. Ask an attendant what rides or shows are closed that day. Adjust the touring plan accordingly.

4. When you're admitted, go right on Hollywood Boulevard, pass Mel's Diner (on your left), and keep the lagoon on your left. Arrive at Men in Black. Ride.

5. After Men in Black, backtrack to Back to the Future and ride.

6. Exit left and pass the International Food Bazaar. Bear left past the *Animal Actors Stage* to E.T. Adventure. Ride.

7. Retrace your steps toward Back to the Future. Keeping the lagoon on your left, cross the bridge to Amity. Ride Jaws.

8. Exit left down the Embarcadero to Kongfrontation in the New York set. Go ape.

9. Ride Earthquake in San Francisco.

10. Head toward the main entrance and ride The Funtastic World of Hanna-Barbera. Expect to wait 25–40 minutes. If you've had enough simulator rides for the moment, skip to Step 11.

11. Return to New York for *Twister.*

12. This is a good time for lunch. King Jester's in Hollywood serves Creole cuisine, and Mel's Diner nearby has good milkshakes. The International Food Bazaar adjacent to Back to the Future has gyros, bratwurst, pizza, and other ethnic foods. Louie's Italian Restaurant in New York serves pizza, calzones, and salads. Sandwiches and pastries are specialties of the Beverly Hills Boulangerie near the park entrance. Upscale and relaxed Lombard's Landing on the waterfront, across from Earthquake, offers prime rib, creative seafood entrees, and an exceptional hamburger at a fair price.

13. You have six major attractions left to see:

   - *Terminator 2: 3-D*
   - *The Gory Gruesome & Grotesque Horror Make-Up Show*
   - *Animal Actors Stage*
   - *Wild, Wild, Wild West Stunt Show*

- "Alfred Hitchcock: The Art of Making Movies"
- *Beetlejuice's Rock 'N Roll Graveyard Revue*
  Animal Actors Stage, the *Beetlejuice* show, and the stunt show are performed several times daily. Check the entertainment schedule, and plan the remainder of your itinerary according to their show times. The *Horror Make-Up Show* runs continuously. Try to see *Terminator 2: 3-D* after 3:30 p.m.; whatever you do, don't miss it. Save "Alfred Hitchcock" for last.

14. We haven't included the Nickelodeon Studios Tour, Woody Woodpecker's Kidzone, or *A Day in the Park with Barney.* If you have school-age children, consider experiencing Nickelodeon in late afternoon or on a second day at the park. If you're touring with preschoolers, see *Barney* after you ride E.T., and then head for the Kidzone.

15. This concludes the touring plan. Spend the remainder of your day revisiting favorite attractions or inspecting sets and street scenes you may have missed. Also, check the schedule for live performances.

Universal's Islands of Adventure

When Islands of Adventure opened in 1999, it provided Universal with enough critical mass to actually compete with Disney. For the first time, Universal has on-site hotels, a shopping and entertainment complex, and two major theme parks. Plus, the new Universal park is a direct competitor with Disney's Magic Kingdom.

How direct a competitor is it? Check this out:

Islands of Adventure	Magic Kingdom
Six Islands (includes Port of Entry)	Seven Lands (includes Main Street)
Two adult roller coaster attractions	Two adult roller coaster attractions
A Dumbo-type ride	Dumbo
One flume ride	One flume ride
Toon Lagoon character area	Mickey's Toontown Fair character area

The clash of the titans is once again hot. Universal is coming on strong with the potential of sucking up three days of a tourist's week (more if you include Universal's strategic relationship with Sea World and Busch Gardens). That's more time than anyone has spent off the Disney campus in a long time.

Publicly, Disney and Universal have downplayed their fierce competition, pointing out that any new theme park makes central Florida more marketable. Behind closed doors, however, it's a Pepsi/Coke–type rivalry that will undoubtedly keep both companies working hard to gain an edge. The good news is this competition translates into better and better attractions for you to enjoy.

BEWARE OF THE WET AND WILD

Although we have described Universal's Islands of Adventure as a direct competitor to the Magic Kingdom, there is one major qualification you should know. Where most Magic Kingdom attractions are designed to be enjoyed by guests of any age, attractions at Islands of Adventure are largely created for an under-40 population. The roller coasters at Universal are serious with a capital "S," making Space Mountain and Big Thunder Mountain look about as tough as Dumbo. In fact, seven out of nine top attractions at Islands are thrill rides, and of these, there are three that not only scare the bejeebers out of you but also drench you with water.

In addition to thrill seekers, families with young children will also find a lot to do at Islands of Adventure. There are three interactive playgrounds for little ones, as well as six rides that young children will enjoy. Of the thrill rides, only the two in Toon Lagoon (described later) are marginally appropriate for young children, and even on these rides your child needs to be fairly stalwart.

Not to Be Missed at Universal's Islands of Adventure

The Incredible Hulk Coaster

The Adventures of Spider-Man

Jurassic Park River Adventure

Dueling Dragons

Poseidon's Fury!

GETTING ORIENTED

Both Universal theme parks are accessed via Universal CityWalk entertainment complex. Crossing CityWalk from the parking garages, bear right to Universal Studios Florida or left to Universal's Islands of Adventure.

Islands of Adventure is arranged much like the World Showcase section of Epcot, that is, in a large circle surrounding a lake. Unlike Epcot, however, the Islands of Adventure theme areas evidence the sort of thematic continuity pioneered by Disneyland and the Magic Kingdom. Each island is self-contained and visually consistent in its theme, though you can see parts of the other islands across the lake.

Passing through the turnstiles, you first encounter the Moroccan-style Port of Entry, where you will find Guest Services, lockers, stroller and wheelchair rentals, ATM banking, lost and found, and, of course, shopping. From the Port of Entry, moving clockwise around the lake, you can access Marvel Super Hero Island, Toon Lagoon, Jurassic Park, Lost Continent, and Seuss Landing. You can crisscross the lake on small boats, but otherwise there is no in-park transportation.

MARVEL SUPER HERO ISLAND

This island, with its futuristic and retro-future design and comic book signage, offers shopping and attractions based on Marvel Comics characters.

The Adventures of Spider-Man

What It Is: Indoor adventure simulator ride based on Spider-Man

Scope & Scale: Super headliner

When to Go: Before 10 a.m.

Special Comments: Must be 40" tall to ride

Author's Rating: Our choice for the best attraction in the park;
    ★★★★★

Appeal by Age Group:

Pre-School	Grade School	Teens	Young Adults	Over 30	Senior Citizens
★★★	★★★★★	★★★★★	★★★★★	★★★★★	★★★★

Duration of Ride: 4½ minutes

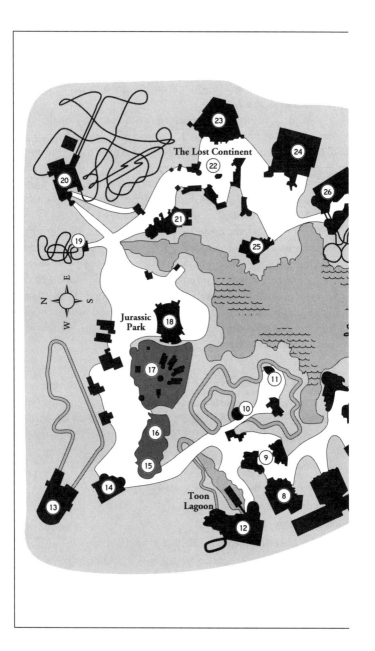

The Lost Continent

Jurassic Park

Toon
Lagoon

N
W E
S

Islands of Adventure

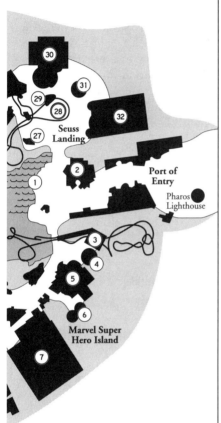

Port of Entry
1. Island Skipper Tours
2. Confisco's Grill

Marvel Super Hero Island
3. Incredible Hulk Coaster
4. Storm Force
5. Cafe 4
6. Dr. Doom's Fearfall
7. The Adventures of Spider-Man

Toon Lagoon
8. Comic Strip Café
9. Comic Strip Lane
10. Popeye & Bluto's Bilge-Rat Barges
11. Me Ship, *The Olive*
12. Dudley Do-Right's Ripsaw Falls

Jurassic Park
13. Jurassic Park River Adventure
14. Thunder Falls Terrace
15. Camp Jurassic
16. Pteranodon Flyers
17. Triceratops Encounter
18. Jurassic Park Discovery Center

The Lost Continent
19. The Flying Unicorn
20. Dueling Dragons
21. The Enchanted Oak Tavern (and Alchemy Bar)
22. Sinbad's Village
23. *The Eighth Voyage of Sinbad*
24. *Poseidon's Fury! Escape from the Lost City*
25. Mythos Restaurant

Seuss Landing
26. Sylvester McMonkey McBean
27. If I Ran the Zoo
28. Caro-Seuss-El
29. The Once-ler's House
30. Circus McGurkus Cafe Stoo-pendous
31. One Fish Two Fish Red Fish Blue Fish
32. The Cat in the Hat

Loading Speed: Fast

Description and Comments   Covering one and a half acres and combining moving vehicles, 3-D film, and live action, Spider-Man is frenetic, fluid, and astounding. The visuals are rich and the ride is wild, but not jerky.

The story line is that you are touring the offices of the *Daily Bugle* newspaper (where Peter Parker, a.k.a. Spider-Man, works as a mild-mannered reporter), when it's discovered that evil villains have stolen (I promise I'm not making this up) the Statue of Liberty. You are drafted on the spot to join a posse to save Ms. Liberty. After being thrust into "a battle between good and evil," you experience a "sensory drop" of 400 feet into darkness. You'll want to ride again and again.

Touring Tips   Ride first thing in the morning after The Incredible Hulk Coaster or in the hour before closing.

The Incredible Hulk Coaster

What It Is: Roller coaster
Scope & Scale: Super headliner
When to Go: Before 9:30 a.m.
Special Comments: Must be 54" tall to ride
Author's Rating: A coaster lover's coaster; ★★★★½
Appeal by Age Group:

Pre-School	Grade School	Teens	Young Adults	Over 30	Senior Citizens
½	★★★★★	★★★★★	★★★★★	★★★★	★★½

Duration of Ride: 1½ minutes
Loading Speed: Moderate

Description and Comments   You will be launched like a cannonball shot from 0 to 40 mph in 2 seconds, then flung upside down 100 feet off the ground. From there it's a mere seven rollovers punctuated by two plunges into holes in the ground before you're allowed to get out and throw up. Seriously, the Hulk is a great roller coaster, perhaps the best in Florida. Plus the ride is smooth.

Touring Tips   The Hulk gives Spider-Man a run as the park's most popular attraction. Ride first thing in the morning. Universal provides electronic lockers near the entrance of Hulk for any items you might lose during the coaster's seven inversions. *Note:* there is a separate line for those who want to ride in the front row.

Dr. Doom's Fearfall

What It Is: Lunch liberator
Scope & Scale: Headliner
When to Go: Before 9:15 a.m.
Special Comments: Must be 52" tall to ride
Author's Rating: More bark than bite; ★★★
Appeal by Age Group:

Pre-School	Grade School	Teens	Young Adults	Over 30	Senior Citizens
—	★★★	★★★★	★★★½	★★★	—

Duration of Ride: 40 seconds
Loading Speed: Slow

Description and Comments   Here you are (again) strapped into a seat with your feet dangling and blasted 200 feet in the air and then allowed to partially free-fall down. The good news is this ride looks much worse than it actually is. The scariest part by far is the apprehension that builds as you sit, strapped in, waiting for the thing to launch.

Touring Tips   We've seen glaciers that move faster than the line to Dr. Doom. If you want to ride without investing half a day, be one of the first in the park to ride.

Storm Force Accelatron

What It Is: Indoor spinning ride
Scope & Scale: Minor attraction
Special Comments: May induce motion sickness
When to Go: Before 10:30 a.m.
Author's Rating: Teacups in the dark; ★★★
Appeal by Age Group:

Pre-School	Grade School	Teens	Young Adults	Over 30	Senior Citizens
★★★½	★★★	★★★	★★★	★★★	★★★

Duration of Ride: 1½ minutes
Loading Speed: Slow

Description and Comments   Storm Force is a spiffed-up indoor version of Disney's nausea-inducing Mad Tea Party. Here you spin to the accompaniment of a simulated thunderstorm and swirling sound and light. There's a story line that loosely ties this midway-type ride to the Marvel Super Hero theme area, but it's largely irrelevant and offers no advice on keeping your lunch down.

Touring Tips   Ride early or late to avoid long lines. If you're prone to motion sickness, keep your distance.

TOON LAGOON

Toon Lagoon is cartoon art translated into real buildings and settings. Whimsical and gaily colored, with rounded and exaggerated lines, Toon Lagoon is Universal's answer to Mickey's Toontown Fair. The main difference between the two toon lands is that you have about a 60% chance of going into a state of hypothermia at Universal's version.

Dudley Do-Right's Ripsaw Falls

What It Is: Flume ride
Scope & Scale: Headliner
When to Go: Before 11 a.m.
Special Comments: Must be 48" tall to ride
Author's Rating: A minimalist Splash Mountain; ★★★½
Appeal by Age Group:

Pre-school	Grade School	Teens	Young Adults	Over 30	Senior Citizens
★★½	★★★★	★★★½	★★★	★★★½	★★½

Duration of Ride: 5 minutes
Loading Speed: Moderate

Description and Comments   Inspired by the *Rocky and Bullwinkle* cartoon series, this ride features Canadian Mountie Dudley Do-Right as he attempts to save Nell from evil Snidely Whiplash. Story line aside, it's a flume ride, with the inevitable big drop at the end. Universal claims this is the first flume ride to "send riders plummeting 15 feet below the surface of the water." We're not exactly sure how this works, but it sounds like you better bring your diving gear.

Touring Tips   This ride will get you wet, but on average not as wet as you might expect (it looks worse than it is). If you want to stay dry, arrive prepared with a poncho or at least a big garbage bag with holes for your head and arms. After riding, take a moment to gauge the timing of the water cannons that go off along the exit walk. This is where you can really get drenched. Younger children are often intimidated by the big drop. Ride first thing in the morning after experiencing the Marvel Super Hero rides.

Popeye & Bluto's Bilge-Rat Barges

What It Is: Whitewater raft ride
Scope & Scale: Headliner
When to Go: Before 10:30 a.m.
Special Comments: Must be 48" tall to ride
Author's Rating: Bring your own soap; ★★★★
Appeal by Age Group:

Pre-school	Grade School	Teens	Young Adults	Over 30	Senior Citizens
★★★	★★★★½	★★★★	★★★★	★★★½	★★½

Duration of Ride: 4 ½ minutes
Loading Speed: Moderate

Description and Comments   This sweetly named attraction is a whitewater raft ride that includes an encounter with an 18-foot-tall octopus. Engineered to ensure everyone gets drenched, the ride even provides water cannons for highly intelligent nonparticipants ashore to fire at those aboard. The rapids are rougher and more interesting and the ride longer than the Animal Kingdom's Kali River Rapids.

Touring Tips   You'll get a lot wetter from the knees down on this ride, so use your poncho or garbage bag and ride barefoot with your britches rolled up. Ride the barges in the morning after experiencing the Marvel Super Hero attractions and Dudley Do-Right. If you don't have raingear or forgot your trash bag, you might want to put off riding until last thing before leaving. Most preschoolers enjoy the raft ride; those who are frightened react more to the way the rapids look as opposed to the roughness of the ride.

Me Ship, The Olive

What It Is: Interactive playground

Scope & Scale: Minor attraction

When to Go: Anytime

Author's Rating: Colorful and appealing for kids; ★★★

Appeal by Age Group:

Pre-school	Grade School	Teens	Young Adults	Over 30	Senior Citizens
★★★★	★★★½	½	½	½	—

Description and Comments   The Olive is Popeye's three-story boat as an interactive playground. Younger children can scramble around in Swee' Pea's Playpen, while older sibs shoot water cannons at riders trying to survive the adjacent Bilge-Rat raft ride.

Touring Tips   If you are into the big rides, save the playground for later in the day.

Comic Strip Lane

What It Is: Walk-through exhibit and shopping/dining venue

Scope & Scale: Diversion

When to Go: Anytime

Description and Comments   This is the main street of Toon Lagoon. Here you can visit the domains of Beetle Bailey, Hagar the Horrible, Krazy Kat, the Family Circus, and Blondie and Dagwood, among others. Shops and eateries tie into the cartoon strip theme.

Touring Tips   A great place for photo ops with cartoon characters in their own environment.

JURASSIC PARK

Jurassic Park (for anyone who's been asleep for 20 years) is a Steven Spielberg film about a fictitious theme park with real dinosaurs. Jurassic Park at Universal's Islands of Adventure is a real theme park (or at least a section of one) with fictitious dinosaurs.

Jurassic Park River Adventure

What It Is: Indoor/outdoor adventure ride based on *Jurassic Park*

Scope & Scale: Super headliner

When to Go: Before 11 a.m.

Special Comments: Must be 42" tall to ride

Author's Rating: Better than its Hollywood cousin; ★★★★

Appeal by Age Group:

Pre-school	Grade School	Teens	Young Adults	Over 30	Senior Citizens
★★★	★★★★½	★★★★	★★★★	★★★★	★★★½

Duration of Ride: 6 ½ minutes

Loading Speed: Fast

Description and Comments   Guests board boats for a water tour of Jurassic Park. Everything is tranquil as the tour begins, but as word is received that some of the carnivores have escaped their enclosure, the tour boat is accidentally diverted into Jurassic Park's maintenance facilities. Here, the boat and its riders are menaced by an assortment of hungry meat eaters led by the ubiquitous T-Rex. At the climax, the boat and its passengers escape by plummeting over an 85-foot drop billed as the "longest, fastest, steepest water descent ever built."

Touring Tips   Though the boats make a huge splash at the bottom of the 85-foot drop, you don't get that wet. Before the boat leaves the dock, however, you must sit in the puddles left by previous riders. Once underway there's a little splashing, but nothing major until the big drop at the end of the ride. Young children must endure a double whammy on this ride. First, they are stalked by giant, salivating reptiles, then they're sent catapulting over the falls. Unless your children are stalwart, wait a year or two before you spring Jurassic Park on them.

Triceratops Encounter

What It Is: Prehistoric petting zoo

Scope & Scale: Minor attraction

When to Go: Before 11:30 a.m.

Author's Rating: Well executed; ★★★

Appeal by Age Group:

Pre-School	Grade School	Teens	Young Adults	Over 30	Senior Citizens
★★★★	★★★★	★★★½	★★★½	★★★½	★★★½

Duration of Show: 5 minutes

Probable Waiting Time: 15–25 minutes

Description and Comments   Guests are ushered in groups into a "feed and control station," where they can view and pet a 24-foot-long, animatronic triceratops dinosaur. While the trainer lectures about the creature's behaviors, habits, and lifestyle, the triceratops breathes, blinks, chews, and flinches at the touch of the guests.

Touring Tips   Nothing is for sure, but this may be the only attraction in the park where you won't get wet. Though not a major attraction, Triceratops Encounter is popular and delevops long lines. Make it your first show/exhibit after experiencing the rides.

Discovery Center

What It Is: Interactive natural history exhibit

Scope & Scale: Minor attraction

When to Go: Anytime

Author's Rating: ★★★

Appeal by Age Group:

Pre-school	Grade School	Teens	Young Adults	Over 30	Senior Citizens
★★½	★★★½	★★★	★★★	★★★	★★★

Description and Comments   The Discovery Center is an interactive, educational exhibit that mixes fiction from the movie, such as using fossil DNA to bring dinosaurs to life, with various skeletal remains and other paleontological displays. One exhibit allows guests to watch an animatronic raptor being hatched. Another allows you to electronically "fuse" your DNA with a dinosaur to see what the resultant creature would look like.

Touring Tips   Cycle back after experiencing all the rides or on a second day. Most folks can digest this exhibit in 10–15 minutes.

Pteranodon Flyers

What It Is: Dinosaur version of Dumbo the Flying Elephant

Scope & Scale: Minor attraction

When to Go: When there's no line

Author's Rating: All sizzle, no steak; ½

Appeal by Age Group:

Pre-School	Grade School	Teens	Young Adults	Over 30	Senior Citizens
★★★	★★	★	★½	★	★½

Duration of Ride: 1¼ minutes

Loading Speed: Slower than anyone thought possible

Description and Comments This attraction is Islands of Adventure's biggest blunder. Engineered to accommodate only 170 persons per hour (about half the hourly capacity of Dumbo!), the ride swings you along a track that passes over a small part of Jurassic Park. We recommend you skip this one.

Touring Tips Photograph the pteranodon as it flies overhead. You're probably looking at something that will soon be extinct.

Camp Jurassic

What It Is: Interactive play area

Scope & Scale: Minor attraction

When to Go: Anytime

Author's Rating: Creative playground, confusing layout; ★★★

Appeal by Age Group:

Pre-school	Grade School	Teens	Young Adults	Over 30	Senior Citizens
★★★	★★★	—	—	—	—

Description and Comments A great place for children to let off steam. It's sort of a Jurassic version of Tom Sawyer Island. Kids can explore lava pits, caves, mines, and a rain forest.

Touring Tips Camp Jurassic will fire the imaginations of the under-13 set. If you don't impose a time limit on the exploration, you could be here awhile. The layout of the play area is confusing and intersects the queuing area for the Pteranodon Flyers.

LOST CONTINENT

This theme area is an exotic mix of Silk Road bazaar and ancient ruins, with Greco-Moroccan accents. And you thought your decorator was nuts. Anyway, this is the land of mythical gods, fabled beasts, and expensive souvenirs.

Poseidon's Fury! Escape from the Lost City

What It Is: High-tech theater attraction

Scope & Scale: Headliner

When to Go: After experiencing all the rides

Special Comments: Audience stands throughout

Author's Rating: Packs a punch; ★★★★

Appeal by Age Group:

Pre-School	Grade School	Teens	Young Adults	Over 30	Senior Citizens
★★	★★★★	★★★★	★★★★	★★★★	★★★★

Duration of Presentation: 17 minutes including preshow

Probable Wait: 25 minutes

Description and Comments   Poseidon, the Greek god of the sea, dukes it out with Zeus, the supreme deity of the ancient Greeks. All this happens with you in the middle, but with less subtlety than in the average dysfunctional family quarrel. The operative word in this brawl is special effects. Poseidon fights with water while Zeus uses fire. Though the production is a little slow and plodding at first, it wraps up with quite an impressive flourish. There's some great technology at work here. *Poseidon* is the best of the Islands of Adventure theater attractions.

Touring Tips   You will probably be pulling for Zeus in hopes you might finally dry out, but our money is on Poseidon. It's legal in Florida for theme parks to get you wet, but setting you on fire is somewhat frowned upon. The explosions and noise may frighten younger children, so exercise caution with preschoolers. Shows run continuously; we recommend catching *Poseidon* after experiencing the rides.

Dueling Dragons

What It Is: Roller coaster

Scope & Scale: Headliner

When to Go: Before 10:30 a.m.

Special Comments: Must be 54" tall to ride

Author's Rating: Almost as good as the Hulk Coaster; ★★★★

Appeal by Age Group:

Pre-School	Grade School	Teens	Young Adults	Over 30	Senior Citizens
—	★★★★	★★★★	★★★★	★★★★	★★

Duration of Ride: A minute and 45 seconds

Loading Speed: Moderate

Description and Comments This high-tech coaster launches two trains (Fire and Ice) at the same time on tracks that are closely intertwined. Each track, however, is configured differently so you get a different experience on each. Several times a collision with the other train seems imminent, a catastrophe that seems all the more real because the coasters are inverted. Because this is an inverted coaster, your view of the action is limited unless you are in the front row. Dueling Dragons is the highest coaster in the park and claims the longest drop at 115 feet, not to mention five inversions. And it's a nice smooth ride. We prefer the front row on either train, but the coaster loonies hype the front row of Fire and the last row of Ice.

Touring Tips The good news is that you won't get wet unless you wet yourself. The bad news is that wetting yourself comes pretty naturally. The other bad news is that the queuing area for Dueling Dragons is the longest, most convoluted affair we've ever seen, winding endlessly through a maze of subterannean passages. Once you reach the loading area, you must choose between riding Fire or Ice. Try to ride during the first 90 minutes the park is open. Warn anyone waiting for you that you might be a while. Finally, if you don't have time to ride both Fire and Ice, be advised that the *Unofficial* crew unanimously prefers Fire.

The Eighth Voyage of Sinbad

What It Is: Theater stunt show

Scope & Scale: Major attraction

When to Go: Anytime as per the daily entertainment schedule

Author's Rating: Not inspiring; ★★

Appeal by Age Group:

Pre-School	Grade School	Teens	Young Adults	Over 30	Senior Citizens
★★★	★★★½	★★½	★★★	★★★	★★½

Duration of Presentation: 17 minutes
Probable Waiting Time: 15 minutes

Description and Comments   A story about Sinbad the Sailor is the glue that (loosely) binds this stunt show featuring water explosions, ten-foot-tall circles of flame, and various other daunting eruptions. Even if you bear in mind that it's billed as a stunt show, the production is so vacuous and redundant it's hard to get into the action.

Touring Tips   See *Sinbad* after you've experienced the rides and the better-rated shows. The theater seats 1,700.

The Flying Unicorn

What It Is: Children's roller coaster
Scope & Scale: Minor attraction
When to Go: Before 11 a.m.
Special Comments: Must be 36" tall to ride
Author's Rating: A good beginner's coaster; ★★★
Appeal by Age Group:

Pre-School	Grade School	Teens	Young Adults	Over 30	Senior Citizens
★★★★	★★★½	★★	★★	★	★

Duration of Ride: 1 minute
Loading Speed: Slow

Description and Comments   A child-sized roller coaster through a forest setting, the Flying Unicorn provides a nonthreatening way to introduce young children to the genre.

Touring Tips   This one loads very slowly. Ride before 11 a.m.

SEUSS LANDING

A ten-acre theme area based on Dr. Seuss's famous children's books. Like at Mickey's Toontown in the Magic Kingdom, the style of the buildings and attractions mimic a whimsical, brightly colored cartoon with exaggerated features and rounded lines.

The Cat in the Hat

What It Is: Indoor adventure ride
Scope & Scale: Major attraction
When to Go: Before 11:30 a.m.

Author's Rating: Seuss would be proud; ★★★½
Appeal by Age Group:

Pre-School	Grade School	Teens	Young Adults	Over 30	Senior Citizens
★★★★	★★★★	★★★	★★★½	★★★½	★★★½

Duration of Ride: 3½ minutes
Loading Speed: Moderate

Description and Comments   Guests ride on "couches" through 18 different sets inhabited by animatronic Seuss characters, including The Cat in the Hat, Thing 1, Thing 2, and the beleaguered goldfish who tries to maintain order in the midst of mayhem. Well done overall, with nothing that should frighten younger children.

Touring Tips   This is fun for all ages. Try to ride early.

One Fish, Two Fish, Red Fish, Blue Fish

What It Is: Wet version of Dumbo the Flying Elephant
Scope & Scale: Minor attraction
When to Go: Before 10 a.m.
Author's Rating: Who says you can't teach an old ride new tricks?; ★★★½
Appeal by Age Group:

Pre-School	Grade School	Teens	Young Adults	Over 30	Senior Citizens
★★★★	★★★★	★★★	★★★	★★★	★★★

Duration of Ride: 2 minutes
Loading Speed: Slow

Description and Comments   Imagine Dumbo with Seuss-style fish instead of elephants and you've got half the story. The other half involves yet another opportunity to drown. Guests steer their fish up or down 15 feet in the air while traveling in circles. At the same time, they try to avoid streams of water projected from "squirt posts." A catchy song provides clues for avoiding the squirting. Though ostensibly a children's ride, the song and the challenge of steering your fish away from the water jets make this attraction fun for all ages.

Touring Tips   We don't know what it is about this theme park and water, but you'll get wetter than at a full-immersion baptism.

Caro-Seuss-El

What It Is: Merry-go-round
Scope & Scale: Minor attraction
When to Go: Before 10:30 a.m.
Author's Rating: Wonderfully unique; ★★★½
Appeal by Age Group:

Pre-school	Grade School	Teens	Young Adults	Over 30	Senior Citizens
★★★★	★★★★	—	—	—	—

Duration of Ride: 2 minutes
Loading Speed: Slow

Description and Comments Totally outrageous, the Caro-Seuss-El is a full-scale, 56-mount merry-go-round made up exclusively of Dr. Seuss characters.

Touring Tips Even if you are too old or don't want to ride, this attraction is worth an inspection. Whatever your age, chances are good you'll see some old friends. If you are touring with young children, try to get them on early in the morning.

Sylvester McMonkey McBean's Very Unusual Driving Machines

What It Is: Indoor/outdoor track ride
Scope & Scale: Major attraction
When to Go: Before 10:30 a.m.
Author's Rating: Not open at press time
Appeal by Age Group: Not open at press time
Duration of Ride: 5 minutes
Loading Speed: Slow

Description and Comments This ride offers a tour of Seuss Landing on an elevated track, passing in and out of various attractions, shops, and restaurants. The inspiration, a Seuss book about discrimination, is sort of lost in the translation. Also lost is whatever it takes to get the ride up and running. As the park entered its second year the attraction still was not operational.

Touring Tips Visually appealing. You can cover the same territory on foot.

If I Ran the Zoo

What It Is: Interactive playground

Scope & Scale: Minor attraction

When to Go: Anytime

Author's Rating: Eyecatching; ★★★

Appeal by Age Group:

Pre-School	Grade School	Teens	Young Adults	Over 30	Senior Citizens
★★★★	★★★	—	—	—	—

Description and Comments   Based on Dr. Seuss's *If I Ran the Zoo*, this playground is divided into three distinct areas, Hedges, Water, and the New Zoo. Each area features various interactive elements, including, of course, another opportunity for a good soaking.

Touring Tips   Visit this playground after you've experienced all the major attractions.

Universal's Islands of Adventure One-Day Touring Plan

There are an inordinate number of attractions in this park that will get you wet. If you want to experience them, come armed with ponchos, large plastic garbage bags, or some other protective covering. Failure to follow this prescription will make for a potentially squishy, sodden day.

This plan is for groups of all sizes and ages and includes thrill rides that may induce motion sickness or get you wet. If the plan calls for you to experience an attraction that does not interest you, simply skip that attraction and proceed to the next step. The plan calls for some backtracking. If you have young children in your party, customize the plan to fit their needs and take advantage of switching off at thrill rides (page 54).

1. Call (407) 363-8000 the day before your visit for the official opening time. Try to purchase your admission prior to the day you intend to tour.

2. On the day of your visit, eat breakfast and arrive at Universal Florida 50 minutes before opening time. Park, buy your admission (if you did not purchase it in advance),

and wait at the turnstiles to be admitted.

3. While at the turnstile, ask an attendant whether any rides or shows are closed that day. Adjust the touring plan accordingly.

4. When the park opens, go straight through the Port of Entry and take a left, crossing the bridge into Marvel Super Hero Island. At Super Hero Island, bear left to the Incredible Hulk Coaster.

5. Ride Incredible Hulk.

6. Exiting Hulk, hustle immediately to The Adventures of Spider-Man, also in Marvel Super Hero Island.

7. Dr. Doom's Fearfall, to the left of Spider-Man, is sort of a poor man's Tower of Terror. What's more, it loads about as fast as molasses on a shingle. We suggest you skip it. However, if you're bound and determined to ride, now's the time.

Note: Steps 8–10 involve attractions where you will get wet. If you're not up for a soaking this early in the morning, skip ahead to Step 11, but be advised that you may have a bit of a wait at the Toon Lagoon attractions later in the day.

8. Continuing clockwise around the lake, depart Super Hero Island and cross into Toon Lagoon.

9. In Toon Lagoon, ride Dudley Do-Right's Ripsaw Falls.

10. Also in Toon Lagoon, subject yourself to Popeye & Bluto's Bilge-Rat Barges.

11. After the barge ride, continue clockwise around the lake, passing through Jurassic Park without stopping. Continue to the Lost Continent.

12. At Lost Continent, ride both tracks of Dueling Dragons.

13. While at Lost Continent, experience *Poseidon's Fury! Escape from the Lost City*.

14. Depart Lost Continent, moving counterclockwise around the lake, and enter Jurassic Park.

15. In Jurassic Park, try the Jurassic Park River Adventure.

16. Also in Jurassic Park, check out the Triceratops Encounter.

17. Return to Lost Continent. Check the daily entertainment schedule for the next performance of *The Eighth Voyage of Sinbad* stunt show. If a show is scheduled to begin

within 30 minutes or so, go ahead and check it out. Otherwise, skip ahead to Step 18 and work *Sinbad* in later.

18. From Lost Continent, move clockwise around the lake to Seuss Landing. Ride The Cat in the Hat.

19. While in Seuss Landing, ride Sylvester McMonkey if it's operating.

20. At this point you will have done all the big stuff. Spend the rest of your day experiencing attractions you bypassed earlier or repeating ones you especially enjoyed.

Part Thirteen

The Water Theme Parks

Short-timers are unlikely to spend their hours at Walt Disney World's three swimming theme parks or the Orlando area's two independent water parks, but they should know what they are. Making up Disney's trio are River Country, the oldest and smallest; Typhoon Lagoon, the most diversified; and Blizzard Beach, which has the most slides and most unusual theme. Outside the World are Wet 'n Wild and Water Mania. (The full-sized *Unofficial Guide to Walt Disney World* has expanded descriptions. For Disney details, call (407) 824-4321.)

Each Disney water park rents water gear (even towels) and lockers and sells food, swimming gear, and footwear. Picnics are welcome (no alcoholic beverages or glass containers allowed). Admission to Blizzard Beach and Typhoon Lagoon is about $29 per day for adults, $23 for children ages three to nine, and free for kids younger than three. River Country charges $18 and $14.

Blizzard Beach and Typhoon Lagoon fill early, and gates close by 11 a.m. The parks are widely scattered: Blizzard Beach is near the All-Star Resorts; Typhoon Lagoon is east of Epcot; and River Country is near Fort Wilderness Campground. Disney transportation reaches all, but it's a time-gobbling commute for River Country. Each park has a parking lot.

Thunderstorms, common in the afternoon, may close the parks. Lines for water slides can seem endless; ride early or return to an uncrowded park when it reopens after a storm.

BLIZZARD BEACH

Blizzard Beach conjures a ski resort in Florida. Alas for the make-believe adventurer, the ice of savage storms is melting, the palms have grown back, and the Alpine lodge and ski lifts survive among dripping icicles. Ski slopes and bobsled runs have become water slides, and a great lagoon is fed by gushing mountain streams.

This wild story has spawned a wave pool, 17 slides (2 long), a children's swimming area, and a tranquil stream for tubing. Picnic areas and sunbathing beaches dot the park. Summit Plummet, the world's longest speed slide, begins with a steep 120-foot descent. Teamboat Springs is 1,200 feet long.

TYPHOON LAGOON

Typhoon Lagoon evokes the "aftermath of a typhoon." The landmark is a boat beached atop the 100-foot Mount Mayday. Caves, dinosaur "fossils," a ramshackle tropical town, geysers, and a misty rain forest add to the adventure. The park is about the size of Blizzard Beach and four times as big as River Country. It has ten water slides and streams, activity pools, and tube rapids. Two attractions—the surf pool and Shark Reef—are unique.

Shark Reef

At Shark Reef, snorkelers (equipped and instructed for free) swim with tropical fish, small stingrays, and a few harmless sharks. It's fun in early morning before lines become intolerable and attendants must enforce the 60-foot direct route across the crowded pool. There is also an underwater viewing chamber.

Surf Pool

The world's largest inland surf facility, this pool is swept by five-to six-foot waves about every 90 seconds. They're perfectly formed, ideal for riding and larger than most folks encounter in the ocean. Unlike ocean waves, they don't slam you down. Still, watch other riders' technique before you try it.

Club Typhoon

On Friday nights from mid-June to mid-August Typhoon Lagoon reopens from 7 p.m. until 11 p.m. as "Club Typhoon." Live music and organized activities augment the park's water attractions. Adult admission is about $15. Not only is the price right, but the park is less crowded than during the day.

RIVER COUNTRY

For pure and simple swimming and splashing, River Country gets high marks. Rocky canyons and waterfalls blend with white-sand beaches in this beautifully landscaped park. It has only two slides, and lines become long. Sunbathing and tubing are more relaxed.

Access to River Country by car is a hassle. You must bus from the parking lot, and the long ride can be crowded. *Solution:* Catch the bus to Pioneer Hall (loads in the River Country parking lot) and walk from the hall to River Country. It's also walking distance from much of Fort Wilderness Campground.

DISNEY VS. WET 'N WILD AND WATER MANIA THEME PARKS

Wet 'n Wild, on International Drive in Orlando, is open until 11 p.m. during summer. (Disney parks and Water Mania close between 5 and 8 p.m.) Live music is featured in the evenings.

Water Mania, on US 192 south of I-4, is the only water park that offers a stationary surfing wave. The facility is less crowded than its competitors.

Wet 'n Wild costs about the same as Typhoon Lagoon and Blizzard Beach. River Country and Water Mania are less expensive. Look for discount coupons in visitor magazines.

For slides, Wet 'n Wild is on par with Blizzard Beach and beats Typhoon Lagoon, River Country, and Water Mania. Headliners are the Black Hole, the Surge, and the Fuji Flyer. At the Black Hole, guests descend on a two-person tube down a totally enclosed corkscrew slide, a sort of wet version of Space Mountain—only much darker. The Surge launches groups of five down a twisting, 580-foot course. The Fuji Flyer is a 450-foot water-toboggan course.

The independents can't compete with Disney's attention to detail, variety, adventure, and impact. Water Mania is nicely landscaped but themeless. Wet 'n Wild, though clean, is cluttered and not very appealing to the eye.

Typhoon Lagoon's surf pool wins hands down, with Wet 'n Wild taking second. Each park has an area for young children, and all except River Country feature unique attractions.

WHEN TO GO

Weekends (except Sunday morning) are tough because they're popular with locals. Go Monday or Tuesday, when most other tourists will be in the Magic Kingdom, Epcot, the Animal Kingdom, or Disney-MGM Studios. Locals will be at work. Friday also is good because people traveling by car routinely start home then. Be at the gates a half hour before opening.

Part Fourteen

Beyond the Parks

DOWNTOWN DISNEY

Downtown Disney is a shopping, dining, and entertainment development strung out along the banks of the Buena Vista Lagoon. On the far right is the Downtown Disney Marketplace (formerly known as the Disney Village Marketplace). In the middle is the gated (admission required) Pleasure Island nighttime entertainment, and on the far left is Disney's West Side.

Marketplace   The Marketplace is primarily a shopping and dining venue. The centerpiece of shopping is the World of Disney, the largest Disney trademark merchandise store in the world. Another noteworthy retailer is the LEGO Imagination Center, showcasing a number of huge and unbelievable sculptures made entirely of LEGO "bricks." Rounding out the selection are stores specializing in resort wear, athletic attire and gear, Christmas decorations, Barbie dolls, Disney art and collectibles, and handmade craft items.

Rainforest Cafe is the headliner restaurant at the Marketplace. There is also Cap'n Jack's Oyster Bar, Wolfgang Puck pizza kitchen, a soda fountain, a deli and bakery, and a McDonald's. Full-service restaurants are listed by cuisine in Part 8: Dining in Walt Disney World.

Pleasure Island   Pleasure Island is a nighttime entertainment complex. Though admission is charged after 7 p.m., shops and restaurants are open with no admission required during the day. More information on the nightspots is provided in Part 15: Nightlife Inside Walt Disney World. There are four full-service restaurants at Pleasure Island. Fulton's Crab House and the Portobello Yacht Club can be accessed at any time without paying admission to Pleasure Island. The Wild Horse Saloon, a country music club and barbecue restaurant, and the Pleasure Island Jazz Club are within the gated part of Pleasure Island.

Disney's West Side   The West Side is the newest addition to Downtown Disney and offers a broad range of entertainment, dining, and shopping. Restaurants include House of Blues (Cajun), Planet Hollywood (American); Bongos Cuban Cafe, serving Cuban favorites; and Wolfgang Puck Cafe, featuring California cuisine.

West Side shopping is some of the most interesting in Walt Disney World. For starters, there's a Virgin (records and books) Megastore. Across the street is the Guitar Gallery by George's Music, specializing in custom, collector, rare, and unique guitars. Other specialty shops include a cigar shop, a rock 'n' roll and movie memorabilia store, and a western apparel boutique.

In the entertainment department, there is DisneyQuest, an interactive theme park contained in a building; the House of Blues, a concert and dining venue; and a 24-screen AMC movie theater. The West Side is also home to *Cirque du Soleil,* a not-to-be-missed production show with a cast of almost 100 performers and musicians.

THE DISNEY INSTITUTE

Launched in 1996, the Disney Institute offers team-building programs and courses on the Disney style of management to companies and business groups. Its campus is in the Villas section of Disney World and includes lodging, classrooms, and recreational facilities.

DISNEY'S WIDE WORLD OF SPORTS

Disney's Wide World of Sports is a 200-acre competition and training complex with a 7,500-seat ballpark; a field house; and venues for baseball, softball, tennis, track and field, beach volleyball, and 27 other sports. Amateur and professional competitions abound. Spectators must pay.

To check the schedule, call (407) 828-3267. Fast food is available. The complex is off Osceola Parkway between World Drive and where the parkway crosses I-4 (no interstate access). The complex has a parking lot and is accessible via the Disney Transportation System.

WALT DISNEY WORLD SPEEDWAY

Adjacent to the Transporation and Ticket Center parking lot, the one-mile tri-oval course hosts several races each year. Between competitions, the Richard Petty Driving Experience lets you ride in a two-seat stock car ($90) or learn to drive one. Lessons are by reservation. The cost ranges from $330 (8 laps) to $1,100 (30 laps). You must be age 18 or older, have a valid driver's license, and know how to drive a stick shift to take a course. For information, call (800) 237-3889.

DISCOVERY ISLAND

As anticipated, after the opening of the Animal Kingdom, Disney closed Discovery Island. At this time, it is used for private parties and special events.

WALT DISNEY WORLD RECREATION

Most Walt Disney World guests never make it beyond the theme parks, the water parks, and Downtown Disney. Those who do, however, discover an extraodinary selection of recreational opportunities ranging from guided fishing expeditions and water skiing outings to hay rides, horseback riding, fitness center workouts, and miniature golf. If it's something you can do at a resort, it's probably available at Walt Disney World.

Boating, biking, and fishing equipment rentals are handled on an hourly basis. Just show up at the rental office during operating hours and they'll fix you up. The same goes for various fitness centers in the resort hotels. Golf, tennis, fishing expeditions, waterski excursions, hayrides, trail rides, and most spa services must be scheduled in advance. Though every resort features an extensive selection of recreational options, those resorts located on a navigable body of water offer the greatest variety. Also, the more upscale a resort, the more likely it is to have such amenities as a fitness center and spa. In addition to the resorts, you can rent boats and other recreational equipment at the Marketplace in Downtown Disney.

WALT DISNEY WORLD GOLF

Disney World has six golf courses, all expertly designed and meticulously maintained. The Magnolia, the Palm, and the Oak Trail courses are across Floridian Way from the Polynesian Resort. They envelop the Shades of Green recreational complex, and the pro shops and support facilities adjoin it. Lake Buena Vista Golf Course is at the Disney Institute, near Walt Disney World Village and across the lake from Pleasure Island. The Osprey Ridge and

Eagle Pines courses are part of the Bonnet Creek Golf Club near Fort Wilderness Campground. Each location includes driving ranges and putting greens.

Oak Trail is a nine-hole course for beginners. The other five courses are designed for the mid-handicap player and are quite forgiving. All courses are popular, with morning tee times at a premium, especially January–April. To avoid the crowds, play on a Monday, Tuesday, or Wednesday and book a late-afternoon tee time.

Peak season for all courses is September–April; off-season is May–August. Off-season and afternoon twilight rates are available. Carts are required and are included in the greens fee. Tee times may be reserved 60 days in advance by Disney resort guests, 30 days in advance for day guests with a credit card, and 7 days in advance without a guarantee. Proper attire is required: a collared shirt and slacks or Bermuda shorts.

MINIATURE GOLF

Fantasia Gardens Miniature Golf is an 11-acre complex with two 18-hole dink-and-putt golf courses ($9 for adults and $8 for children). One course is an "adventure" course, themed after Disney's animated film *Fantasia.* The other course, geared to older children and adults, is an innovative approach-and-putt course with sand traps and water hazards.

Fantasia Gardens is beautifully landscaped and creatively executed. It's on Epcot Resort Boulevard, across from the Walt Disney World Swan. To reach Fantasia Gardens via Disney transportation, take a bus or boat to the Swan Resort. For more information, call (407) 560-8760.

In 1999, Disney opened Winter Summerland, a second miniature golf facility located next to the Blizzard Beach water park. Winter Summerland offers two 18-hole courses—one has a blizzard in Florida theme, while the other sports a tropical holiday theme. The Winter-Summerland courses are much easier than the Fantasia Courses, making them a better choice for families with preteens.

Part Fifteen

Nightlife inside Walt Disney World

Walt Disney World at Night

Anybody still standing after touring the theme parks all day will find a lot to do in the evening at Walt Disney World.

In the Parks

At Epcot, the major after-dark event is *IllumiNations,* a laser and fireworks show on World Showcase Lagoon. Show time is listed in the daily entertainment schedule.

In the Magic Kingdom there are evening parade(s) and *Fantasy in the Sky* fireworks. See the schedule for times.

When the park is open late, Disney-MGM Studios offers Sorcery in the Sky, a laser and fireworks spectacular, and *Fantasmic!,* a laser, special effects water spectacular. Check the schedule for show times.

At present, there is no nighttime entertainment at the Animal Kingdom.

At the Hotels

The Floating Electrical Pageant is a parade of barges on Seven Seas Lagoon. One of our favorite Disney productions, the short show of light and music starts at 9 p.m. nightly off the Polynesian Resort docks. It circles, then repeats at 9:15 p.m. at the Grand Floridian. Afterward, it goes to Fort Wilderness, Wilderness Lodge, and the Contemporary Resort.

At Fort Wilderness Campground

The free nightly campfire program is open only to Disney resort guests. It begins with a sing-along led by Disney characters, and progresses to viewing a Disney feature movie.

At Disney's BoardWalk

Jellyrolls at the BoardWalk features dueling pianos and sing-alongs in the tradition of New Orleans' Pat O'Brien's. The BoardWalk has Disney's first and only brew pub. A sports bar, an upscale dance club, and several restaurants complete the BoardWalk's entertainment mix. Access is by foot from Epcot, by launch from Disney-MGM Studios, and by bus from other Disney World locations.

At Downtown Disney

For nighttime entertainment options in Downtown Disney, see pages 287–288.

WALT DISNEY WORLD DINNER THEATERS

Several dinner-theater shows are staged each night at Disney World. Call (407) 824-8000 for same-day reservations. Disney resort guests can book at their hotel or up to 60 days in advance by calling (407) 939-3463. Getting seats at the *Polynesian Luau* isn't too tough—not so for the *Hoop-Dee-Doo Revue.*

Polynesian Luau

Presented nightly at the Polynesian Resort, the evening consists of a "Polynesian-style" all-you-can-eat meal followed by South Sea native dancing. The dancing is interesting and largely authentic, but we consider the evening average. The cost is about $46 for adults, $24 for children ages 3 to 11. Sea World presents a similar dinner show each evening.

At the Polynesian Resort's Luau Cove is *Mickey's Tropical Revue,* which features Disney characters. This show starts at 4:30 p.m.—too early to be hungry and too hot to be outdoors. The cost is about $40 for adults, $20 for children ages 3–11.

Hoop-Dee-Doo Revue

Presented nightly at Pioneer Hall at Fort Wilderness Campground, this is the most popular Disney dinner show. The meal includes barbecued ribs, fried chicken, corn on the cob, and baked beans. Most dishes are satisfactory.

Western dance-hall song, dance, and humor are presented by a talented, energetic, and memorable cast. The cost of the evening is $46 for adults, $24 for children ages 3–11. Show times are 5, 7:15, and 9:30 p.m.

Unfortunately for last-minute guests, *Hoop-Dee-Doo Revue* is sold out months in advance to lodgers at Disney properties who booked it when they reserved their rooms. Nonetheless, try (407) 824-2748 at 9 a.m. each morning while you're at Disney World for same-day reservations. Generally, 3 to 24 people are admitted.

Pleasure Island

Pleasure Island, Disney World's nighttime entertainment complex, offers eight nightclubs for one admission price (about $20). Located on a man-made island in Walt Disney World Village, it's accessible by shuttle bus from the theme parks and the Transportation and Ticket Center.

The six-acre playground also has restaurants and shops. A few of the restaurants and shops are open during the day, but the nightclubs don't start opening until 7 p.m. Some of the clubs may not open until 8 p.m. or later, and Pleasure Island doesn't fully come alive until after 9 p.m. or even 10 p.m. Guests younger than age 18 must be accompanied by a parent after 7 p.m.

Have It All   It's possible to visit all of the island's clubs in one night. Nightclub shows outside Disney World are an hour or more long; Pleasure Island's (except at the Comedy Warehouse) are shorter and more frequent. Guests can circulate without missing much. The music clubs (Rock 'n' Roll Beach Club, 8TRAX, Wildhorse Saloon, BET Soundstage Club, Mannequins Dance Palace, and Pleasure Island Jazz Company) go nonstop. The Adventurers Club and Comedy Warehouse offer scheduled shows.

In a Nutshell, Here's a One-Night Touring Plan   Arrive at 6 p.m. if you want to eat on the island, 8 p.m. if you don't. Catch the first or second performance at the tough-ticket Comedy Warehouse. See the library show at the Adventurers Club. Enjoy rap, soul, and R&B at BET Soundstage. Grab the '70s beat at 8TRAX. Backtrack to Mannequins Dance Palace for techno-pop. Step out at Pleasure Island Jazz Company, then move to Rock 'n' Roll Beach Club for oldies. Scoot a boot at Wildhorse Saloon (country music and line dancing). Stop by the jumping West End Stage.

Alcoholic Beverages   All Pleasure Island nightclubs serve alcohol. Guests not obviously older than age 21 must provide proof of age if they wish to buy alcoholic beverages. To avoid repeated checking, color-coded eligibility wristbands are issued.

Dress Code   Casual is in. Shirts and shoes are required.

Good News for the Early-to-Bed Crowd   All bands, dancers, comedians, and showmen come on like gangbusters from the very beginning of the evening.

Invited Guests Only   Occasionally before 9 p.m. selected clubs will be closed for private parties.

Parking Hassle   Pleasure Island has its own parking lot, which often fills up. Jot your location down to find your car quickly.

Advice   Park adjacent to the movie theaters and Disney's West Side and enter via the bridge connecting the movie complex to Pleasure Island. An admissions booth is on the bridge; you don't have to go to the main gate. The Disney bus system is also a good option.

Restaurants   Though noisy, crowded, and expensive, restaurants here serve a variety of well-prepared dishes. You must buy club admission to eat at the Jazz Company and Wildhorse Saloon, but no admission is required for West Side or Marketplace restaurants. Most are open during the day.

The new headliner is the Wildhorse Saloon, replacing the Fireworks Factory as the barbecue capital of Walt Disney World. The Jazz Company now serves Cajun and Creole food. Other restaurants include Fulton's Crab House, on the *Empress Lily* riverboat, specializing in shellfish and fresh Florida seafood, and the Portobello Yacht Club, serving seafood, pasta, and pizza. Food at Planet Hollywood, at the entrance to Disney's West Side, is pretty good, but waits are long unless you eat at odd hours. The decor of Hollywood memorabilia is the draw.

Sandwiches and snacks are served in the clubs.

Shopping   Pleasure Island has some shops that are attractions in themselves. At Cover Story, guests dress up to be photographed for the mock cover of a major magazine. Superstar Studio lets you star in your own music video. At either, it's almost as much fun just to watch.

There's no admission fee for daytime shoppers. At night, however, the island is gated.

A Word about Universal CityWalk

CityWalk is Universal's version of Pleasure Island. In addition to a number of themed restaurants, you'll find a jazz club, a reggae club, a Pat O'Briens dueling-pianos club, a Hard Rock Cafe and concert venue, a Motown Cafe with live R&B, Jimmy Buffett's Margaritaville, and a high-tech dance club called The Groove.

There's no admission charge to enjoy the shops, restaurants, and street entertainment. You can buy a pass for about $8 that admits you to all the clubs (like at Pleasure Island), or if you prefer, you can pay a cover charge (usually about $4) at each club you visit. In addition to the clubs, shops, and restaurants, there's a 20-screen Cineplex movie theater.

CityWalk vs. Pleasure Island

Just as Universal's Islands of Adventure theme park allows for more direct competition with Disney's Magic Kingdom, City-Walk squares off with Pleasure Island in the field of nightlife entertainment. As the underdog, CityWalk tries to catch the wave of the hottest fads in nightclubs and dining, while Pleasure Island tends more toward themes and trends with long-established general appeal. Here's a comparison of the high points of each:

How CityWalk and Pleasure Island Compare	
CityWalk	**Pleasure Island**
Adjacent to Universal's parks	Adjacent to Downtown Disney
Parking decks free after 6 p.m.	Parking is hectic; use Disney transport
About $8 for pass to all clubs	About $19 for admission to complex
Half local/half tourist; mostly ages 20–30	Mostly teens or curious older adults
Ten restaurants	Four restaurants
Four dance clubs	Five dance clubs
Six live music venues	Three live music venues
Upscale mall fare shopping	Disney memorabilia; hipster clothing

Appendix

Small Child
Fright-Potential Chart

Our "Fright-Potential Chart" is a quick reference to identify attractions to be wary of, and why. The chart represents a generalization, and all kids are different. It relates specifically to kids ages three to seven. On average, children at the younger end of the range are more likely to be frightened than children in their sixth or seventh year.

MAGIC KINGDOM

Main Street, U.S.A.

Walt Disney World Railroad: Not frightening in any respect.
Main Street Vehicles: Not frightening in any respect.

Adventureland

Swiss Family Treehouse: Not frightening in any respect.
Jungle Cruise: Moderately intense, some macabre sights. A good test attraction for little ones.
Enchanted Tiki Birds: A thunderstorm momentarily surprises very young children.
Pirates of the Caribbean: Slightly intimidating queuing area; intense boat ride with gruesome (though humorously presented) sights and a short, unexpected slide down a flume.

Frontierland

Splash Mountain: Visually intimidating from outside, with moderately intense visual effects. The ride, culminating in a 52-foot plunge down a steep chute, is somewhat hair-raising for all ages. Switching off option provided (page 54).
Big Thunder Mountain Railroad: Visually intimidating from outside, with moderately intense visual effects. The roller coaster is wild enough to frighten many adults, particularly seniors. Switching off provided (page 54).
Tom Sawyer Island: Some very young children are intimidated by dark, walk-through tunnels that can be easily avoided.

Country Bear Jamboree: Not frightening in any respect.
Frontierland Shootin' Arcade: Not frightening in any respect.
Diamond Horseshoe Saloon Revue: Not frightening in any respect.

Liberty Square

The Hall of Presidents: Not frightening, but boring for young ones.
Liberty Belle Riverboat: Not frightening in any respect.
Mike Fink Keelboats: Not frightening in any respect.
The Haunted Mansion: Name raises anxiety, as do sounds and
  sights of waiting area. Intense attraction with humorously pre-
  sented macabre sights. The ride itself is gentle.

Fantasyland

Mad Tea Party: Can induce motion sickness in all ages.
The Many Adventures of Winnie the Pooh: Not frightening in any
  respect.
Snow White's Adventures: Moderately intense spook-house-genre
  attraction with some grim characters. Absolutely terrifies
  many preschoolers.
Legend of the Lion King: Certain special effects frighten some
  young children.
Dumbo the Flying Elephant: A tame midway ride; a great
  favorite of most young children.
Cinderella's Golden Carrousel: Not frightening in any respect.
It's a Small World: Not frightening in any respect.
Peter Pan's Flight: Not frightening in any respect.

Mickey's Toontown Fair

All attractions except roller coaster: Not frightening in any respect.
The Barnstormer at Goofy's Wiseacres Farm: May frighten some
  young children.

Tomorrowland

Alien Encounter: Extremely intense. Capable of frightening all
  ages. Not for young children. Switching off provided (page
  54).
The Timekeeper: Realistic cinematic technique may frighten
  some young children.
Buzz Lightyear's Space Ranger Spin: Spinning and intense effects
  may frighten preschoolers.

Tomorrowland Transit Authority: Not frightening in any respect.

Space Mountain: Very intense roller coaster in the dark; the Magic Kingdom's wildest ride and a scary roller coaster by any standard. Switching off provided (page 54).

Astro Orbiter: Visually intimidating from the waiting area. The ride is relatively tame.

Walt Disney's Carousel of Progress: Not frightening in any respect.

Tomorrowland Speedway: Noise of waiting area slightly intimidates preschoolers; otherwise, not frightening.

EPCOT

Future World

Spaceship Earth: Dark and imposing presentation intimidates a few preschoolers.

Innoventions East and West: Not frightening in any respect.

Universe of Energy: Dinosaur segment frightens some preschoolers; visually intense, with some intimidating effects.

Wonders of Life—Body Wars: Very intense, with frightening visual effects. Ride causes motion sickness in susceptible riders of all ages. Switching off provided (page 54).

Wonders of Life—Cranium Command: Not frightening in any respect.

Wonders of Life—The Making of Me: Not frightening in any respect.

Test Track: Intense thrill ride may frighten any age.

Journey into Your Imagination Ride: Loud noises and unexpected flashing lights startle younger children.

Journey into Your Imagination—Honey, I Shrunk the Audience: Extremely intense visual effects and loudness frighten many young children.

The Land—Living with the Land: Not frightening in any respect.

The Land—Circle of Life Theater: Not frightening in any respect.

The Land—Food Rocks: Not frightening in any respect, but loud.

World Showcase

Mexico—El Río del Tiempo: Not frightening in any respect.

Norway—Maelstrom: Visually intense in parts. Ride ends with a plunge down a 20-foot flume. A few preschoolers are frightened.

China—Wonders of China: Not frightening in any respect, but audience must stand.
Germany: Not frightening in any respect.
Italy: Not frightening in any respect.
The American Adventure: Not frightening in any respect.
Japan: Not frightening in any respect.
Morocco: Not frightening in any respect.
France—Impressions de France: Not frightening in any respect.
United Kingdom: Not frightening in any respect.
Canada—O Canada!: Not frightening in any respect, but audience must stand.

DISNEY-MGM STUDIOS

The Twilight Zone Tower of Terror: Visually intimidating to young children; contains intense and realistic special effects. The plummeting elevator at the ride's end frightens many adults.
The Great Movie Ride: Intense in parts, with very realistic special effects and some visually intimidating sights.
Doug Live!: Not frightening in any respect.
Sounds Dangerous: Noises in the dark frighten some preschoolers.
Indiana Jones Epic Stunt Spectacular!: An intense show with powerful special effects, including explosions. Presented in an educational context that young children generally handle well.
Rock 'n' Roller Coaster: The wildest coaster at Walt Disney World. May frighten guests of any age. Switching off is provided (page 54).
Star Tours: Extremely intense visually for all ages. Not as likely to cause motion sickness as Body Wars at Epcot. Switching off is provided (page 54).
Disney-MGM Studios Backlot Tour: Sedate and nonintimidating except for "Catastrophe Canyon," where an earthquake and a flash flood are simulated. Prepare younger children for this part of the tour.
Backstage Walking Tours: Not frightening in any respect.
MuppetVision 4D: Intense and loud, but not frightening.
"Honey, I Shrunk the Kids" Movie Set Adventure: Everything is oversized, but nothing is scary.
Voyage of the Little Mermaid: Not frightening in any respect.
The Magic of Disney Animation: Not frightening in any respect

ANIMAL KINGDOM

Boneyard: Not frightening in any respect.

Conservation Station: Not frightening in any respect.

Dinosaur: High-tech thrill ride rattles riders of all ages.

Festival of the Lion King: A bit loud, but otherwise not frightening in any respect.

Flights of Wonder: Swooping birds alarm a few small children.

Pangani Forest Exploration Trail: Not frightening in any respect.

Pocahontas and Her Forest Friends: Not frightening in any respect.

It's Tough to Be a Bug!: Very intense and loud with special effects that startle viewers of all ages and potentially terrify young children.

Kilimanjaro Safaris: A "collapsing" bridge and the proximity of real animals make a few young children anxious.

Maharaja Jungle Trek: Some children may balk at the bat exhibit.

The Oasis: Not frightening in any respect.

Kali River Rapids: Potentially frightening and certainly wet for guests of all ages.

Theater in the Wild: Not frightening in any respect.

Wildlife Express Train: Not frightening in any respect.

Index

If you would like to express your opinion about Walt Disney World or this guidebook, complete the following survey and mail it to:

> *Unofficial Guide* Reader Survey
> P.O. Box 43673
> Birmingham, AL 35243

Inclusive dates of your visit _____

Members of your party:	Person 1	Person 2	Person 3	Person 4	Person 5
Gender (M or F)	_____	_____	_____	_____	_____
Age	_____	_____	_____	_____	_____

How many times have you been to Walt Disney World? _____

On your most recent trip, where did you stay? _____

Concerning accommodations, on a scale with 100 best and 0 worst, how would you rate:

The quality of your room? _____   The value for the money? _____

The quietness of your room? _____   Check-in/checkout efficiency? _____

Shuttle service to the parks? _____   Swimming pool facilities? _____

Did you rent a car? _____   From whom? _____

Concerning your rental car, on a scale with 100 best and 0 worst, how would you rate:

Pickup processing efficiency? _____   Return processing efficiency? _____

Condition of the car? _____   Cleanliness of the car? _____

Airport shuttle efficiency? _____

Concerning your touring:

Who in your party was most responsible for planning the itinerary? _____

What time did you normally get started in the morning? _____

Did you usually arrive at the theme parks prior to opening? _____

Did you return to your hotel for rest during the day? _____

What time did you normally go to bed at night? _____

If a Disney Resort guest, did you participate in early entry? _____

On a scale with 100 best and 0 worst, rate how the touring plans worked:

Park	Name of Plan	Rating
Magic Kingdom	_____	_____
EPCOT	_____	_____
Disney-MGM	_____	_____
Animal Kingdom	_____	_____
Universal	_____	_____

Concerning your dining experiences:

How many restaurant meals (including fast food) did you average per day? ____

How much (approximately) did your party spend on meals per day? ____

Favorite restaurant outside of Walt Disney World? ____

Did you buy this guide: Before leaving? ____ While on your trip? ____

How did you hear about this guide?

Loaned or recommended by a friend ____   Radio or TV ____

Newspaper or magazine ____   Bookstore salesperson ____

Just picked it out on my own ____   Library ____

Internet ____

What other guidebooks did you use on this trip? _____

On the 100 best and 0 worst scale, how would you rate them? _____

Using the same scale, how would you rate the *Unofficial Guide?* _____

Are *Unofficial Guides* readily available in bookstores in your area? _____

Have you used other *Unofficial Guides?* ____ Which one(s)? _____

Comments about your Walt Disney World vacation or about the *Unofficial Guide:* Page 62 - Rides